An Encomium for Jesus

New Testament Monographs, 40

AN ENCOMIUM FOR JESUS

LUKE, RHETORIC, AND THE STORY OF JESUS

Jerome H. Neyrey

SHEFFIELD PHOENIX PRESS

2020

Copyright © 2020 Sheffield Phoenix Press

Published by Sheffield Phoenix Press
Sheffield Institute for Interdisciplinary Biblical Studies (SIIBS),
University of Sheffield, S10 2TN

www.sheffieldphoenix.com

A CIP catalogue record for this book
is available from the British Library

Typeset by Forthcoming Publications

ISBN 978-1-910928-73-8 (hardback)

CONTENTS

Contents

ABBREVIATIONS

ABD	Anchor Bible Dictionary
ANRW	*Aufstieg und Niedergang der römischen Welt*
BDAG	Frederick W. Danker, Walter Bauer, William Arndt, and F. Wilbur Gingrich. *Greek–English Lexicon of the New Testament and Other Early Christian Literature*. 3rd edn. Chicago: University of Chicago Press, 2000
BTB	*Biblical Theology Bulletin*
CBQ	*Catholic Biblical Quarterly*
ConNT	Coniectanea Novi Testamenti
DR	*Downside Review*
HTR	*Harvard Theological Review*
HUCA	*Hebrew Union College Annual*
HvTSt	*Hervormde teologiese studies*
JBL	*Journal of Biblical Literature*
JHS	*Journal of Hellenic Studies*
JJS	*Journal of Jewish Studies*
JSJ	*Journal for the Study of Judaism in the Persian, Hellenistic, and Roman Period*
JSNT	*Journal for the Study of the New Testament*
JTS	*Journal of Theological Studies*
NovT	*Novum Testamentum*
NTS	*New Testament Studies*
PRS	*Perspectives in Religious Studies*
RB	*Revue Biblique*
SBLDS	Society of Biblical Literature Dissertation Series
SBLSP	*Society of Biblical Literature Seminar Papers*
ST	*Studia theologica*
TAPA	*Transactions and Proceedings of the American Philological Association*
TDNT	*Theological Dictionary of the New Testament*
ZNW	*Zeitschrift für die neutestamentliche Wissenschaft*

Chapter 1

FOLLOWING THE RHETORICAL THREAD

> This is the division of the encomion. You should elaborate it with the
> following headings...you will state the person's origin, which you will
> divide into nation, homeland, ancestors, and parents; then upbringing, which
> you will divide into habits and acquired skills; then you will compose the
> greatest heading of the encomion, deeds, which you will divide into those of
> mind and body and fortune (Aphthonius, *Preliminary Exercises* 36).[1]

Because of the quality of his Greek composition, we know that Luke
received the education of a high-status person, which meant that he
was trained to write adult prose based on the 'preliminary exercises' he
learned. These exercises were the stuff of the rhetorical handbooks called
the *progymnasmata*, extant at his time.[2] Utilizing this scholarship, we
argue that Luke himself was educated by means of the exercises in the
progymnasmata, in particular the genre called the encomium, and that
he employed it in composing his narrative about Jesus. He redacted the

---

1. Translation by George A. Kennedy, *Progymnasmata: Greek Textbooks of Prose
Composition and Rhetoric* (Atlanta, GA: Society of Biblical Literature Press, 2003),
p. 108.
2. The *progymnasmata* are slowly entering New Testament scholarship. The most
significant in this is Kennedy, *Progymnasmata*, a book of significance because it was
published by a biblical press. See also Ronald Hock and Edward O'Neill, *The Chreia
in Ancient Rhetoric* (Atlanta, GA: Scholars Press, 1986); and most recently, Mikeal
C. Parsons and Michael Wade Martin, *Ancient Rhetoric and the New Testament*
(Waco, TX: Baylor University Press, 2018). Use of them in scholarship includes:
Jerome H. Neyrey, *Honor and Shame in the Gospel of Matthew* (Louisville, KY:
Westminster/John Knox Press, 1998), and Neyrey, 'Encomium versus Vituperation:
Contrasting Portraits of Jesus in the Fourth Gospel', *JBL* 126 (2007), pp. 529-52; and
Bruce J. Malina and Jerome H. Neyrey, *Portraits of Paul: An Archaeology of Ancient
Personality* (Louisville, KY: Westminster/John Knox Press, 1996), pp. 19-63, 80-83.

materials which he received according to this rhetorical form, thus using a model that was both ancient, current, and highly consistent. The encomium contained traditional topics from which to find praise for the subject of an oration or a literary work. The typical encomium, thus, consisted of conventional sources of praise, which had enjoyed currency from before Aristotle, down through the Hellenistic period and into Roman rhetoric. The encomium consisted of the search for praise in someone's origins, his nurture, education and training, his accomplishments, which were categorized as 'deeds of the body', 'deeds of the soul' (virtues), and 'deeds of fortune'. Another category, 'noble death', was occasionally urged, but it was considered part of the encomium's treatment of the person's deeds of the soul.[3]

But what are the *progymnasmata*? Have serious scholars studied them? What profit does study of them offer? 'Be not the first by which the new is tried…' In investigating the *progymnasmata*, we stand in a line of scholarship which builds on the pioneering work of formidable scholars who have discussed *progymnasmata* and the genre of the gospels. Only the high points of this scholarly investigation can be noted, and not necessarily in chronological order. In the third quarter of the last century, individual texts of various *progymnasmata* were edited and translated[4]—a necessary foundation for rhetorical study. Then followed a period when these texts were introduced to scholars, both of classics and Bible. We cannot present a precise history of the discovery and use of the *progymnasmata*, but certain publications proved to be significant, such as the publication in 1986 of Ronald Hock and Edward O'Neil's *The Chreia in Ancient Rhetoric. I. The Progymnasmata*.[5] Doors and windows, however, flew open with the publication by George Kennedy of the extant texts of the *progymnasmata*.[6]

3. See Michael W. Martin, 'Progymnastic Topic Lists: A Compositional Template for Luke and Other *Bioi*', *NTS* 54 (2008), pp. 18-41.

4. C.S. Baldwin, *Medieval Rhetoric and Poetic* (New York: Sedgwick, 1928), pp. 23-38; Ray Nadeau, 'The Progymnasmata of Aphthonius in Translation', *Speech Monographs* 19 (1952), pp. 264-85; Stanley F. Bonner, *Education in Ancient Rome* (Berkeley, CA: University of California Press, 1977), pp. 250-74; H.I. Marrou, *A History of Education in Antiquity* (Madison WI: University of Wisconsin Press, 1982), pp. 196-200. The as-yet unpublished dissertation in 1986 of James R. Butts, 'The Progymnasmata of Theon: A New Text with Translation and Commentary', caused much attention to be paid to the *progymnasmata* for use by New Testament scholars.

5. Published in Atlanta by Scholars Press, an apposite venue.

6. Kennedy, *Progymnasmata*.

Even before Kennedy's edition, considerable interest developed in regard to various genres found in the *progymnasmata*, in particular, the *chreia*. As rhetorical criticism grew apace among scholars of the gospels, the '*chreia*' or the 'pronouncement story' was admired, examined, and became integral to study of Jesus' words and deeds.[7] In time, another genre, encomium, attracted attention.[8] Likewise 'speech in character' and syncrisis. Most recently, Mikeal Parsons and Michael Wade published a detailed study of seven of the genres found in the *progymnasmata*, which will surely get the attention of serious scholars.[9] Interest in the *progymnasmata*, moreover, went in another scholarly direction, namely, consideration of the genre of the gospels. Philip L. Shuler's tidy book forced a conversation on a particular genre in the *progymnasmata*, the encomium.[10] When the dust of controversy over his proposal settled, it had gained acceptance among experts in the field, such as Richard Burridge.[11] It is not academic heresy, then, to consider a gospel in terms of an 'encomium biography'.

Therefore, this study is not the first in time to study ancient rhetoric, the *progymnasmata*, the genre encomium, and the gospels. Several studies have appeared which employed the categories of the *progymnasmata* for interpretation of a gospel. Shuler considered Matthew in the light of an encomium (only origins and death) and the genre of comparison.[12] I myself

7. Burton Mack and Vernon Robbins, *Patterns of Persuasion in the Gospels* (Sonoma, CA: Polebridge Press, 1989). Vernon Robbins alone made well known this important item: 'Classifying Pronouncement Stories in Plutarch's Parallel Lives', *Semeia* 20 (1981), pp. 33-42; 'Pronouncement Stories and Jesus' Blessing of the Children: A Rhetorical Approach', *Semeia* 29 (1983), pp. 43-74; and 'Introduction: Using Rhetorical Discussions of the Chreia to Interpret Pronouncement Stories', *Semeia* 64 (1994), pp. vii-xvii. See also Jerome H. Neyrey, 'Questions, Chreiai, and Honor Challenges: The Interface of Rhetoric and Culture in Mark's Gospel', *CBQ* 60 (1998), pp. 657-81.

8. Jerome H. Neyrey, 'Josephus' Vita and the Encomium: A Native Model of Personality', *JSJ* 25 (1994), pp. 177-206.

9. Parsons and Martin, *Ancient Rhetoric*.

10. Philip L. Shuler, *A Genre for the Gospels: The Biographical Character of Matthew* (Philadelphia, PA: Fortress Press, 1982).

11. Richard A. Burridge, *What Are the Gospels? A Comparison with Graeco-Roman Biography* (Waco, TX: Baylor University Press, 2018). Much criticism was given Shuler's proposal because his data base was considered too meagre; but Burridge's extensive survey of types of *bioi* resurrected Shuler's argument.

12. Shuler, *A Genre for the Gospels*, pp. 88-106.

applied all of the formal topics of an encomium to understand Matthew.[13] Recently, Michael Martin published an article of great significance. After examining the various *progymnasmata*, he gathered his observations on typical topics found there and proffered them as a template for inter-preting Luke.[14] Furthermore, Mikeal Parson's commentary on Luke[15] has given serious attention to several genres of the *progymnasmata* in Luke, namely, narrative and syncrisis; curiously, however, not the encomium. Thus, some scholarship has been given to the relationship of *progym-nasmata*, encomium, and Luke.

We argue that Luke knew the *progymnasmata* and in particular the rhetorical genre encomium because he learned it through progymnastic 'preliminary exercises'.[16] It was such a common way of drawing honor and praise for someone, that it was readily understood by Luke's audience accustomed to hearing its use. Therefore, we argue that Luke, an appropri-ately educated person of high status, shaped his narrative according to the topics of the encomium, thus indicating that at least one rhetorical purpose for his work was the drawing of praise for Jesus from categories which

13. Neyrey, *Honor and Shame in the Gospel of Matthew*; he employed the topics 'Origins, Birth, Nurture, Training' (Chapter 4), 'Accomplishments and Deeds' (Chapter 5), and 'A Noble Death' (Chapter 7). The genre encomium was employed to display the treatment of Jesus in terms of the pivotal value of 'honor' (or praise).

14. Michael Wade Martin ('Progymnastic Topic Lists') not only cites progymnastic authors but examines various *bioi* in terms of the topic lists. He begins with Plutarch's parallel lives, and so privileges the progymnastic genre of comparison. The grand comparisons are then illustrated in terms of the typical topics of an encomium (origins, nurture, deeds, death).

15. Mikeal C. Parsons, *Luke* (Grand Rapids, MI: Baker Academic Press, 2015).

16. One might inquire whether Luke studied any formal rhetorical theory, such as is found in Cicero and Quintilian. But it seems reasonable to begin with the rhetoric according to which a person of Luke's social standing would have been trained, namely, the 'preliminary exercises' taught in the rhetorical handbooks called the *progymnasmata*. The reasons for starting here are two: first, anyone learning to write prose at the level which Luke can began schooling with the progymnastic handbooks; and second, these exercises were as good an education Luke was likely to get. In Martin's article cited above, he argues this: 'Mastery of the lists and all the progym-nastic forms was regarded as essential preparation not only for the practice of decla-mation (hence, the name *progymnasmata*), but also for written composition, a point about which Theon is emphatic' ('Progymnastic Topic Lists', p. 20). Aelius Theon says, 'The preliminary exercises, in fact, constituted the highest level of training for written composition in Greco-Roman education, as all subsequent training focused strictly on oratory' (Theon, *Exercises* 70 [Murray, p. 13].

all agreed were the right places to find data for praise. Luke's use of this general rhetorical form does not preclude any other theme or topic which might shape his narrative.

Luke's Education

How literate was Luke's world?[17] Who received an education to read and to write for civic purposes?[18] Of what did that education consist? Robert Kaster has conveniently summarized the model of education in Roman times. As he notes, it has been generally thought that ancient education consisted of:

> ...the 'primary' school overseen by the 'primary' teacher, where one learned 'letters'—the elements of reading and writing—and some arithmetic; the 'secondary' or 'grammar' school, where one received thorough and systematic instruction in language and literature, especially poetry, under the grammarian; and the school of rhetoric.[19]

To this Kaster offers the following correction: ancient education was 'a socially segmented system laid out along two essentially separate tracks. The most important formal distinction here is the division between the two tracks or segments: the *ludus literarius*, providing common literacy for students of relatively humble origins, and the *scholae liberales*, catering to the more privileged part of the population'. He continues, 'The *scholae liberales* began with instruction in writing for a public or

17. The primary study on literacy in the ancient world is that of William V. Harris, *Ancient Literacy* (Cambridge, MA: Harvard University Press, 1989), pp. 3-42 and 323-37; Raffaella Cribiore, *Writing, Teachers, and Students in Graeco-Roman Egypt* (Atlanta, GA: Scholars Press, 1996), pp. 3-152. Of considerable worth are the studies of Catherine Hezser, *Jewish Literacy in Roman Palestine* (Tübingen: Mohr/Siebeck, 2001); and Douglas E. Oakman, 'Jesus, Q, and Ancient Literacy in Social Perspective', in his *Jesus and the Peasants* (Eugene, OR: Cascade Books), pp. 298-308.

18. See Jerome H. Neyrey, 'The Social Location of Paul: How Paul Was Educated and What He Could Compose as Indices of His Social Location', in David B. Gowler, L. Gregory Bloomquist, and Duane F. Watson (eds.), *Fabrics of Discourse: Essays in Honor of Vernon K. Robbins* (Harrisburg, PA: Trinity Press International, 2003), pp. 126-64.

19. Robert A. Kaster, 'Notes on "Primary" and "Secondary" Schools in Late Antiquity', *TAPA* 113 (1983), pp. 323-46, here 323. The prevailing model is found in Marrou, *A History of Education in Antiquity*; while regularly cited, it is out of date.

municipal audience, especially epideictic rhetoric so necessary for civic life'.[20] Skill in rhetoric was taught through a collection of exercises, namely, the *progymnasmata*, which in particular contained the cultural rules and values for the encomium, the literary expression of the rhetoric of praise and blame. Luke, then, received instruction in writing for a public or municipal audience; this instruction generally consisted of mastery of the exercises found in progymnastic handbooks for learning appropriate rhetoric.[21]

Progymnasmata

Educated elites such as Luke began learning to write adult prose by mastery of the 'preliminary exercises' contained in the typical handbooks of rhetoric called a *progymnasmata*.[22] George Kennedy produced an important tool for scholars with his publication of the extant texts of most of the *progymnasmata*.[23] Each handbook consisted of 'a series of set exercises of increasing difficulty', whose aim was to produce in someone 'the source of facility in written and oral expression for many persons and training for speech in public life'.[24] Kennedy, a premier student of

20. Kaster, 'Notes on "Primary" and "Secondary" Schools', p. 323.

21. Scholars such as Talbert and Burridge pass over the issue of education in antiquity, in particular, the training of a writer such as Luke. One solid reason for this lies in their unfamiliarity with the rhetorical handbooks called *progymnasmata* or their downplaying of their significance. Martin ('Progymnastic Topic Lists') likewise ignores education, although he knows much about *progymnasmata*. Literacy for a writer such as Luke began with progymnastic rhetorical handbooks.

22. Whether orator or writer, this person began from the beginning. One progymy nastic author attests to the fundamental and essential skills learned from mastering the 'preliminary exercises' in the *progymnasmata*: 'Now I have included these remarks, not thinking that all are useful to all beginners, but in order that we may know that training in exercises is absolutely useful not only to those who are going to practice rhetoric but also is one wishes to undertake the function of poets or historians or any other writers. These things are, as it were, the foundations of every kind of discourse...' (Theon 70 [Kennedy, p. 13]).

23. Kennedy, *Progymnasmata*; not included, Menander Rhetor (D.A. Russell and N.G. Wilson, *Menander Rhetor* [Oxford: Clarendon Press, 1981]).

24. Scholarly consideration of the *progymnasmata* would include: Katherine Thaniel, 'Quintilian and the Progymnasmata' (unpublished dissertation, McMaster University, 1973); Hock and O'Neil, *The Chreia in Ancient Rhetoric*. I. *The Progymnasmata*; Ian H. Henderson, 'Quintilian and the *Progymnasmata*', *Antike und Abendland* 36 (1934), pp. 82-99; and W. Stegemann, 'Theon', *RE* 5A (1934), pp. 2037-54.

rhetoric, claims for the 'preliminary exercises' in the *progymnasmata* this honor: 'Not only in the secular literature of the Greeks and Romans, but the writings of early Christians beginning with the gospels and continuing through the patristic age, and of some Jewish writers as well, were molded by the habits of thinking and writing learned in schools'.[25]

Of what 'preliminary exercises' did a typical *progymnasmata* consist? Extant handbooks typically contain the following exercises: (1) myths/fable, (2) narration, (3) *chreia*/anecdote, (4) maxim/proverb, (5) refutation, (6) confirmation, (7) topos/common-place, (8) encomium, (9) invective, (10) syncrisis/comparison, (11) ethopoeia/characterization, (12) ecphrasis/description, (13) thesis proposal, and (14) law.[26] We propose that Luke employed the exercises of the encomium to structure the materials in his writing which we call a 'gospel'.[27]

The argument of this book, therefore, has two parts. First, we must establish that those educated for a civic or public forum began to compose by means of the 'preliminary exercises' taught in the ancient rhetorical handbooks called *progymnasmata*. Second, it must be shown that Luke, educated via such common rhetorical handbooks, employed the formal topics of the encomium as a recognizable template[28] for narrating a story about Jesus. He used, therefore, a conventional form and its traditional parts as the typical and natural way for finding praise for someone, namely, Jesus of Nazareth. In his narrative, he articulates events in the life of Jesus as instructed in the rules which he was taught on how to compose a progymnastic encomium, specifically the topics: Origins, Nurture and Training, Accomplishments (the canon of four virtues), and Noble Death.

25. Kennedy, *Progymnasmata*, p. ix.

26. Synopses of the progymnastic genres are available in Kennedy, *Progymnasmata*, p. xiii, and Martin, 'Progymnastic Topic Lists', p. 22, and Parsons and Martin, *Ancient Rhetoric*, pp. 4-5.

27. 'Gospel' became a technical term for the narratives constructed by the four evangelists; but naming it such should not mean that it was innocent of the literary forms and genres taught in rhetorical handbooks, such as *chreia* and maxim.

28. 'Compositional Template' is Martin's term for the topics consistently found in progymnastic encomia ('Progymnastic Topic Lists', pp. 18-20). He sees his task as supporting Shuler by extending the encomiastic topic list: 'This study does so in support of a thesis similar to and at the same time more encompassing than Shuler's, namely, that progymnastic topic lists are employed in *bioi* generally and Luke specifically as a compositional template, guiding the narrative in its overall structure and content' (p. 20).

Encomium: Form and Content

A while back, scholars debated about the form of a 'gospel', whether
it had its own distinctive, i.e., Christian, literary form. We need not go
back over that conversation, because we are making a new proposal for
a rhetorical reading of Luke, namely, in terms of the progymnastic genre
of an 'encomium'. As all know, 'epideictic' rhetoric concerns itself with
giving praise or blame to someone. This general type of rhetoric, moreover,
eventually contained prescribed topics where an orator or author might
find conventional materials to praise someone.[29] These topics became
well known and highly conventional. But eventually they were gathered
together into a recognizable literary genre called 'encomium', which
became one of the important exercises in a typical *progymnasmata*. They
continued to develop into a recognizable template which served as a guide
to investigate particular areas in a man's life which would provide data for
the praising and honoring of that person.

The individual topics are themselves ancient, and semblances of their
being gathered as a template equally ancient. The Athenian Funeral
Orations are ready examples of both topics and compositional structures.[30]
From Aristotle to Cicero to Quintilian, we find both recognition of these
topics and acceptance of them as an adequate template for collecting data
for the praise of an honorable person. All of this is historical fact and
not under dispute. It is possible to argue that writers of New Testament
documents were trained using these handbooks.[31] The proof of this lies
in the successful application of the form and template of 'encomium' for
interpreting gospels,[32] letters,[33] a writing such as Hebrews. Throughout
this book, we will argue that Luke knew this literary form and that it
served as a recognized template for him to gather and organize data about
Jesus available to him.

29. Aristotle's remarks (*Rhet.* 1.9.33) were cited in the 'Introduction' to this book,
to which readers are urged to return.

30. On the use of funeral orations as sources of epideictic rhetoric, see Jerome
H. Neyrey, 'The "Noble" Shepherd in John 10: Cultural and Rhetorical Background',
JBL 120 (2001), pp. 267-91.

31. The best evidence is the widespread use of the *chreia* and maxims in all of
the gospels.

32. Neyrey, *Honor and Shame in the Gospel of Matthew*, and Neyrey, 'Encomium
versus Vituperation'.

33. Malina and Neyrey, *Portraits of Paul*, pp. 19-63 and 80-83.

Since this book focuses on the common materials available for Luke to tell his story of Jesus, we turn our attention to what both rhetoricians and progymnastic authors said about the form of the encomium and its prescribed topics. Therefore, we begin with a gathering of materials from the Greco-Roman world which refer to and describe the contents of the literary genre of the encomium. Many passages from the *progymnasmata* will be cited here and throughout this book, which we consider essential for appreciating how Luke followed the conventions for writing prose.

The Common Categories for Praise found in the Encomium

As noted, encomiastic topics can be found in miscellaneous places in classical literature. But contemporary scholars now possess in the rhetorical handbooks, called the *progymnasmata*, formal expositions of the genre encomium and what typically constitutes one. Inasmuch as these handbooks borrow from one another, they are remarkably consistent both in their individual presentations of an encomium, and in other rhetorical descriptions of them. What follows is a composite sketch of the contents of a typical encomium drawn from the extant discussions found in the *progymnasmata*.

First of all, what is an encomium? It is one of twelve or fourteen genres taught to a student of rhetoric. Hermogenes, defines it: 'Encomion is the exposition of the good qualities of a person or thing, in general or individually; for example, an encomion of a man, an encomion of Socrates' (*Preliminary Exercises* 16 [Kennedy, p. 81]). Hermogenes goes on to list the topics in an encomium from which it is possible to draw praise, which consist of:

> ...(a subject's) national origin, such as a Greek city, such as Athens, family, such as Alcmaeonid...marvelous occurrences at birth, for example from dreams or signs or things like that...nurture...upbringing, how he was trained or how educated...the nature of mind and body will be examined and each of these divided into several qualities...about his body (beautiful, large, swift), about his mind (just, temperate, wise, brave)...pursuits (philosopher, orator, general)...most important are deeds...manner of death (Hermogenes, *Preliminary Exercises* 16 [Kennedy, p. 81]).

Although we quote only one progymnastic author about the contents of an encomium, Aristotle earlier cited them, gathering material from his predecessors. When schematized, the topics look like this:

   A.   Origins
       1. Geographical: country, polis, etc.
          Generational: ancestors, parents, genealogies
       2. Phenomena accompanying birth: celestial events, earthly prophecies
   B. Nurture, Upbringing, Education, and Training
   C. Accomplishments
       1. Deeds of the body
       2. Deeds of the soul (i.e., virtues)
       3. Deeds of Fortune
   D. Noble Death

It is not enough, of course, simply to have these categories before us. Nor can we presume that we understand them accurately, as the ancients did, because we are so far removed from their cultural world. We need, therefore, for the authors of the *progymnasmata* to define these topics and tell us what they mean, a task worthy of our time.

Origins

It has always proved helpful to view comparable materials in some form of a synopsis, which applies as well to the progymnastic contents of 'origins' in the encomium. As noted above, 'origins' refers to geographical and genealogical materials.

Hermogenes	Aelius Theon	Aphthonius
ethnic affiliation (*ethnos*)	ethnic affiliation (*ethnos*)	ethnic affiliation(*ethnos*)
nation/city-state (*polis*)	nation/city-state (*polis*)	home locale (*patris*)
clan/tribe (*genos*)	government (*politeia*)	ancestors (*progonoi*) fathers (*pateres*)

As just stated, these terms must also be understood in terms of the culture of their authors, for which purpose we quote one of them, namely, Theon: 'External goods are, first, good birth, and that is twofold, either from the goodness of (a man's) city and tribe and constitution, or from ancestors and other relatives' (*Preliminary Exercises* 110 [Kennedy, p. 50]). But this is itself an example of ancient stereotypical thinking, which itself needs to be unpacked. Quintilian's remarks on 'birth' can help here:

> 'Birth', for persons are generally regarded as having some semblance to their *parents and ancestors*, a resemblance which sometimes leads to their living

disgracefully or honorably, as the case may be; then, there is *nationality* for races have their own their own character, and the same action is not probable in the case of a barbarian, a Roman and a Greek; *country* is another, for there is a like diversity in the laws, institutions and opinions of different states (*Inst. Orat.* 5.10.23-25, italics added).

Stereotypical thinking, moreover, is a characteristic of the ancient world: *ab uno disce omnes.*[34]

Nurture, Upbringing, Education, and Training

Not all progymnastic authors considered 'nurture and training' in their rules. Moreover, they differed from one another both in terminology and content. In fact, there appears to be a tendency to combine them, which seems to focus on education and upbringing in general, but especially that of elites.

Aphthonius	Hermogenes	Menander Rhetor
[T]hen you will take up education, which you will divide into inclination to study, talent, and rules. (*Preliminary Exercises* 36 [Kennedy, p. 108]).	Next, nurture, as in the case of Achilles, that he was reared on lions' marrow and by Chiron. Then training, how he was trained and how educated. (*Preliminary Exercises* 16 [Kennedy, p. 82])	Next comes 'nurture'. Was he reared in [a] palace? Were his swaddling clothes of purple? Was he brought up in [the] lap of royalty...discuss his education. Observing here: 'I wish to describe [the] quality of his mind'. Then you must speak of his love of learning, his quickness, his enthusiasm for study, his easy grasp of what is taught him. If he excels in literature, philosophy, knowledge of letters, you must praise him (*Treatise* II.371.17–372.2)[35]

---

34. See Malina and Neyrey, *Portraits of Paul*, pp. 23-26, and Neyrey, *Honor and Shame in the Gospel of Matthew*, pp. 91-101; John J. Pilch, *A Cultural Handbook to the Bible* (Grand Rapids, MI: Eerdmans, 2012), pp. 76-82.

35. Menander Rhetor in Russell and Wilson, *Menander Rhetor*, pp. 80-82.

Aphthonius seems to have the simplest and clearest categories: 'education', 'study', 'talent', and 'rules'. Yet even here, these categories befit a
person in training for some elite role and status, not some general understanding of education. We add the comments of Cicero, whose remarks
clearly reflect the encomiastic materials:

> Under manner of life should be considered with whom he was reared, in
> what tradition and under whose direction, what teachers he had in the liberal
> arts, what instructors in the art of living, with whom he associates on terms
> of friendship, in what occupation, trade or profession he is engaged, how he
> manages his private fortune, and what is the character of his home life (*Inv.*
> 1.24.35; see Quintilian, *Inst. Orat.* 3.7.10-18).

The progymnastic authors themselves used a variety of terms, which
does not mean that they were confused about what they were talking. Let
us take those used by Aphthonius and examine them more carefully to see
what they are expressing. Our lexicon is the New Testament itself, which
uses them in this way.[36]

1. *Technē*: skill, trade, what one learns professionally: 'He was of the
   same trade, he stayed with them…by trade they were tentmakers'
   (Acts 18.3)
2. *Nomos*: custom, rule, principle, norm
   a) any legal system: 'One who has become a priest, not through
      a legal requirement concerning physical descent' (Heb. 7.16);
      'Do you know—for I am speaking to those who know *the
      law*—that *the law* is binding on a person only during that
      person's lifetime?' (Rom. 7.1-4, italics added).
   b) Moses' system: 'When the time came for their purification
      according to the law of Moses' (Lk. 2.22); 'If a man receives
      circumcision on the Sabbath that the law of Moses may not be
      broken…' (Jn 7.23; see Acts 15.5 and Eph. 2.15).
3. *Agōgē*: conduct of life: '…my teaching, my conduct, my aim in life,
   my faith, my patience, my love, my steadfastness' (2 Tim. 3.10).
4. *Ēthos*: custom or tradition: 'He went to the synagogue on the
   Sabbath day, as was his custom' (Lk. 4.16).[37]

---

36. The meaning of Aphthonius' terms is controlled by the following works:
Michael Darton, *Modern Concordance to the New Testament* (London: Longman &
Todd, 1976), and Johannes Louw and Eugene Nida, *Greek–English Lexicon of the New
Testament based on Semantic Domains* (New York: American Bible Society, 1986).
37. See Jerome H. Neyrey, '"How Does This Man Have Learning, since He is
without Education?" (John 7:15)', *BTB* 48 (2018), pp. 85-96 (90).

Accomplishments

When progymnastic authors developed the next topic in an encomium, they regularly instructed students to look for praise in the deeds of the person being investigated. They divided these into three categories: deeds of the body, deeds of the soul, and deeds of fortune.

Aelius Theon	Hermogenes	Aphthonius
Goods of the body are health, strength, beauty, and acuteness of sense. Important ethical virtues are goods of the mind and the actions resulting from these; for example, that a person is prudent, temperate, courageous, just, pious, and the like (*Preliminary Exercises* 110 [Kennedy, p. 50]).	The nature of mind and body will be examined and each of these divided into several qualities. You will say of his body that it was beautiful, large, swift, strong; about his mind that it was just, temperate, wise, brave (*Preliminary Exercises* 16 [Kennedy, p. 82]).	...then you will compose the greatest heading of the encomion, deeds, which you will divide into those of mind and body and fortune: mind, as courage or prudence; body, as beauty or swiftness of strength; and fortune, as power and wealth and friends (*Preliminary Exercises* 36 [Kennedy, p. 108]).

For our purposes, we will examine only 'deeds of the soul', since Luke's narrative about Jesus seems silent about 'deeds of the body' or 'deeds of fortune'. Furthermore, these authors and many rhetoricians consider 'deeds of the soul' under the category of 'virtue', in particular the canon of four virtues identified earlier by Plato and followed by most other writers: wisdom (prudence), justice, courage (fortitude) and self-control (temperance). Each of these in turn must be explained according to the culture of the Greco-Roman world, because we must expect that they understood them differently than we do. Furthermore, the ancient rhetoricians spoke with one voice when they instructed others to *portray deeds* expressive of these virtues, rather than label a deed as 'just' or 'courageous'.[38] This last item alerts us that in the telling of a narrative, an author like Luke would expect his audience to put the correct label on various actions of Jesus. Because they were socialized to know the canon of four virtues and to recognize them, Luke could expect them to do what persons in our culture cannot—easily identify what is being said. Much could be assumed in the 'high context' world of Luke,[39] which is so foreign to

---

38. See Aristotle, *Rhet.* 3.6.1-3 and 3.17.12.

39. Anthropologist Edward T. Hall (*Beyond Culture* [New York: Doubleday, 1981], pp. 105-16) distinguished cultures in terms of what must be explicit and

our modern 'low context' world where everything must be spelled out in detail, which means for scholars, footnotes.

Noble Death

Athens developed a rhetorical way of praising and honoring the noble heroes who died in battle for her defense,[40] which some consider the cradle of epideictic rhetoric. The shape of funeral orations quickly became conventional, in that a recognized group of reasons for praise developed, as a template according to which the orations should be composed and readily appreciated. Ideally, a warrior would survive combat and be honored by the *polis* with distinguished material expressions of honor. But most did not, alas, and their funeral oration was the first way of honoring these fallen warriors. Orators eventually settled on six aspects of a soldier's death that warranted it being labeled 'noble'.

(1) First of all, they considered a death 'noble' if it *benefitted* the city, as described by Hyperides: 'Their courage in arms...reveals them as the authors of many benefits conferred upon their country and the rest of Greece' (Hyperides, *Funeral Speech* 9). (2) Then their death was noble because they were *virtuous*, virtuous according to the convention appreciation of the canonical virtues, particularly *justice and courage*. 'For they deemed that it was the way of wild beasts to be held subject to one another by force, but the duty of men to delimit justice by law, to convince by reason, and to serve these two in act by submitting to the sovereignty of law and the instruction of reason' (Lysias, *Funeral Oration* 17-19). (3)

---

what may be presumed. He contrasted American and Japanese culture, considering American culture 'low context' because so much has to be specified and in detail, and Japanese culture 'high context' where so many things can be presumed or assumed. The Greco-Roman world is correctly understood as 'high context', illustrated by it conventional learning, rhetoric, and use of stereotypes. 'Low context' is exemplified by the list of instructions attached to medicines, details of a contract, and exact specifications of law. Kathy Reiko Maxwell's dissertation comes at the same material from reader response criticism: 'I propose that narrative gaps in Luke and Acts are examples of an ancient, intentional, sophisticated rhetorical tool intended to encourage audience participation in the narrative' (*Hearing Between Lines: The Audience as Fellow-Worker in Luke–Acts and its Literary Milieu* [Waco, TX: Baylor University Press, 2007) published online at baylor-ir.tdl.org/handle/2104/5142.

40. John E. Ziolkowski, *Thucydides and the Tradition of Funeral Speeches at Athens* (Salem, NH: The Ayer Company, 1981); Nicole Loraux, *The Invention of Athens: The Funeral Oration in the Classical City* (Cambridge, MA: Harvard University Press, 1986).

Only a death *voluntarily chosen* or accepted was virtuous, which distinguished these citizens from slaves or other mean groups. So says Plato: 'We, who might have ignobly lived choose rather to die nobly before we bring you and those after you to disgrace or before we shame you with our fathers and all our earlier forebearers' (Plato, *Menex.* 246d). (4) Although a soldier or warrior died in battle, in the imagination of the orators it could be argued that they died *unconquered or victorious*. As Lycurgus wrote: '*Unconquered,* they fell in the defense of freedom, and if I may use a paradox, they *triumphed in* their death' (*Leocrates* 48-49). (5) An orator might argue that a death was *unique* in some way, namely, he achieved what 'no one' else had ever achieved or that he was the 'first' and maybe the 'only' person to act so. Thus Hyperides said: 'Never before did men strive for a nobler cause, either against stronger adversaries or with fewer friends, convinced that valour gave strength and courage superiority as no mere numbers could' (Hyperides, *Funeral Speech* 19). (6) *Posthumous honors* attended the burial of great heroes, such as games, feasts, and the like. A monument commemorating the battle in which the soldiers died might be erected, and a celebration held on the anniversary of the battle. The greatest posthumous honor was 'everlasting remembrance', fame, and glory.

The genre of the encomium comes to us in the *progymnasmata* in a very succinct form, but it was employed to give structure to large writings. For example, after stating the naked topics of an encomium, Aphthonius describes how this might be employed to write an encomium for Thucydides. Likewise, Plutarch structured his parallel lives accordingly. We are arguing in this book that Luke employs it to tell the story of Jesus.

Presuppositions: A Totally Different Cultural World

The theses of this book imply certain assumptions which should be acknowledged from the start. The rhetorical purpose of an encomium was to find reasons to give praise and honor to a person. This, of course, presumes that they had an active appreciation of the premier value of the ancient world, 'honor' or 'praise'. Writers and audiences at that time did not need to be informed about this, as modern folk do. Furthermore, they understood human persons quite differently from modern folk. Whereas we currently prize independence and individuality, they thought of a person as embedded in social institutions (politics and kinship), who may then be described as a 'group-oriented' person. This means that persons regularly looked to others to tell them what to think, what to value, and so how to behave. Luke lived in a cultural world where all of these materials were known, simply because all were socialized into the same culture. This means that modern readers need to be warned that their cultural world is utterly foreign to that of Luke and Jesus.

Progymnasmata: *Esoteric Knowledge?*

Were ancient authors generally instructed in the rhetoric of praise,[41] and in particular, an encomium? Did they write narratives and *bioi* using the structure and topics of an encomium?[42] Yes, as a matter of fact.[43] Take for example, Josephus. When Louis Feldman began examining what he called 'portraits' of Israelite heroes, at first he used an intuitive approach whereby he collected various items, not labeling these individual groupings by any particular name or identifying any genre. Along the way, he discovered the rhetorical form of encomium, which confirmed what he had been doing and instructed him on how to read other 'portraits'. His study of Josephus proves two things: first, Josephus himself was regularly using the rhetorical genre known as an encomium to draw praise for the persons he was considering; and second, a respected scholar had made a significant discovery in finding that rhetorical form.[44] Moreover, among gospel writers, it has been argued that both John and Matthew employed

41. William S. Kurz ('Hellenistic Rhetoric in the Christological Proof of Luke–Acts', *CBQ* 42 [1980], pp. 171-95) discussed for half of his article whether Luke knew rhetoric. Scholarship since then has endorsed Kurz's argument; this monograph is one more proof.

42. David J. Balch, 'Two Apologetic Encomia: Dionysius on Rome and Josephus on the Jews', *JSJ* 13 (1982), pp. 102-22; Shuler, *A Genre for the Gospels*; and Martin, 'Progymnastic Topic Lists'.

43. The topics in the encomium are generally found in biographies in antiquity. See Arnaldo Momigliano, *The Development of Greek Biography* (Cambridge, MA: Harvard University Press, 1971), p. 17; David E. Aune, 'Greco-Roman Biography', in his *Greco-Roman Literature and the New Testament: Selected Forms and Genres* (Atlanta, GA: Scholars Press, 1988), pp. 109-10; Christopher Pelling, *Character and Individuality in Greek Literature* (Oxford: Clarendon Press, 1990).

44. A catalogue of Louis Feldman's 'portraits' of Israelite heroes includes: 'Josephus as an Apologist to the Greco-Roman World: His Portrait of Solomon', in Elizabeth Schüssler-Fiorenza (ed.), *Aspects of Religious Propaganda in Judaism and Early Christianity* (Notre Dame, IN: University of Notre Dame Press, 1976), pp. 69-98; 'Josephus' Portrait of Saul', *HUCA* 53 (1982), pp. 45-99; 'Hellenizations in Josephus' *Jewish Antiquities*: The Portrait of Abraham', in Louis Feldman and Gohei Hata (eds.), *Josephus, Judaism and Christianity* (Detroit, MI: Wayne State University Press, 1987), pp. 133-53; 'Josephus' Portrait of Jacob', *JQR* 79 (1988), pp. 101-51;

the rhetorical form of an encomium in the writing of their works.[45] And the encomium topics have been applied for a fresh reading of Paul's Letter to the Galatians.[46]

Each of the subsequent chapters in this book will cite one of the conventional categories according to which the ancients would search for data for praising someone. This means that there will be seven chapters, each dedicated to a detailed study of encomiastic topics: Chapter 2, origins; Chapter 3, nurture, training, and education; Chapter 4, accomplishments: the virtue of wisdom; Chapter 5, accomplishments: the virtue of justice; Chapter 6, accomplishments: the virtue of courage; Chapter 7, accomplishments: the virtue of self-control; and finally, Chapter 8: noble death. The treatment of each will begin with native definitions of the encomiastic topic and then illustrations from progymnastic sources. Building on this, we will examine Luke's narrative to see if and to what extent each category was recognized by Luke and employed. Finally, readers will find in the Appendix a catalogue of many of the rhetorical materials found in Luke-Acts, confirmation that Luke was well trained in Greco-Roman rhetoric, which should then give substance to the thesis of this book.

'Josephus' Portrait of David', *HUCA* 60 1989), pp. 129-74; 'Josephus' Portrait of Hezekiah', *JBL* 111 (1992), pp. 597-610. To this should be added, Neyrey, 'Josephus' Vita and the Encomium'.

45. For the Gospel of John, see Neyrey, 'Encomium versus Vituperation'. And for Matthew, see Neyrey, *Honor and Shame in the Gospel of Matthew*, pp. 90-162.

46. Malina and Neyrey, *Portraits of Paul*, pp. 19-63. See also George Lyons, *Pauline Autobiography: Toward a New Understanding* (SBLDS, 73; Atlanta, GA: Scholars Press, 1985), whose study depends heavily on the study of Theodore Burrows, 'Epideictic Literature', *Studies in Classical Philology* 3 (1902), pp. 89-261.

Chapter 2

ENCOMIUM: THE ORIGINS OF JESUS

'External goods are, first, good birth, and that is twofold, either from the goodness of (a man's) city and tribe and constitution, or from ancestors and other relatives' (Theon, *Exercises* 110 [Kennedy, p. 50]).

'"Birth", for persons are generally regarded as having some semblance to their parents and ancestors, a resemblance which sometimes leads to their living disgracefully or honorably, as the case may be; then, there is nationality for races have their own character, and the same action is not probable in the case of a barbarian, a Roman and a Greek; country is another, for there is a like diversity in the laws, institutions and opinions of different states' (Quintilian, *Inst. Orat.* 5.10.23-25).

In keeping with the argument of this book, we now examine Luke's infancy narratives, but from the vantage point according to which the ancients instructed an author to investigate them. Our aim remains to discover what rhetorical resources Luke used that groomed him to tell the narrative of Jesus' infancy in a certain rhetorical way. In short, what rhetorical conventions might Luke be following in the way he shaped the data available to him, so as to write a narrative that his audience would recognize? What were they expecting? What are we looking at?

From many extant examples of the lives of great figures in the ancient world and from the instructions in rhetorical handbooks, we are now able to identify the conventions for honoring a person according to the information marshaled about a man's 'origins', that is, his honorable birth. First of all, the ancients were schooled to talk about 'origins', i.e., 'good birth' according to two complementary ideas: geographical origins and generational descent. Both of these report on the ascribed honor of a person, that is, the honor which inevitably belongs to a person of noble global positioning and of noble descent. Thus 'origins' should be construed in two basic ways, geography and generation. There is, moreover, a third category, 'marvelous occurrences at birth, for example from dreams or signs or things like that'.

The commonplace about honorable origins is very, very old. We are fortunate to have a consolidation of that tradition in the remarks about 'origins' found in the *progymnasmata*.[1] We noted briefly in the first chapter what the ancients understood about 'origins', but now we must examine that material more closely.

Origins: Geography and Generation

We turn again to our native informants for their emic comments on the encomiastic topic of 'origins'. As usual, it seems profitable to view them synoptically.

Theon	Hermogenes	Aphthonius
External goods are,	Encomiastic topics are	This is the division of the encomium. You should elaborate it with the following headings…
first, good birth, and that is twofold, either from the goodness of (a man's) city and tribe and constitution, or from ancestors and other relatives (*Preliminary Exercises* 110 [Kennedy, p. 50]).	(the subject's) national origin, such as Greek, city, such as Athenian, family, such as Alcmaeonid. You will mention also any marvelous occurrences at birth, for examples, dreams or signs or things like that (*Preliminary Exercises* 15 [Kennedy, p. 82]).	You will state the person's origins, which you will divide into nation, homeland, ancestors, and parents (*Preliminary Exercises* 36 [Kennedy, p. 108]).

These encomiastic remarks about generation can be further elaborated. needed:

1. Much scholarly attention has been given to 'origins', such as David L. Dungan and David R. Cartlidge, *Sourcebook of Texts for the Comparative Study of the Gospels* (Missoula, MT: Scholars Press, 1974), pp. 7-40; Shuler, *A Genre for the Gospels*, pp. 53-55, 92-94; Thomas R. Lee, *Studies in the Form of Sirach 44–50* (SBLDS, 74; Atlanta, GA: Scholars Press, 1986), pp. 113-16; Neyrey, *Honor and Shame in the Gospel of Matthew*, pp. 91-101. See Parsons and Martin, *Ancient Rhetoric*, pp. 175-230.

Theon	Hermogenes	Aphthonius
ethnic affiliation (*ethnos*)	ethnic affiliation (*ethnos*)	ethnic affiliation (*ethnos*)
nation/city-state (*polis*)	nation/city-state (*polis*)	home locale (*patris*)
clan/tribe (*genos*)	clan/tribe (*genos*)	ancestors (*progonoi*) fathers (*pateres*)

They employ more or less the same vocabulary, which, of course, mean one thing to them, but probably another thing to modern readers. Nevertheless, the distinction between geographical and generational 'origins' is clear, and can be shown to be very conventional. Quintilian's remarks illustrate this clearly:

> 'Birth', for persons are generally regarded as having some semblance to their *parents and ancestors*, a resemblance which sometimes leads to their living disgracefully or honorably, as the case may be; then, there is *nationality* for races have their own character, and the same action is not probable in the case of a barbarian, a Roman and a Greek; *country* is another, for there is a like diversity in the laws, institutions and opinions of different states (*Inst. Orat.* 5.10.23-25, italics added).

Geographical Honor

It mattered greatly where a person was born. Paul was born in 'Tarsus, a not insignificant city' (Acts 21.39). An Israelite born in Jerusalem has reason for boasting (Ps. 87.5-6). And for Romans, the center of the world was Rome. One rhetorician stated this clearly:

> You will come to the topic of his native country. Here you must ask yourself whether it is a distinguished country or not [and whether he comes from a celebrated and splendid place or not]. If his native country is famous, you should place your account of it first, and mention it before his family… If the city has no distinction, you must inquire whether his nation as a whole is considered brave and valiant, or is devoted to literature or the possession of virtues, like the Greek race, or again is distinguished for law, like the Italian, or is courageous, like the Gauls or Paeonians. You must argue that *it is inevitable that a man from such a [city or] nation should have such characteristics* (Menander Rhetor, *Treatise* II.2.369.18–370.5, italics added).

Snobbery, of course, but a window into that elite world. Among the ancients, cities had certain cachets—ones they themselves promoted, but also others used to demote or satirize them, such as:

> Whenever I looked at the country of the Getae I saw them fighting; whenever I transferred my gaze to the Scythians, they could be seen roving about on their wagons: and when I turned my eyes aside slightly, I beheld the

Egyptians working the land. The Phoenicians were on trading-ventures, the
Cilicians were engaged in piracy, the Spartans were whipping themselves
and the Athenians were attending court (Lucian, *Icaromenippus* 17).

These are mild compared to Cicero's remarks about the Carthaginians
(*Agrarian Laws* 2.95). Two conventions, moreover, greatly elevated the
honorable status of a city: it might be considered the *navel* of the world or
heralded as a *metropolis* (mater-polis). In the course of time, the Greeks
considered Delphi the navel; Israelites, Jerusalem;[2] and Romans, Rome.[3]
The cities of Asia bitterly contested the right to be called a 'metropolis'.[4] All know, moreover, the slur, 'Can anything good can come out of
Nazareth?' (Jn 1.46).

Generational Honor
It was essential for an honorable man to enjoy a distinguished pedigree, as
Aristotle noted: 'Noble Birth in the case of a nation or State, means that
its members or inhabitants are sprung from the soil, or of long standing;
that its first members were famous as leaders, and that many of their
descendants have been famous for qualities that are highly esteemed'
(*Rhet.* 1.5.5). And Aristotle, again, 'Noble birth is a heritage of honor
from one's ancestors' (*Rhet.* 2.15.2). His opinion was commonplace,
and it continued to be employed by later writers, such as Plutarch. In
the following remarks, Plutarch clearly contrasts the disadvantages and
advantages of 'noble birth', which aptly expresses the importance of
search for the generational honor in 'origins' in the encomium:

2. 'Just as the navel is found at the center of a human being, so the land of Israel
is found at the center of the world...and it is the foundation of the world. Jerusalem
is at the center of the land of Israel, the Temple is at the center of Jerusalem, the Holy
of Holies is at the center of the Temple, the Ark is at the center of the Holy of Holies
and the Foundation Stone is in the front of the Ark, which spot is the foundation of
the world' (*Tanhuma*, Kedoshim 10).

3. Pliny writes: 'The one race (*gens*) of outstanding eminence in virtue of all the
races in the whole world is undoubtedly the Roman' (*H.N.* 7.40.130).

4. David Magie, *Roman Rule in Asia Minor, to the End of the Third Century after
Christ* (Princeton, NJ: Princeton University Press, 1950), I, p. 1636 and II, p. 1496.
Philo of Alexandria made the same claim about Jerusalem: 'As for the holy city...
While she is my native city she is also the mother city not of one country Judaea but of
most of the others in virtue of the colonies sent out at diverse times to the neighboring
lands Egypt, Phoenicia, the part of Syria...as well as the lands lying far apart,
Pamphilia, Cilicia, most of Asia up to Bithynia and the corners of Pontus, similarly
also into Europe, Thessaly, Boeotia, Macedonia, Aetolia, Attica, Argos, Corinth and
most of the best part of the Peloponnese' (*Gaius* 281).

For those who are *not well-born*, whether on the father's or the mother's side, have an *indelible disgrace* in their low birth, which accompanies them throughout their lives, and offers anyone desiring to use it *a ready subject of reproach and insult*... A *goodly treasure*, then, is honorable birth, and such a man may speak his mind freely, a thing which should *be held of the highest account by those who wish to have issue lawfully begotten*. In the nature of things, the spirit of those whose blood is base or counterfeit are constantly brought down and humbled, and quite rightly does the poet declare:

A man, though bold, is made a slave whene're
He learns his mother's or his sire's disgrace
(Plutarch, *Moralia* 1.1.2, italics added).[5]

Pedigree matters in humans, as in animals.

Origins: Cosmic Markers of Importance
The importance of the birth of a mortal on earth could be expressed by heavenly phenomenon attesting to it, such as celestial signs, dreams, portents, prophecies and the like.[6] Menander Rhetor provides an encomiastic summary of this:

If any divine sign occurred at the time of his birth, either on land or in the heavens or on the sea, compare the circumstances of those of Romulus, Cyrus, and similar stories, since in these cases also there were miraculous happenings connected with their birth—the dream of Cyrus' mother, the suckling of Romulus by the she-wolf (*Treatise* II.371.5-14).[7]

Dreams, to be sure, were significant and functional, but we will pass over them because they do not occur in Luke's narrative about Jesus. A comet

5. This citation from Plutarch and many other relevant remarks about the importance of 'noble birth' are from the article of Richard L. Rohrbaugh, 'The Social Function of Genealogies in the New Testament and its World', in Stephen K. Black (ed.), *To Set at Liberty: Essays on Early Christianity and its Social World in Honor of John H. Elliott* (Sheffield: Sheffield Phoenix Press, 2014), pp. 311-27.

6. See Charles H. Talbert, 'Prophecies of Future Greatness: The Contribution of Greco-Roman Biographies to an Understanding of Luke 1:5–4:15', in James Crenshaw and Samuel Sandmel (eds.), *The Divine Helmsman* (New York: KTAV, 1980), pp. 129-41.

7. On the relationship of heavenly phenomena to events on earth, see Bruce J. Malina, *On the Genre and Message of Revelation: Star Visions and Sky Journeys* (Peabody, MA: Hendrickson, 1995), pp. 12-22. See also Bruce J. Malina, 'Apocalyptic and Territoriality', in Fredrick Manns and Eugenio Alliata (eds.), *Early Christianity in Context: Monuments and Documents: Essays in Honour of Emmanuel Testa* (Jerusalem: Franciscan Printing, 1993), pp. 369-80.

was said to pass over Rome at the birth of Julius Caesar, suggesting that the heavens signaled the birth of an important earthly person (see Mt. 2.1-10). In addition, the appearance of celestial phenomena in general was expected in history and encomia.[8] In this regard, the ancients were attuned to and expected prophecies of future greatness at the birth of an important person, such as was reported at the birth of Augustus. Suetonius prefaces his lengthy catalogue with the summary statement: 'Since we are upon this subject, it may not be improper to give an account of the omens, before and at his birth, as well as afterwards, which gave hopes of his future greatness, and the good fortune that constantly attended him' (*Augustus* 94).[9]

8. We are focusing on 'origins', but the tradition of celestial phenomena might reflect other historical events. For example, Josephus related that a star in the shape of a sword stood over Jerusalem for about a year, presaging its destruction (*War* 6.289). He interpreted this as an indication of divine benevolence: 'Reflecting on these things one will find that God has a care for men, and by means of all kinds of premonitory signs shows His people the way to Salvation' (*War* 6.310).

9. Of all mentions of such phenomena in ancient literature, Suetonius's account is the most complete, and deserves to be cited:

> [*pre-birth*] A part of the wall of Velletri having in former times been struck with thunder, the response of the soothsayers was, that a native of that town would some time or other arrive at supreme power... At last it appeared that the omen had portended the elevation of Augustus...a few months before his [Augustus's] birth, there happened at Rome a prodigy, by which was signified that Nature was in travail with a king for the Roman people; and that the senate, in alarm, came to the resolution that no child born that year should be brought up; but that those amongst them, whose wives were pregnant, to secure to themselves a chance of that dignity, took care that the decree of the senate should not be registered in the treasury...
>
> *Upon the day he was born*, the senate being engaged in a debate on Catiline's conspiracy, and Octavius, in consequence of his wife's being in childbirth...it is a well-known fact, that Publius Nigidius, upon hearing the occasion of his coming so late, and the hour of his wife's delivery, declared that the world had got a master.
>
> [*post-birth*] Afterwards, when Octavius...consulted the oracle in the grove of father Bacchus concerning his son, he received from the priests an answer to the same purpose... And the next night he dreamt that he saw his son under more than human appearance, with thunder and a sceptre, and the other insignia of Jupiter Optimus Maximus, having on his head a radiant crown, mounted upon a chariot decked with laurel, and drawn by six pair of milk-white horses (Suetonius, *Augustus* 94).

Luke, Encomium: Origins and Birth

Luke, it should be noted, does not use any of the encomiastic vocabulary ('origins' or geography or generation), but he clearly has them in view as he fills in each topic with appropriate data. Luke, it would seem, knows them and knows that his audience knows and expects them.

Geographical Honor

Jesus was raised in Nazareth in Galilee, which did not enjoy a particularly honorable cachet: 'Can anything good come out of Nazareth?' (Jn 1.46). But Luke emphatically emphasizes that Jesus was born in an honorable place, 'the *city of David* called Bethlehem' (2.4), which note is repeated by the heavenly messengers, 'To you is born this day in the *city of David* a Savior (2.11).[10] Bethlehem, then, is the nest where rulers of Israel were born—a noble site indeed. Moreover, Luke reports that from his infancy Jesus was associated with the principal civic shrine of the chief city of Israel, the Temple in Jerusalem. It is one thing to connect the priest Zechariah with the Temple, but quite another matter to have the infant-child Jesus associated with this place. The Temple is the appropriate place for Jesus to be administered the rite of dedication to the Lord (2.22-24), for prophets—male and female—to declare his significance for the house of Israel (2.25-38), and for his annual celebration of Passover (2.41-42). For those who do not know of the rhetorical form of the encomium, the significance of these items may be difficult to appreciate. But according to the traditional sources of honor in the various encomistic topics, these communicate significant information about the honorable child, Jesus.

Generational Honor

'Origins' also includes data about the *genealogical* background of a person to be praised. The author of Luke-Acts not infrequently mentions the 'tribes' to which some persons belonged, which gives them some sort of status. To appreciate what it meant for an Israelite to state and boast of generational origins, we pause to note Paul's custom in this regard. He cites his pedigree twice, because, to Paul, it matters.

---

10. Matthew seemed quite aware of the potential dishonor of being born in a mere village. He narrated that the professional class of Israel appreciated the true honor which could accrue to someone being born in Bethlehem: 'And you, Bethlehem, in the land of Judah, are by no means least among the rulers of Judah; for from you shall come a ruler who is to shepherd my people Israel' (Mt. 2.6/Mic. 5.2).

Rom. 11.1

I myself am an Israelite
descendant of Abraham
a member of the tribe of Benjamin

Phil. 3.5

a member of the people of Israel
of the tribe of Benjamin
a Hebrew born of Hebrews

He boasts of his blood lines, and names his tribe, Benjamin. It is hard to know what specific honor was claimed by stemming from 'the tribe of Benjamin', except that he was belonged to one of the official tribes, and so was not a generic Israelite and Hebrew.[11]

In regard to Jesus, we know several things. His tribal ancestry could not be more honorable, because he is descended from 'the house of David'. Indeed Joseph is regularly labeled as 'of the house of David' (1.27; 2.4), and Mary was told by a heavenly messenger that her son would inherit 'the throne of his ancestor David' (1.32). This is formally expressed in Jesus' genealogy, 'son of Mattatha, son of Nathan, son of David' (3.29; see also 18.38; 20.44). Zechariah concurs with this: 'He [God] has raised up a mighty savior for us in the house of his servant David' (1.69). Luke, however, has another tribe in view as part of Jesus' genealogy, namely, Levi. Jesus, it is claimed, is 'son of Matthat, *son of Levi*' (3.29). Scholars have little to say about this, preferring to stress Jesus' descent from the tribe of Judah via David; nor is there any conversation about Jesus' descent from the two most important tribes, the Levi/priestly clan[12] and the Judah/royal clan. Figures who were both priests and kings were not unknown in Israel's history (Melchizedek; Hasmoneans); all know, moreover, that monarchs often functioned as priest and king.

---

11. Except for Jacob's blessing in Gen. 49, the twelve tribes of Israel are not itemized and cited collectively. All twelve tribes of Israel, however, are named in Rev. 7.4-8, whose tribal names are later described as being inscribed over the twelve gates (21.12). Luke himself records that the twelve disciples will judge the twelve *tribes* (*phylas*) of Israel (22.30).

12. Some have argued that Mary, who was cousin to Elizabeth, 'descendant of Aaron' (Lk. 1.5), was of a priestly clan herself. The argument would look like this: Mary is cousin to a member of a priestly clan, who is married to a member of a priestly clan. Pure bloodlines are presumed. Mary, it is implied, has bloodline connections to priestly people. See Raymond E. Brown, *The Birth of the Messiah* (New York: Doubleday, 1993), pp. 266, 449.

Generational Honor and Genealogy[13]

Jesus, moreover, enjoys a genealogy. We pass over the scholarly investigation of its source, original language, and historicity, to focus on the
fact that there is one in Luke to honor Jesus. Genealogies befit patriarchs
(Gen. 11.10-27), kings, and priests (Ezra 2.59-63), and serve to establish
identity, status and legitimacy. It greatly matters that the genealogy of
Jesus climaxes with his being 'the son of Adam, the son of God' (3.38).[14]
Jesus stems from the significant ancestors of Israel.[15]

At this point we do well to consider the conclusion of Charles Talbert
in his article on prophecies of future greatness; he prefers the genre of
'biography', whereas we prefer that of 'encomium'. His argument, we
recall, is to describe how Greco-Roman audiences of Luke would have
understood Lk. 1.5–4.15, about which we are both in agreement:

> Virtually the totality of the material about Jesus in 1.5–4.15 would have been
> regarded as an anticipation of his later public greatness. The angelophanies,
> the prophecies of a Jewish type, the portent plus its interpretation, the vision
> plus its audition, the two stories of childhood prodigies, the genealogy (and
> miraculous conception) would combine to foretell/foreshadow the type
> of person Jesus would be in his public ministry... By writing in this way,
> the Evangelist was simply following the conventions of Greco-Roman
> biographical literature.[16]

Summary and Conclusions

1. Evidence that Luke knew and employed the genre of encomium
argues that he began his elite training by mastering the materials of the
progymnasmata. Writers of Greek prose began learning their craft from
mastering the exercises of these handbooks. Luke knows this material
about 'origins', at least as far as following the conventions for narrating
this. Luke was formally aware of what he was doing.

2. Who else knows these rhetorical rules? In addition to Paul's remarks
in Rom. 11.1 and Phil. 3.5, the following figure is very persuasive.

---

13. For a recent and excellent treatment of this, see Rohrbaugh, 'The Social
Function of Genealogies in the New Testament World'.

14. John Nolland, *Luke 1–9:20* (Dallas, TX: Word Books, 1989), p. 173; he offers
an interesting parallel to Luke's 'son of God' from Philo, *On the Virtues* 204-205.

15. William S. Kurz, 'Luke 3:23-38 and Greco-Roman and Biblical Genealogies',
in Charles H. Talbert (eds.), *Luke–Acts: New Perspectives from the Society of Biblical
Literature Seminar* (New York: Crossroads, 1984), pp. 169-87.

16. Talbert, 'Prophecies of Future Greatness', p. 137.

Lk. 1.26–2.38	Mt. 1.1–2.23
1. Geographical: '…from the town of Nazareth in Galilee to Judea, to the city of David called Bethlehem' (2.4)	1. Geographical: 'In Bethlehem of Judea; for so it has been written by the prophet: "And you, Bethlehem, in the land of Judah, are by no means least among the rulers of Judah; for from you shall come a ruler who is to shepherd my people Israel"' (2.5-6)
2. Generational: – genealogy (3.23-38) – tribe of Judah, house of David: 'Joseph went…Judea, to the city of David, because he was descended from the house and family of David' (2.4); 'To you is born in the city of David a Savior, who is the Messiah' (2.11) – ascribed honor based on generational descent (role and status): 'Savior, Messiah' ('son of David' implies 'king')	2. Generational: – genealogy (1.1-17) – tribe of Judah, house of David: 'Joseph, son of David' (1.20); 'Where is the child…born king of the Jews' (2.2); 'Bethlehem, in the land of Judah…from you shall come a ruler who is to shepherd my people Israel' (2.5-6) – ascribed honor based on generational descent (role and status): 'Emmanuel' (1.20); 'king of the Jews' (2.2); 'ruler who is to shepherd Israel' (2.6); 'my son' (2.15)
3. Special events at birth – heavenly proclamation: '"The angel said to them… I am bringing you good news of great joy for all the people: to you is born this day in the city of David a Savior, who is the Messiah, the Lord". And suddenly there was with the angel a multitude of the heavenly host, praising God and saying, Glory to God in the highest heaven, and on earth peace among those whom he favors!' (2.10-14) – prophecies of greatness: 'My eyes have seen your salvation, which you have prepared in the presence of all peoples, a light for revelation to the Gentiles and for glory to your people Israel' (2.30-32); '…a prophet, Anna the daughter of Phanuel, of the tribe of Asher…she came, and began to praise God and to speak about the child to all who were looking for the redemption of Jerusalem' (2.36-38)	3. Special events at birth – new star in heaven '"For we observed his star at its rising, and have come to pay him homage"' (2.2); 'There, ahead of them, went the star that they had seen at its rising, until it stopped over the place where the child was. When they saw that the star had stopped, they were overwhelmed with joy' (2.9-10) – prophecy fulfilled: '…to fulfil what had been spoken through the prophet: "Look, the virgin shall conceive and bear a son…name him Emmanuel"' (1.22-23); '…it has been written by the prophet: "And you, Bethlehem, in the land of Judah"' (2.5-6); 'Then was fulfilled what had been spoken through the prophet Jeremiah: "A voice was heard in Ramah, wailing and loud lamentation…"' (2.17-18) – dreams: 'an angel of the Lord appeared to Joseph in a dream…' (2.13); 'an angel of the Lord appeared in a dream to Joseph in Egypt' (2.17)

3. Acknowledging that Luke is formally employing the conventions about origins might ease a shift in the scholarly consideration of Luke 1–2 in terms of concerns about issues of historicity, chronology, and source to include insights from rhetoric. What Luke is doing by employing encomiastic topics should help readers to appreciate Luke's rhetorical focus. This, alas, does not happen when scholars are unacquainted with rhetoric, the encomium and the *progymnasmata*.

4. Thus, it may be safely concluded that Luke is talking about Jesus in rhetorical terms that were conventionally employed by other narrators of ancient lives. Luke has a plan for talking honorably about Jesus, a plan also known to his audience. They might be said to expect that Luke would inform them in terms of these conventional topics.

Chapter 3

ENCOMIUM:
THE NURTURE AND TRAINING OF JESUS

> I am a Jew, born in Tarsus in Cilicia, but brought up in this city at the feet
> of Gamaliel, educated strictly according to our ancestral law, being zealous
> for God, just as all of you are today (Acts 22.3).

> This is the division of the encomium...then upbringing, which you will
> divide into habits and acquired skills and principles of conduct (Aphthonius,
> *Preliminary Exercises* 36 [Kennedy, p. 108]).

Readers might be tempted to go immediately to studies of education in
antiquity, but such a general approach does not fit the focus of this book.[1]
We began inquiring how Luke was trained to write prose, that is, how
he was educated. This has much to say about how he wrote his narrative
about Jesus in topics both recognized and expected by his audience. We
are following the hypothesis that Luke was trained first in progymnastic
rhetoric, one of whose genres was the encomium.[2] Thus, we shrink our
focus to what is contained in the rules for an encomium which have to do
with 'nurture and training'. The pattern of this book thus far, moreover,
has been to let the progymnastic authors speak for themselves.

Not all progymnastic authors considered 'nurture and training' in their
rules.[3] Moreover, they differed from one another both in terminology

---

1. Marrou, *A History of Education in Antiquity*; Bonner, *Education in Ancient
Rome*.

2. At issue are questions such as, *who* was educated? at *what age* and *how*? *what*
did they learn? what would their *social location* be, and *why* are they educated at
all? Although slaves could be educated by their masters, what about elites and their
retainers? See Kaster, 'Notes on "Primary" and "Secondary" Schools'.

3. An important issue is implied here, the identity of teachers and pupils in
antiquity. Just as we observed generational pedigree, so also did the ancients pride
themselves on their educational pedigree. But a digression into teachers and their

and content, depending on whether they were describing elites and civic leaders. In fact, there seems to be a tendency to combine two different categories into one, which seems to focus on education and upbringing in general. Although we have seen this material earlier, its importance warrants further attention.

Aphthonius	Hermogenes	Menander Rhetor[4]
[T]hen you will take up education (*paideia*), which you will divide into inclination to study (*epitēdeumata*), talent (*technē*), and rules (*nomous*) (*Preliminary Exercises* 36 [Kennedy, p. 108]).	Next, nurture (*trophē*), as in the case of Achilles, that he was reared on lions' marrow and by Chiron. Then training (*agōgē*), how he was trained (*ēchthē*) and how educated (*epipaideuthē*) (*Preliminary Exercises* 16 [Kennedy, p. 82]).	Next comes 'nurture' (*anatrophē*). Was he reared in [a] palace? Were his swaddling clothes of purple… discuss his education (*paideia*)… Then you must speak of his love of learning, his quickness, his enthusiasm for study, his easy grasp of what is taught him. If he excels in literature, philosophy, knowledge of letters, you must praise him (*Treatise* II.2.371.17–372.2).

Aphthonius seems to have the simplest and clearest categories: 'education', 'study', 'talent', and 'rules'. These categories befit a person of high status in training for a public role, and do not describe a general education. We add the comments of Cicero, whose remarks clearly reflect the encomiastic materials: 'Under manner of life (*in victu*) should be considered with whom he was reared, in what tradition and under whose direction, what teachers he had in the liberal arts, what instructors in the art of living, with whom he associates on terms of friendship, in what occupation, trade or profession he is engaged, how he manages his private fortune, and what is the character of his home life' (*Inv.* 1.24.35). As noted, this education was available only for persons of high status in training for a political role. As we saw earlier, these are the important topics:

students stands outside the parameters of this chapter. Nevertheless, see Vernon K. Robbins, *Jesus, the Teacher: A Socio-rhetorical Interpretation of Mark* (Philadelphia, PA: Fortress Press, 1984), pp. 87-108. See W.C. van Unnik, *Tarsus or Jerusalem* (London: Epworth Press, 1962).

   4. Menander Rhetor (*Treatise* II.2.371.17–372.2) in Russell and Wilson, *Menander Rhetor*.

1. *Technē*: skill, trade, craft, what one learns professionally: 'As he was of the same trade, he stayed with them...by trade they were tentmakers' (Acts 18.3; cf. Mk 6.3)
2. *Nomos*: custom, rule, principle, norm
   a) *any legal system*: 'One who has become a priest, not through a legal requirement concerning physical descent' (Heb. 7.16) is 'the law is binding on a person only during that person's lifetime?' (Rom. 7.1-4).
   b) Moses' system: 'When the time came for their purification according to the law of Moses' (Lk. 2.22)
3. *Agōgē*: conduct of life: '...my teaching, my conduct...' (2 Tim. 3.10).
4. *Ethos*: custom or tradition: 'He went to the synagogue on the Sabbath day, as was his custom' (Lk. 4.16).

Jesus according to the Encomium: Nurture and Training

The chief episode in Luke's narrative about Jesus' 'nurture and training' occurs in 2.41-52. None of the quasi-technical terms noted above are present here, but that does not mean that Luke is not making some comment on Jesus' nurture and training. We propose to consider the episode from these perspectives: (1) as an event in the socialization of Jesus; (2) as a *chreia*; (3) as a statement about 'nurture and training' commensurate with encomiastic criteria, and (4) as an expression of precociousness.[5]

Socialization

As noted, the thrust of the remarks in the *progymnasmata* about a person's 'nurture and training' seem slanted toward his education, i.e., formal schooling. But Hermogenes focuses on another aspect, namely, 'training', which might be called 'socialization': 'Then training, how he was trained (*ēchthē*) and how educated (*epipaideuthē*)'. Conceding that Jesus did not go to any school and so was not taught by a recognized teacher, he was nevertheless 'trained' in the ways appropriate for a boy to mature into an adult Israelite. If socialized, then new questions arise: (1) What is socialization? (2) Who (parents, kin) trained him? (3) If not book learning, what was he taught? and how? (4) What was the purpose of this training? (5) Was his training publicly recognized?

---

5. Was Jesus literate? Those who recognize Jesus' status as a peasant, argue against it. Others argue for it, but their arguments lack sophistication in terms of the social location of the peasant Jesus; see Paul Foster, 'Educating Jesus: The Search for a Plausible Context', *Journal for the Study of the Historical Jesus* 4 (2006), pp. 7-33.

What is socialization?[6] This term, which developed in the social sciences, describes the many sources of instruction which a person might receive, primarily in the family and immediate social groups (i.e., village and synagogue).

> 'Socialization', refers to very general knowledge of many various, common and typical things that make up a cultural world. It refers to what 'everybody knows' in that world, their 'high context' understanding of the world. Socialization includes tips on social skills, whom to trust or avoid, maxims to channel behavior, and narratives on which to depict the large canvas of one's world and one's place in life, in short, all one needs to function successfully.[7]

Socialization might come from many directions. How did Jesus become an observant Israelite?[8] Primarily he learned by experience and observation how to keep rituals and customs. For example, we consider that Luke, of all the evangelists, described how his parents raised Jesus— whether he was conscious of it or not. Luke affirms that Jesus was socialized from birth in terms of Israelite observance: circumcision on the eighth day and dedication on the fortieth day. Luke continues: 'Now every year his parents went to Jerusalem for the festival of the Passover. And when he was twelve years old, they went up as usual for the festival' (2.41-42). Passover is more than a personal rite such as circumcision or dedication, for it brings the boy Jesus beyond the primary social institution of family/kinship into the civic or political institution of the House of Israel. Moreover, the family went annually to Jerusalem to celebrate it. Thus it is said that Jesus had made pilgrimage every year before this,

---

6. John A. Clausen, *Socialization and Society* (Boston, MA: Little, Brown & Co., 1968), p. 7; Clausen offered this observation about socialization: '...the kinds of social learning that lead the individual to acquire the personal and group loyalties, the knowledge, skills, feelings, and desires that are regarded as appropriate to a person of his age, sex, and particular social status, especially as these have relevance for adult role performances'. We consider this an excellent description about what the encomia are concerned.

7. Neyrey, 'How Does This Man Have Learning?', p. 87.

8. An observant Israelite would 'keep' all the Commandments (Mt. 19.18-19) or a specific one, such as circumcision (Acts 15.5). Keeping all of them was very important (Jas 2.10). Moreover, keeping them perfectly was charged on Timothy, '...to keep the commandment without spot or blame until the manifestation of our Lord Jesus Christ' (1 Tim. 6.14). The disciples of Jesus required Gentile members to keep certain commands (Acts 21.25).

and so Luke's audience would presume that Jesus knew the feast, its ritual, and history. Luke, then, should be understood as stressing Jesus' socialization into proper Israelite 'observance', both in the institutions of kinship and of politics. His 'training' included learning to act and think as an observant Israelite. His 'training' obviously was not book learning, so much as social training.

But socialization extends beyond rituals which Jesus learned to cultural things such as obedience. How should a mature Israelite comport himself? The issue, then, is not information, but what values and virtues Jesus must learn so that he comports with the expectations of his peers. Derrett summarizes what proper socialization here would mean:

> A list of what we might call 'gentlemanly' qualities as the educated Hebrew understood them would be very short. 'Good conduct', 'deportment' was conveyed by the characteristic phrase *derek erets*, not quite 'the way of the world'...but rather 'conformity with the ideal norm, behaving oneself with propriety'—a complacent concept offering no challenge: good manners rather than good morals.[9]

What this meant, in fact, was 'learning obedience'. As Derrett remarked further: 'After a child reached the age of 5 he began to learn that the society was duty-oriented, not right-oriented...not one concerned about his rights; everyone wanted to know his duties and wished to be thought "worthy to fulfil them"...'[10] But obedience to whom? concerning what? In this chapter, we consider 'obedience' to be synonymous with 'socialization'.

What cultural meanings are contained in the term 'obedience?' In a subsequent article, Derrett elaborated on his earlier treatment of Lk. 2.41-52.[11] As many have noted, much is crowded into the Lukan remark that 'He went down with them and came to Nazareth, and was obedient to them' (2.51). It is often observed that 'obedience' is owed to two figures in 2.41-52: (1) 'I must be in my Father's house' and (2) 'He was obedient to them'. However we rank these duties of Jesus, Luke states that Jesus had much more to learn to be a respectable man, namely, the premier habit of filial obedience. Derrett speaks of a commonplace, a generality, about the importance of filial obedience: 'Society's requirement of obedience

---

9. J. Duncan M. Derrett, *Jesus' Audience: The Social and Psychological Environment in which He Worked* (New York: Seabury Press, 1974), p. 67.

10. Derrett, *Jesus' Audience*, pp. 34-35.

11. J. Duncan M. Derrett, 'An Apt Student's Matriculation (Lk 2,39-52)', *Estudios Biblicos* 58 (2000), pp. 101-22.

was stricter than the biblical text... Unquestioning obedience being the norm... Obedience, no matter how achieved, was what mattered'.[12] This does not require much support, as all know statements such as, '...Not my will but yours be done' (Lk. 22.42); 'Although he was a Son, he learned obedience through what he suffered' (Heb. 5.8); and 'Children, obey your parents in the Lord, for this is right. 'Honor your father and mother'— this is the first commandment with a promise' (Eph. 6.1; see Col. 3.11). As Jesus grew, he also 'increased...in divine and human favor', that is, obedient to God and parents. As Lk. 2.39-40 and 51-52 indicate, Jesus had much to learn from his parents, that is, proper socialization.

Can we indicate to what degree Jesus remained to be socialized when this episode ended? Obviously his nurture and training were incomplete, a judgment which Luke's audience will easily make about further need for his socialization. Luke communicates this in a narrative way through the juxtaposition of many contrasts and opposites in the story. Luke and his audience knew what was appropriate for a boy twelve years old, which serves as a foil for how the narrative tells a story of conflict and things out of place.

1. Place and time: while it was appropriate for Jesus to be in Jerusalem to celebrate Passover, at its conclusion he should have been on the road to Nazareth with his family; he remained and they travelled.

2. Conflicting rituals: while Passover was an appropriate ceremony[13] for Jesus to celebrate, the same cannot be said about his engagement in a challenge–riposte ritual with the Teachers in the temple. At Passover, membership in the House of Israel was generally confirmed, which contrasts with a particular status transformation ritual of challenge and riposte. Different players are found in each: Passover was celebrated by kin, whereas in the 'listen and question' episode, Jesus engages strangers; thus different interests are at stake; and different results occur.

3. *Dramatis personae*: peasant parents are juxtaposed with 'the Teachers' in the Temple, a contrast between kinsfolk vs. elites or countryside vs. city; moreover, they represent two different institutions (kinship vs. politics).

12. Derrett, *Jesus' Audience*, p. 35.

13. We are drawing on the anthropological distinction made between ceremony (a regularly repeated event, confirming role and status) and ritual (a once-and-for-all event, changing a person's role and status). See Jerome H. Neyrey, 'The Footwashing in John 13:6-11: Transformation Ritual or Ceremony?', in L.M. White and O.L. Yarbrough (eds.), *The Social World of the First Christians: Essays in Honor of Wayne A. Meeks* (Minneapolis, MN: Fortress Press, 1995), pp. 198-213.

4. Conflicting interests: Jesus seems unclear about whose interests he should serve, those of his Father or those of his kin. Shall we say, moreover, that each 'father' expected different things from this one son.
5. Duties owed, but to whom? Jesus has two sets of duties, to God and to family: 'Did you not know that I must be in my Father's house?' vs. 'Why have you treated us like this? Your father and I have been searching for you in great anxiety.' But he does not know how to accommodate both, nor has he yet any understanding of the appropriate priority of duties owed (see Acts 4.19 and 5.29).
6. Conflict of two institutions: in regard to the two institutions contrasted (kinship vs. politics), each requires an appropriate socialization and training. Jesus has superior knowledge suited to the political institution, but imperfect knowledge appropriate to his kinship institution. His parents know their duties, but do not understand Jesus' alleged duty to another Father. His performance before 'the Teachers' suggest suitable training for success in that institution, but his training for success in the kinship institution is demonstrably inadequate.
7. Tenor of Jesus' behavior: Jesus' self-assurance contrasts with the anxiety of his parents. Initially Jesus was in control, but they were not, which should not be so in the dynamics of a child–parent relationship. They searched for him 'with anxiety', only to be rebuffed with a remark which they do not understand, which is certain to keep them anxious.

Therefore, Luke and his audience, when considering the socialization of Jesus who is growing in maturation, would clearly see that Jesus still has much to learn. The arena of his incomplete training is that of learning obedience in his family, fulfilling their commands, finding his proper role and status there, and generally knowing what his parents, neighbors, and villagers expect of him.

Chreia

We refer readers to the important discussions of the genre *chreia* that were so prevalent and productive in the 1980s.[14] This literary genre proceeded according to a predictable choreography: (1) a wise or prominent person

---

14. The *chreia* enjoyed a long history in Greek literature; see Jan F. Kindstrand, 'Diogenes Laertius and the Chreia Tradition', *Elenchos* 7 (1986), pp. 219-43. Important current studies include Hock and O'Neil, *The Chreia in Ancient Rhetoric*, pp. 3-60; Mack and Robbins, *Patterns of Persuasion in the Gospels*; see also Burton Mack, 'Decoding the Scripture: Philo and the Rules of Rhetoric', in Frederick E. Greenspahn, Earle Hilgert, and Burton L. Mack (ed.), *Nourished with Peace: Studies*

(a claim implies), (2) is challenged by another, (3) whose challenge aims to demote the status and honor of the wise/prominent person, but (4) which is rebuffed by the clever response of the person challenged, (5) who retains his honorable status. As all know, such *chreiai* are considered the building blocks of the various episodes in the gospel narratives about Jesus. The story in 2.41-52 deserves to be considered in this light.

In fact, Luke's narrative in 2.41-52 is structured by means of two *chreiai*, one of which is incomplete, and the other narrated in full form. The first *chreia* (2.36-37) describes Jesus in a very formal setting, 'in the temple', in discourse with the temple's elite. Luke knows that his audience knows that such discourse is by no means neutral in tone: rabbinic traditions consist of asking critical questions and responding with defensive answers. The scene, then, is one of challenge–riposte.[15] We suggest that 'listening to them' means hearing their challenging opinions, and 'asking questions', the normal way in which challenge–riposte exchanges are described: a hostile question is answered with a hostile question. What we are not told is the claim of Jesus to be wise enough to engage in this conflictual discourse.

	First Chreia (2.46-47)	**Second Chreia (2.41-45, 48-52)**
Presentation of a prominent person	'After three days they found him in the temple...'	'Now every year his parents went to Jerusalem for the festival of the Passover. And when he was twelve years old, they went up as usual for the festival. When the festival was ended and they started to return, the boy Jesus stayed behind in Jerusalem, but his parents did not know it. Assuming that he was in the group of travelers, they went a day's journey. Then they started to look for him among their relatives and friends. When they did not find him, they returned to Jerusalem to search for him...'

in Hellenistic Judaism in Memory of Samuel Sandmel (Chico, CA: Scholars Press, 1984), pp. 81-115.

15. On challenge and riposte, see Bruce J. Malina, *The New Testament World: Insights from Cultural Anthropology* (Louisville, KY: Westminster/John Knox Press, 3rd edn, 2001), pp. 33-36, 40-53; Bruce J. Malina and Jerome H. Neyrey, 'Honor and Shame in Luke–Acts: Pivotal Values of the Mediterranean World', in Jerome H. Neyrey (ed.), *The Social World of Luke–Acts: Models for Interpretation* (Peabody, MA: Hendrickson, 1991), pp. 25-65 (29-32).

Challenge	'...sitting among the teachers, listening to them and asking them questions'.	'...When his parents saw him they were astonished; and his mother said to him, "Child, why have you treated us like this? Look, your father and I have been searching for you in great anxiety."'
Witty, clever response	'And all who heard him were amazed at his understanding and his answers'.	'He said to them, "Why were you searching for me? Did you not know that I must be in my Father's house?"' (a counter-question in response to a reproaching question)
Winners and losers	-------	'But they did not understand what he said to them'. 'Then he went down with them and came to Nazareth, and was obedient to them'.
Who ends up in control?	-------	'And Jesus increased in wisdom and in years, and in divine and human favor'.

Luke's narrative of the first *chreia* is incomplete, but will be resumed later to become a key element in the narrative. As is typical of Luke, he is preparing his audience for the increasingly hostile attacks which will come upon Jesus. Luke, moreover, does not tell us how and why Jesus was accepted into a controversial exchange with 'the Teachers' in the temple. But maybe Luke is only claiming that Jesus, a mere 'twelve years of age', is in communication with others of importance who recognized the precocious abilities of this mere boy.[16] Luke implies that Jesus was conversing in the temple for at least three days, confirming that 'the Teachers' continued to evaluate him as worthy of serious conversation. Those who know the genre of the *chreia* understand that the conversation with 'the Teachers' was formally a challenge to Jesus. As all know, rabbinic discourse was highly conflictual: one teacher's interpretation of Torah was challenged, and necessarily defended (see 20.27-40, 41-44). Thus when Luke says that Jesus was 'sitting among the teachers, listening

16. The recognition of Jesus' precocious wisdom contrasts starkly with the rejection of the testimony of Peter and John in Acts: 'Now when they saw the boldness of Peter and John and realized that they were *uneducated and ordinary men*, they were amazed and recognized them as companions of Jesus' (Acts 4.13, italics added). Peter and John were officially ordered to silence: 'So they called them and ordered them not to speak or teach at all in the name of Jesus. But Peter and John answered them, "Whether it is right in God's sight to listen to you rather than to God, you must judge; for we cannot keep from speaking about what we have seen and heard"' (4.18-20). Yet no one will doubt that Peter and John 'won' a victory.

to them and asking them questions', he is listening to their claims and challenging them with questions. This conversation is itself a challenge–riposte exchange. Who won? The subsequent remark serves as a referee's verdict on the contest: 'And all who heard him were amazed at his understanding and his answers' (2.47). The first *chreia*, although much compressed, praised Jesus' wisdom, that is, how he went about doing his Father's business.

Luke, however, narrates a second *chreia* in full form (2.41-45, 49-52). The wise person (Jesus) has already been presented to the audience through the telling of the first *chreia*: the precocious Jesus holds his own against the Teachers of the temple. This constitutes his claim to wisdom. But instead of Teachers asking him hostile questions, his mother takes up this role: 'Child, why have you treated us like this? Look, your father and I have been searching for you in great anxiety' (2.48). Make no mistake, according to the conventional genre of a *chreia*, this is a critical question, an attack. Jesus responds, as one would expect, with a counter-question: 'Why were you searching for me? Did you not know that I must be in my Father's house?' In one sense, his response argues that concern for his heavenly Father's affairs trumps his obligation to obedience to his earthly family. Thus, in one sense, Jesus gave an adequate response to the parental challenge: he won, sort of. But he did not win simply because his parents did not understand his answer: 'But they did not understand what he said to them'. The parental challenge to Jesus was *not* about his precocious knowledge, but about his failure to fulfil a very basic commandment, 'Honor your father and your mother'. Luke concludes the story by stating that his parents indeed won. Jesus' duty to his family in this case outranks his claim to be busy about his (heavenly) Father's business. 'Then he went down with them and came to Nazareth, and was obedient to them'. He may be 'obedient' to one Father, but he must learn obedience to earthly parents. After all, a noble boy must be properly trained.

Therefore, by telling the story in 2.41-52 in the form of progymnastic *chreiai*, Luke establishes several things. First, as regards a claim, the 'wisdom' of the boy is on display, and it implies a special source which was not due to any rabbinic training. The narrative characters themselves offer the challenges, by means of questions. Jesus quickly responds to both, answering one challenge but bested by the second one. His defeat, however, is not the destruction of this wise person, but the occasion for Jesus to return to school. His nurture and training are incomplete, but more training will remedy that. At twelve years old, Jesus is precocious beyond measure, but lacks training concerning how to fit into his kinship group. More than a boy, but not yet an adult.

Encomium

As we saw at the chapter's beginning, the encomiastic categories of 'nurture and training' focus on 'education...inclination to study... training...quality of his mind...love of learning, quickness, enthusiasm for study, easy grasp of what is taught'. This generally speaks to the formal education of elites, the recognition of them as qualified, official persons of high status preparing for public roles. Although the encomiastic categories are not formally named in Luke's narrative, this does not in any way argue that Luke is not aware of or is not following them. Luke establishes that Jesus was an apt student: he is learning how to celebrate Passover and how to be trained in proper obedience.[17] We argued above that Jesus was socialized to be an observant Israelite, but Luke and his audience would likely think in terms of 'nurture and training'.

Furthermore, one significant source of information on this topic is found in Paul's description in Acts about his own training and upbringing: 'I am a Jew, *born* in Tarsus in Cilicia, but *brought up* in this city at the feet of Gamaliel, *educated strictly* according to our ancestral law, being zealous for God, just as all of you are today' (Acts 22.3, italics added). Luke, in his report on Paul, definitely uses encomiastic categories about a person's 'origins': (1) origins and geography: 'born in Tarsus in Cilicia'; (2) origins and generation: 'I am a Jew'. Next Luke includes the categories we are investigating: nurture and training: 'educated strictly according to our ancestral law'. Luke also tells us the name of Paul's teacher, 'Gamaliel', who was introduced earlier as 'a teacher of the law, respected by all the people' (Acts 5.34). W.C. van Unnik assembled many literary parallels to these remarks, coming from various times and authors and genres.[18] His collection is the best evidence of the prevalence and significance of what we are studying here. Thus, it would seem that we are in the right place, with the appropriate tools, and observing a worthy use

17. He was properly 'trained'. A family observant enough to make an annual pilgrimage to Jerusalem for Passover implies many things. Because Passover was ideally celebrated in Jerusalem, peasant families from Galilee would mingle with other Israelites observing the feast, which both confirmed its centrality in Israelite piety and communicated information on its proper celebration. The feast was conducted according to a fixed formula, including proper telling of the story from Scripture and conducting the meal in a traditional manner. Jesus was socialized to know this collection of information and praxis. His 'training' presumably included observance of the dietary laws, Sabbath, and some traditional purity regulations, as well as the proper observance of annual festivals such as Rosh ha-Shana, Tabernacles, Hanukkah, Pentecost and the like.

18. Van Unnik, *Tarsus or Jerusalem*, pp. 19-27.

of them.[19] In Luke's actual use in Acts 22 of a technical vocabulary related to encomiastic concerns about 'origins' and 'nurture and training', we have proof that Luke knew them and expected his audience to recognize them.

Precocious

We noted above how all the progymnastic authors instructed writers to learn about the mental capabilities of person they intend to praise. 'Education', of course; but also 'inclination to study', 'quality of mind', 'love of learning', 'enthusiasm for study', etc. Occasionally a person being praised will be presented as precocious.[20] Many doxographers claim this for their subjects,[21] but we focus on one example contemporaneous with Luke, namely, that of Josephus. Of himself Josephus says:

> I made great progress in my education, gaining a reputation for an excellent memory and understanding. While still a mere boy, about fourteen years old, I won universal applause for my love of letters; insomuch that the chief priests and leading men of the city used constantly to come to me for precise information on some particular in our ordinances (*Life* 8-9).

He claims proficiency, 'great memory and understanding', which wins approval when the chief priests and leading men in turn seek 'to know my opinion about the accurate understanding of points of the law'. The topic of his knowledge is also significant, because it is Israelite to the core: 'points of the law'. Interesting, also, are the dates of these achievements, as both speak to 'childhood' and 'about fourteen years of age'. Finally, Josephus is in transition, for later at sixteen years of age, he formally studies the three chief sects, which entailed actually living an appropriate ascetic life. Eventually he chose to conduct himself 'according to the rules

---

19. In Phil. 3.5-6, Paul claims an exceptional nurture and training, but without use of rhetorical tags: '...as to the law, a Pharisee; as to zeal, a persecutor of the church; as to righteousness under the law, blameless'.

20. Although we are concentrating on precocious intelligence, the ancients also praised other aspects of youthful prowess, superiority in stature and strength, for example. See Charles H. Talbert, 'Prophecies of Future Greatness: The Contribution of Greco-Roman Biographies to an Understanding of Luke 1:5–4:15', in James Crenshaw and Samuel Sandmel (eds.), *The Divine Helmsman* (New York: KTAV, 1980), pp. 129-41 (136-37).

21. H.J. De Jonge, 'Sonship, Wisdom, and Infancy: Luke ii:41-51a', *NTS* 24 (1978), pp. 317-54 (322-23).

of the sect of the Pharisees, which is kin to the sect of the Stoics, as the Greeks call them'. Implied here is a status change between fourteen and sixteen years of age. This is, moreover, what precociousness looks like.

It appears that Luke is making similar claims for Jesus, even in terms of the same criteria.

Josephus		Jesus	
1	proficiency claimed	1	proficiency dramatized
2	reputation for great memory and understanding	2	amazement at his understanding
3	topic: points of the law	3	presumed, since interlocutors are 'Teachers'
4	confirmed: his opinion requested	4	listening to them and asking them questions...amazed at his answers
5	age: a boy, about fourteen years of age	5	age: he was twelve years old
6	between boyhood and youth[22]	6	between boyhood and youth

If Josephus is claiming to be precocious, then the same could be said of Luke's claim for Jesus. Josephus, however, was schooled ('progress in my education'); Jesus was not.

This comparison shows the importance of the various items in Luke's presentation of Jesus. They collectively speak to his nurture and training, in which Jesus is outstanding, because he is precocious.

Twelve Years of Age

Did Luke mean anything by stating that Jesus was 'twelve years old'? Does this have anything to do with the encomiastic categories of nurture and training? Some have incorrectly argued that Luke alludes to some sort of bar mitzvah, for which there is no evidence at this early period. Does Luke intend in any way to suggest a status transformation ritual suggesting that Jesus is transitioning from being a boy to a youth?

---

22. Josephus gives two dates. At 'fourteen' he was still a boy: 'While still a mere boy, about fourteen years old, I won universal applause for my love of letters'; but at 'sixteen' he claims to be old enough to make a life-time choice: 'At about the age of sixteen I determined to gain personal experience of the several sects into which our nation is divided' (*Life* 9-10).

Although we are not arguing that 'about twelve years old' indicates a rite of passage, such rites were common in the Greco-Roman world, such as the assumption of the *toga virilis*.[23] But Jesus, an Israelite, was younger than typical Roman boys who attained manhood in this way. Furthermore, any transition would be immediately erased by the remarks that 'He went down with them and came to Nazareth, and was obedient to them... And Jesus increased in wisdom and in years, and in divine and human favor' (Lk. 2.50-51). No, he was not transitioning into the status of a youth, much less an adult. He was not transitioning at all—yet.

Many argue in the literature on 'twelve years of age' that it refers to a time 'in between', that is, an age when a boy is more than a boy but not yet a youth. Several studies have pointed out how accurately Luke uses precise terms for the growth of Jesus from birth to near-adulthood: 'babe' (*brephos*, 2.12), 'child' (*paidian*, 2.40) and 'boy' (*pais*, 2.43).[24] Saburin's article argues that Luke puts great emphasis on the 'growth' of Jesus. In a convenient chart, he lists instances of 'growth' in the gospel and then in Acts, but we cite only those from the gospel:[25]

Luke's Growth Concept:

1.80   'And the child [John] continued to *grow* and to become strong in spirit'.

2.40   'And the child [Jesus] continued to *grow* and become strong, increasing in wisdom, and the grace of God was upon him'.

2.52   'And Jesus *kept increasing* in wisdom and stature, and in favor with God and men'.

On the basis of his study of 'growth' in Luke-Acts, Saburin argues that Luke considered 'twelve years of age' as part of Jesus' development from infant, to child, to youth, and on to adulthood. 'Twelve', however,

---

23. Beryl Rawson, *Children and Childhood in Roman Italy* (Oxford: Oxford University Press, 2003), p. 142: 'At 12 and 14 respectively, girls and boys were eligible to marry. The ages must have been associated with the onset of puberty... From that age, however, a boy might go through the ritual of attaining manhood by changing his boyhood garb (the *toga praetexta*) for the *toga virilis*. Ages known for this ceremony range from 15 to 18.'

24. Michael Golden, '*Pais*, "Child", and "Slave"', *L'Antiquité Classique* 54 (1985), pp. 91-104 (93); and Richard A. Saburin, 'The Growing of Christ: Understanding Luke 2:40, 52, in the Light of the Structural Pattern of Luke–Acts', *Journal of Asia Adventist Seminary* 10 (2007), pp. 15-25 (23).

25. Saburin, 'The Growing of Christ', pp. 20-22.

is a stage of incompletion. Saburin, moreover, is hardly alone in holding this opinion. H. De Jonge also expresses the same: 'The most notable implication of the statement that Jesus was twelve is therefore that he was not fully grown, had not reached the first stage of maturity, but was still in a phase of physical, spiritual, and intellectual development'.[26] Therefore, 'twelve years of age', while not an exact age marker in any of the schemes of development we recognize, can be culturally interpreted with some precision because it is *not* a marker of transition or recognized growth. It is doubtful that Luke's Hellenistic audience would recognize it as a definite year of transition between recognized and accepted developmental markers. And that is the point. More than, but not quite yet.

More than Bookends (2.39-40 and 51-52)

When we view Lk. 2.41-52 from the perspective of a progymnastic encomium, the final remarks in 2.39-40 and 51-52 deserve more critical attention. They are generally taken in a structural sense as a mere conclusions to their stories, a type of literary bookends.[27] But when we examine them in terms of the encomiastic category of 'nurture and training', we learn that much more is implied. Jesus, a 'babe' (*brephos*, 2.12), grew into a 'child' (*paidian*, 2.40), a period of development characterized by careful observance of the law. It began in the Temple after 'they had finished everything required by the law of the Lord', and continued in 'their own town of Nazareth'. But this stage of Jesus' socialization, which began with his family fulfilling the requirements of the Law (circumcision, 2.21; dedication, 2.22), appropriately continued with an annual pilgrimage to Jerusalem. Luke does not specify when this 'babe' (*brephos*, 2.12) was considered a 'child' (*paidian*, 2.40), but he labels that period of growth appropriately: 'The child grew and became strong, filled with wisdom' (2.40). As to his body, Jesus developed as a child would; but 'filled with wisdom' deserves careful consideration.[28] It is doubtful that 'wisdom' here explains the precociousness of the twelve-year-old boy. When Luke

26. De Jonge, 'Sonship, Wisdom, Infancy', p. 321.

27. For example, Bradley Billings, 'At the Age of 12: The Boy Jesus in the Temple (Luke 2:41-52), the Emperor Augustus, and the Social Setting of the Third Gospel', *JTS* 60 (2009), pp. 70-89 (71-72).

28. In encomiastic categories, certain achievements are called 'deeds of the body' and 'deeds of fortune': '...deeds, which you will divide into those of mind and body and fortune: mind, as courage or prudence; body as beauty or swiftness or strength; and fortune, as power and wealth and friends' (Aphthonius, *Preliminary Exercises* 36

says that Jesus, a child who 'grew and became strong', he is only saying what he had said about John, 'the child grew and became strong' (1.80). But John became 'strong in spirit', which is the counterpoint to Jesus' being 'filled with wisdom'. Minimally, both are developing appropriately as children, not as boys, with a village socialization which should not be taken as any kind of formal schooling.

Luke tells his narratives in the Gospel and Acts by means of many parallels, as in the beginning of his gospel with parallel annunciations to Zechariah and Mary.[29] Most who observe this simply identify it as a literary item, a 'parallel'; but we suggest that it be investigated in light of the encomiastic topics we have been considering.[30] When Luke is observed following encomiastic rules for 'origins', then we are justified in asking if he is also following encomistic criteria for 'nurture and training'.

John the Baptist	Jesus
Origins:	**Origins:**
– Geography: village in Judean 'hill country'	– Geography: Nazareth in Galilee
– Generation: Zechariah, priest of the division of Abijah; Elizabeth, a daughter of Aaron	– Generation: Joseph, of the house of David; Mary (tribe unspecified)
– Kinship of John and Jesus confirmed: '…your kinswoman Elizabeth has also conceived a son'	– Kinship of John and Jesus confirmed: '…your kinswoman Elizabeth has also conceived a son…Mary set out and went with haste to a Judean town in the hill country, where she entered the house of Zechariah and greeted Elizabeth'

[Kennedy, p. 108]). These 'deeds' are predicated of adult males, which Jesus certainly is not. Yet, it is not out of order for readers of this book to keep such categories in mind.

29. For a summary of this, see Joseph A. Fitzmyer, *The Gospel according to Luke I–IX* (Garden City, NY: Doubleday, 1981), pp. 313-15; for a more detailed analysis, see A. George, 'Le parallèle entre Jean-Baptiste et Jésus en Lc 1–2', in A. Descamps and A. De Halleux (eds.), *Mélangaes bibliques en hommage au R. P. Béda Rigaux* (Gembloux: Duculot, 1970), pp. 147-71; see also Charles H. Talbert, *Literary Patterns, Theological Themes, and the Genre of Luke–Acts* (Missoula, MT: SBL Press, 1975), pp. 44-45; Brown, *Birth of the Messiah*, pp. 250-52.

30. Rather than 'parallel', Luke is making a comparison (*synchrisis*) between them; see Martin, 'Progymnastic Topic Lists'. This article argues that Luke is employing one more topic from the *progymnasmata*, 'comparison'.

Special Events:	Special Events:
– angelic annunciation, birth by barren wife	– angelic annunciation: birth by virgin maiden
– sign: dumbness for disbelief	– sign: 'your kinswoman Elizabeth…'
– sign: voice restored	– sign: 'As soon as I heard the sound of your greeting, the child in my womb leapt for joy' (1.44)
– prophecy of greatness: 'Zechariah was filled with the Holy Spirit and spoke this prophecy… And you, child, will be called the prophet of the Most High; for you will go before the Lord to prepare his ways, to give knowledge of salvation to his people by the forgiveness of their sins' (1.76-77)	– prophecy of greatness: '…and you will name him Jesus. He will be great, and will be called the Son of the Most High, and the Lord God will give to him the throne of his ancestor David. He will reign over the house of Jacob for ever, and of his kingdom there will be no end' (1.31-33)
– inspired canticle: praise of God, 'He has shown the mercy promised to our ancestors, and has remembered his holy covenant, the oath that he swore to our ancestor Abraham…' (1.72-73).	– inspired canticle: praise of God, 'He has helped his servant Israel, in remembrance of his mercy, according to the promise he made to our ancestors, to Abraham and to his descendants for ever' (1.54-55).
	– angelic announcement of birth: '"Do not be afraid; am bringing you good news of great joy for all the people: to you is born this day in the city of David a Savior, who is the Messiah, the Lord…" And suddenly there was with the angel a multitude of the heavenly host, praising God and saying, "Glory to God in the highest heaven, and on earth peace among those whom he favors!"' (Lk. 2.10-14)
Nurture and Training:	**Nurture and Training:**
– 'the child (*paidion*) grew and became strong in spirit' (1.80).	– 'The child (*paidion*) grew and became strong, filled with wisdom; and the favor of God was upon him' (2.40).[31]

Luke may have safely assumed that 'the child' John remained in his kinship group, under the tutelage of both parents, presumably learning the 'craft' of his priestly father. Becoming a priest was much more a matter of instruction and imitation than book learning, so we do not need to imagine

31. In addition to this syncrisis, one should consult Parsons and Martin, *Ancient Rhetoric and the New Testament*, pp. 265-68.

John in any sort of school. How long should a 'child' remain in his kinship network,[32] especially if there was no specific future role that John would assume? Granted Zechariah prophesied about his prophet son, 'And you, child, will be called the prophet of the Most High' (1.76), Luke offers no indication of what kind of prophet his son would be.[33] John, moreover, never joined a group of prophets, and so we know nothing about how he was socialized into this role. Presumably, his 'nurture and training' occurred in his kinship group. As a youth, John would need nurture (food, clothing, shelter, etc.) for a very long time. Luke does not tell us when John left his kinship network and 'was in the wilderness'.[34] 'Wilderness', moreover, is unlikely a geographical desert place, inasmuch as we next hear of John at a river, performing washing rites, which many consider as a liminal or symbolic place. If these comparisons with Jesus are based on encomiastic topics, then we might assume that as Jesus became a public figure 'about thirty years old', a similar age could be imagined for John until 'the day of his manifestation to Israel' (1.80).

32. In fact, the cultural assumption is that a son would remain in his family compound all of his life.

33. The angel who announced the birth of John said 'With the spirit and power of Elijah he will go before him' (1.17); but the meaning of this is never given (not in 9.8 or 30-31). Concerning which prophet John will resemble, Raymond Brown (*The Birth of the Messiah*, p. 275) makes an important distinction: '...when the career is traced to infancy, the dominating model is that of a prophet like Samson ("a Nazirite to God from my mother's womb", Judg. 16.17; 13.7) or Jeremiah ("Before I formed you in the womb, I knew you...I appointed you a prophet to the nations", Jer. 1.14). In the latter Lucan statement, when the career is traced to the beginning of a preaching ministry, the dominating model is the standard opening of several prophetic books, e.g., "In the second year of Darius, the word of God came to Zechariah, the son of Berechiah" (Zech. 1.1).'

34. Once there was much discussion about whether John was an Essene; J.A.T. Robinson, 'The Baptism of John and the Qumran Community', in his *Twelve New Testament Studies* (London: SCM Press, 1962), pp. 11-27. Nolland, *Luke 1–9:20*, p. 149, summarized the arguments against the association of John with the Essenes: 'Despite John's own detachment from society, he does not stand over against normal life in society. Unlike the classical prophets, he does not address society as such, so there is not here a fundamental questioning of the structures of society, nor the exposure of unjust class behavior, nor a call for community action. However, over against Qumran apocalypticism, there is no call to leave society for a holy remnant, nor to leave behind the normal engagements of life for an exclusive attention to spiritual matters. Repentance bears its fruit in relationships between individuals in society'.

Therefore, when we read Lk. 2.39-40 and 51-52 in terms of encomiastic topics, we might consider them in this way. Luke 2.39-40 would indicate, as noted, the period of Jesus' development from 'babe' (*bephos*) to 'boy' (*pais*), that is, from birth to twelve years old. 'Nurture and Training' appropriate to this period would include: 'growth' in body (weight, height, dexterity) and in kinship behavior (to whom did Jesus owe duties? what was expected of him by family and peers?). We call this his initial socialization into the values, behaviors, expectations of family and kin. 'Filled with wisdom' certainly does not refer to any schooling, and may minimally mean that he was a fast learner of what was expected of a baby-becoming-a-boy, quickly enough to be considered precocious. Nor does it imply any sort of heavenly infusion of knowledge, which would surely have perturbed his family and village, as it later angered his peers in the Nazareth synagogue (4.16-30). In the light of 'nurture and training', God's 'favor' could be considered the grooming which special figures, such as Samuel, experienced.[35] Samuel, a youth under the tutelage of Eli 'did not know the Lord' then; but he enjoyed God's favor. Therefore, when we read Lk. 2.39-40 according to the encomiastic categories of 'nurture and training', Jesus was growing up, as Derrett noted earlier.

In 2.51-52, moreover, we do not find anything new or special proposed: 'He went down with them and came to Nazareth, and was obedient to them... And Jesus increased in wisdom and in years, and in divine and human favor'. Jesus returns to his kinship 'school', i.e., his family, where he learned a most important lesson, '...and was obedient to them'. This is the premier domestic virtue Jesus has definitely not yet learned. As would be expected of all boys, he 'increased' in 'wisdom', which in terms of 'nurture and training' would be skill in his father's craft and maturity in appropriate village behavior. The fact that he increased in 'divine and human favor' minimally expresses that he learned what others expected of him and fulfilled their expectations, thus earning 'favor' or honor. His socialization continued apace, the result of which will be his appearance at thirty years old, now recognized as an adult.

'About Thirty Years of Age' (3.23)

From examination of developmental patterns in the typical life span of ancient persons, we return to 'about thirty years of age', because it has some bearing on how Luke understands the completion of Jesus' 'increasing' in nurture and training. If 2.52 looks to growth and development, the next

35. Fitzmyer, *The Gospel according to Luke I–IX*, pp. 432, 446.

time Jesus appears on stage there is no doubt but that he has wisdom, maturity and heavenly patronage.[36] The next time marker in Luke states, 'Jesus was about thirty years old when he began his work'. Once more, we are inclined not to take this as a chronological marker, but as one that speaks culturally to the adult role of Jesus. 'About thirty years of age' implies that Jesus is now fully grown up, mature both in body and in character. George Buchanan[37] published a pithy note on the meaning of the age of Jesus when he began teaching, in which he remarked: 'The Jews reasoned that he must have been of the proper age to qualify for such a position'.[38]

When scholars isolate episodes in Luke's narrative, they are in danger of separating 2.52 from 3.23. Between these two markers ('twelve years of age' and 'about thirty years old'), Jesus becomes a disciple of John, that is, he went out to John, heard his teaching, and was administered a status transformation ritual by John into a new role and status. Much is implied in the remarks, 'And the Holy Spirit descended upon him... And a voice came from heaven, "You are my Son, the Beloved; with you I am well pleased"' (3.22). This signals a distinct transition into a public role of high status, which presumes that Jesus is now qualified to perform it. If in 2.52 Jesus was becoming 'obedient', and 'increasing in wisdom and in years, and in divine and human favor', this growth was eventually completed. To be sure, Luke portrays Jesus as having adequate nurture and training after his apprenticeship with John and the status transformation ritual in 3.22. 'About thirty years old', therefore, signals that Jesus has sufficiency of education, training, and wisdom for his new role and status. If one considers 3.23 in terms of encomiastic categories relevant to nurture and training, then Jesus is declared as having requisite learning, training and knowledge. Narration of his deeds would surely follow.

36. The very idea that an adult would have a patron is rarely recognized, but it is well described by Richard L. Rohrbaugh, 'Luke's Jesus: Honor Claimed, Honor Tested', in his *The New Testament in Cross-Cultural Perspective* (Eugene, OR: Cascade Books, 2007), pp. 31-44; originally published as Rohrbaugh, 'Legitimating Sonship—A Test of Honour: A Social-scientific Study of Luke 4:1-30', in Philip F. Esler (ed.), *Modelling Early Christianity: Social-scientific Studies in the New Testament and its Context* (London: Routledge, 1994), pp. 183-97.

37. George W. Buchanan, 'The Age of Jesus', *NTS* 41 (1995), p. 297. He is responding to M.J. Edwards, 'Not Yet Fifty Years Old', *NTS* 40 (1994), pp. 449-54.

38. See also George Ogg, 'The Age of Jesus When He Taught', *NTS* 5 (1959), pp. 291-98 (292-93).

Summary and Conclusions

1. We now know the encomiastic topics of 'nurture and training' as found in the *progymnasmata*. Knowledge of these increases our understanding of the conventional contents of an encomium.

2. Although Luke does not identify episodes in Jesus' upbringing according to the typical terms used in the encomium, there is no doubt that Luke is concerned to present an account of Jesus' nurture and training. Of course, he does use technical vocabulary in Acts 22. We who know the encomiastic topics can observe Luke's application of them in the narrative, from 2.39-52. Knowing them proves successful in identifying *what* Jesus knew and *did not know*, *when* he knew it, *who* were his teachers, and in *what institutions* this knowledge was necessary.

3. His 'knowledge', moreover, puts him in conflict with 'Teachers' in the Temple, as well as with his family. It served the interests of his 'Father', but not those of his earthly parents. As regards 'knowledge', Luke portrays Jesus as precocious, learned in the most significant area of knowledge necessary for political life in Israel, namely, knowledge of Torah. As regards socialization as an honorable male, Jesus is far from complete in 2.52; he lacks the primary household virtue of obedience essential for honorable living in his kinship group. His knowledge, moreover, is in the realm of controversy, as it will be later in his controversies with the Pharisees.

4. Both 2.39-40 and 41-52 state that Jesus was 'growing' and 'increasing' in the areas of social knowledge. Completion, however, lay in the future. Thus, times, such as 'twelve years of age' and 'about thirty years old', are not chronologically significant, but culturally so. 'Twelve' denotes that Jesus is more than a boy, but not yet a youth. 'Thirty' suggests that Jesus has attained the maturity and aptitude for his new role and status as teacher. Jesus' training, knowledge, and learning, begun in infancy, are complete by 'thirty years old', when he was an adult.

5. This reasoning urges a more continuous reading of Luke 1–4 as a unit in which important encomiastic topics serve as Luke's guide to his presentation of Jesus in cultural terms accessible to his audience. Inasmuch as it has been shown that Luke adheres to encomiastic rules for narrating 'origins', his following them also in regard to 'nurture and training' argues that he began his education mastering the genres of the *progymnasmata*. The hypothesis holds.

Chapter 4

ENCOMIUM:
ACCOMPLISHMENTS AND VIRTUES: WISDOM

...then you will compose the greatest heading of the encomium, deeds, which you will divide into those of mind and body and fortune; mind, as courage or prudence... (Aphthonius, *Preliminary Exercises* 36 [Kennedy, p. 108]).

You will say about...his mind that it was just, temperate, wise, brave (Hermogenes, *Preliminary Exercises* 16 [Kennedy, p. 82]).

Under wisdom, you should praise his legal experience, education, foresight, capacity for clear decisions about present needs...critical understanding of orators, ability to judge the whole sense of the subject from the prooemium (Menander Rhetor, *Treatise* II.415.26–416.4).

All ancients considered the actions or deeds of a person as the premier source of praise and honor. External circumstances (i.e. origins, physical prowess and fortune), while they influence character, are not determinative of it. What a man does, counts. But we must consider how authors and audiences in antiquity thought about 'deeds' and how they treated them in oratory or writing. In many *bioi*, after consideration of a person's origins and nurture/training, writers moved to the most important part of a biography, the actions, deeds, achievements, and pursuits of the subject. They rightly presumed that a person's character is manifested and displayed by actions and deeds. Biographies, for example, tended to focus on pursuits and accomplishments, namely, those appropriate to the role which the subject played. Thus, if the subject of the *bios* was a soldier or statesman or ruler or philosopher, the task of the author was to argue that his actions and deeds were fitting and praiseworthy. For a soldier, the actions and deeds which mattered were those of prowess, strength, courage, and perhaps command. Similarly, for a statesman, it mattered how he behaved in the assembly, what laws he proposed or opposed, and what was his success in forensic and deliberative matters. Although not a man of action, a philosopher was evaluated in terms of his wisdom expressed in his teaching, speaking and writing.

In the *progymnasmata*, however, students were instructed to follow a different path. After instruction on the conventional treatment of origins and nurture/training, they confronted the most significant part of the encomium, namely, finding praise in the character and behavior of a person, their accomplishments. They were guided here, moreover, by still more conventions reflective of their own cultural world, because they were taught to consider 'deeds' in terms of three topics: physical prowess, good fortune, and character. These three categories were known as 'deeds of the body' (strength, beauty, speed), 'deeds of fortune' (that is, external things, such as wealth, success, friends, etc.), and 'deeds of the mind'. The following examples from three progymnastic authors illustrate this clearly.

Hermogenes	Theon	Aphthonius
The nature of mind and body will be examined and each of these divided into several qualities. You will say about his body that it was beautiful, large, swift, strong; about his mind that it was just, temperate, wise, brave. After this you will draw on his pursuits; for example, what sort of life he led... As for externals, they include relatives, friends...luck etc. (*Preliminary Exercises* 16 [Kennedy, p. 82])	Since good things are praised and some good things relate to the mind and character, others to the body, and some are external to us... Important ethical virtues are goods of the mind and the actions resulting to these; for example, that a person is prudent, temperate, courageous, just, pious, generous, magnanimous, and the like (*Preliminary Exercises* 110 [Kennedy, p. 50]).	...then you will compose the greatest heading of the encomium, deeds, which you will divide into those of mind and body and fortune; mind, as courage or prudence... (*Preliminary Exercises* 36 [Kennedy, p. 108]).

Although we cite these progymnastic rules for an encomium, the triple classification they express is very ancient.[1] In Theon, the earliest extant

---

1. Many have argued that Aristotle's remarks in *Rhet.* 1.9.33-34 already reflect the conventions for collecting and classifying data for praising a person: 'All attendant circumstances, such as noble birth and education, merely conduce to persuasion...we pronounce an encomium upon those who have achieved something... Achievements,

progymnasmata, the convention was already clearly established, indicating that it had been formed previously in rhetorical writers:

> Since the good qualities are especially applauded, and since some of these good qualities are connected with the soul and character, others with the body, and still others are external to us, it is obvious that these three would be the categories on the basis of which we will be able to compose an encomium (*Preliminary Exercises* 110 [Kennedy, p. 50]).

And so there were three. But how were 'deeds of the mind' to be understood? Progymnastic authors regularly instruct their students to consider them in terms of the four canonical virtues, wisdom, justice, courage, and temperance. Nothing is left to chance.

Furthermore, Quintilian proposed two different ways of talking about a person's 'deeds'. They be treated either according to the chronology of the person's life or according to a thematic treatment. But even here, Quintilian follows the convention of praising deeds in terms of the four canonical virtues:

> **Chronology**: 'It has always proved the more effective course to trace a man's life and deeds in due chronological order, praising his natural gifts as a child, then his progress at school, and finally the whole course of his life, including words as well as deeds' (*Inst. Orat.* 3.7.15).

> **Character and Virtue**: 'Praise awarded to character is always just, but may be given in various ways... At times it is well to divide our praises, dealing separately with the various virtues, fortitude, justice, self-control and the rest of them, and to assign to each virtue the deeds performed under its influence' (*Inst. Orat.* 3.7.10-18).

in fact, are signs of moral habit.' In the development of rhetoric, the triple division into 'deeds of body, fortune and mind' became an established tradition. For example, *Rhet. Herr.*, 'The following, then, can be subject to praise: External Circumstances, Physical Attributes, and Qualities of Character' (3.6.10-11); Cicero, '[Praise and Censure] will be derived from the topics that are employed with respect to the attributes of persons; these have been discussed above. If one wishes to treat the subject more methodically, these may be divided into mind, body and external circumstances' (*Inv.* 2.177-178); and Quintilian, 'The praise of the individual will be based on his character, his physical endowments and external circumstances... Praise awarded to character is always just... At times it is well to divide our praises, dealing separately with the various virtues, fortitude, justice, self-control and the rest of them, and to assign to each virtue the deeds performed under its influence' (*Inst. Orat.* 3.7.10-18).

At this point we can see how the conventions of *bioi* differ from those of the progymnastic encomium. *Bioi* seem to be focused on a person's achievements (according to role or office); they attend to 'pursuits' which are, of course, honorable and appropriate for public figures.[2] Encomia, on the other hand, search for praise in a person's character, which is displayed by virtuous actions. And so, the progymnastic encomia focused on 'deeds of the mind', by which they understand the canonical four virtues. Thus, we find two quite different treatment of 'deeds', pursuits (*bioi*) and 'deeds of the mind', i.e. virtues' (*encomia*).[3] Because the encomia regularly interpret 'deeds of the mind' in terms of the canonical virtues, it would seem to be a development of philosophical discourse; thus philosophy influenced rhetoric.

The thesis of this book remains that Luke was using the genre of the encomium as the template for his story about Jesus. As we saw, he is fully and carefully following the encomiastic instructions for origins and nurture/training. This argues that we consider the deeds or Jesus according to the encomiastic instructions for finding praise in a man's deed, that is, in terms of 'deeds of the mind', by which we understand the four canonical virtues.

However, in Luke's narrative of Jesus' deeds, except for a coura-geous and noble death, no particular part of his story seems to contain a gathering of Jesus' virtues and deeds strictly classified by a specific virtue. Only a few ancient authors did such, whereas it was conventional to let the narrative express virtuous deeds, which an audience would appropriately recognize and label. This touches on the conventions of how a character might be described, either directly or indirectly. In his recent book, Burridge repeatedly observed that character was generally presented indirectly, that is, by actions and words which were not themselves labeled virtues or vices. In *What Are the Gospels?*, he consist-ently observed that, although noble actions might be treated directly, in general they were presented indirectly.[4] The proper classification, then,

---

2. Andrew Wallace-Hadrill, *Suetonius* (London: Duckworth, 2004), pp. 142-49.

3. Burridge (*What Are the Gospels?*) regularly classified some actions as 'great deeds' (pp. 142, 174, 201) which he distinguishes from 'virtues'. What he means by 'great deeds' might include one such as this, 'Atticus' greatness consists of avoiding public office and war, continuing his financial transactions and still managing to be a friend of everyone' (p. 142). Burridge's sources are exclusively Graeco-Roman *bioi*, and he seems to ignore rhetoric entirely.

4. Burridge, in *What Are the Gospels?*, repeatedly he remarks in the summaries at the end of his survey of methods of characterization, 'We have seen that character was usually depicted indirectly through words and deeds rather than by direct analysis'

depends on the acumen of the author and the socialization of his audience. Because we have already argued that author and audience were familiar with encomiastic topics such as origins and nurture-training, it is no speculative leap to expect that both would recognize a virtue illustrated by actions and deeds.[5] Much could be assumed in the 'high context' world of Luke,[6] which is so foreign to our modern 'low context' world where everything must be spelled out in detail. But, before we embark on this journey, we are confronted with a serious bump in the road.

The Canonical Virtues: Present, but Absent

Since Plato, most ancient rhetoricians and philosophers acknowledge four canonical virtues: wisdom, justice, courage and self-control. The following chapters will each begin with definitions of the canonical four by ancient authors, to assure us that we are understanding them as ancient authors and auditors did. But as we take up each of the four as mandated in the rules for the encomium in the *progymnasmata*, we face a serious problem: the very words used to list them in rhetoric will be scarce or absent in Luke's narrative. This is not to say that Luke was unaware of these canonical virtues, only that he does not use those four words as identification tags for any of Jesus' words or deeds.

Most commentators on Luke-Acts never treat the topic expressed by the name of any virtue, simply because the words for them are not found in a document. Although commentators generally rely on sources such as Moulton and Milligan, BDAG and *TDNT* for the history and meaning

(p. 139); and 'Character emerges from the vast fund of stories about his subject. Thus, we conclude from all our *bioi* that the methods of characterization were primarily indirect, through narration of the subject's words and deeds' (p. 172). He argues that the same is true of the synoptic gospels (p. 199).

5. Aristotle directed speakers to avoid mere labels because description is more effective: 'Use of the description instead of the name of a thing…use metaphors and epithets by way of illustration' (*Rhet.* 3.6.1-4). 'Do not simply state virtues—e.g. 'he is just'—but treat the topic also by considering the opposite: he is not unjust, nor irascible, nor inaccessible, not judging by favoritism, not a taker of bribes' (Menander Rhetor, *Treatise* I.416.5-17).

6. In Chapter 1, we described the classification system developed by Hall, *Beyond Culture*. He distinguished different types of culture and how they assumed much or little. A 'high context' culture such as that of the Greco-Roman world dealt with the world in terms of conventions, traditions, and assumptions. The classic example is 2 Sam. 11.1, 'In the spring of the year, the time when kings go out to battle'. In a 'high context' culture, all would know what 'spring' meant, that is, the end of the late rains after which the ground had dried sufficiently to facilitate horses and chariots.

of words found in the New Testament, they invariably fail to make the crossing from commonplace classical usage to the biblical document they are considering. *TDNT*, for example, is generous in its treatment of the history of certain terms, but because the formal names of each of the canonical four virtues are rare in the documents under study, there is virtually no connection between background and biblical usage.[7] Therefore, on the one hand, the canonical four are identified individually as 'virtues' in the first part of an article, but that material is absent when the New Testament vocabulary is considered.[8] Rhetorical background yields to 'theological' meanings.

Modern readers, however, are regularly tagging certain behaviors as 'obedience', 'love', 'faith', and the like, even though the precise word is absent in this or that part of a narrative. We do this—correctly—because readers are already socialized to expect such behaviors and to label them appropriately. We argue for the same consideration of the relationship of each of the four canonical virtues to words and actions of Jesus. Because authors and audiences of the gospels were justifiably familiar with the canonical four virtues, we argue that they would understand the documents in terms of their cultural world, which were commonplaces in ancient rhetoric and discourse.[9] We are by no means imposing the labels of the canonical four virtues on the narratives, but only presenting native or emic ways of identification and understanding that permeated the cultural world of antiquity to see what they saw. When we learn the ancient language of the virtues, then we can begin to identify them operating in the narrative.

Rhetoricians will give definitions for a specific virtue, dividing them into parts and sub-parts. But an author narrating the life of a person would never be so wooden as to resort to labeling an action 'just', 'wise', or 'courageous', much less divide it into parts. Luke, moreover, was composing a narrative, not writing a book on rhetoric. He would dramatize the virtue. For example, the author of *Rhet. Herr.* instructs students to 'use the topics of wisdom' by way of illustration:

7. In BDAG 987, only *sōphrosynē* is identified as a virtue; none of the others are given this honor.

8. Albrecht Oepke knows that 'courage' is a canonical virtue (*TDNT*, I, pp. 360-62), but leaves this out of consideration of the New Testament use of the word; likewise, 'justice' by Gottlob Schrenk (II, pp. 192-98), 'self-control' by Ulrich Luck (VII, pp. 1098-1102), and 'practical wisdom' by Georg Bertram (IX, pp. 220-30).

9. For example, Luke does not use the encomiastic label 'origins' to indicate what he is doing in Lk. 1–2; and his audience could follow him, even though 'origins' was not explicitly used; the same would be true of 'nurture and training'. Both author and audience were on the same page, so to speak.

> ...if we compare advantages and disadvantages, counselling the pursuit
> of the one and the avoidance of the other; if we urge a course in a field in
> which we have a technical knowledge of the ways and means whereby each
> detail should be carried out; or if we recommend some policy in a matter
> whose history we can recall either from direct experience or hearsay—in
> this instance we can easily persuade our hearers to the course we wish by
> adducing the precedent. (*Rhet. Herr.* 3.3.4)

Virtues, then, will be shown in deeds and expressed in speech.

'Wisdom' (aka 'Prudence')

The first virtue in the quartet is called in English 'wisdom' or 'prudence'.
While there are two Greek words used to express it, only one of them
needs our attention, namely, 'wisdom' which aptly translates *phronēsis*.
It is up to scholars to translate *phronēsis* as 'prudence', or 'knowledge',
or 'wisdom'.[10] Moreover, it can be expressed by a variety of synonym
or shades of meaning. In Greco-Roman culture practical wisdom might
imply sagacity or street smarts, as well as knowledge to plan a course of
action, and as ability to distinguish good from evil. It is, then, much more
than the precociousness of a twelve-year old boy, that is, *sophia* (Lk.
2.40, 52). We do well to let native informants define this for us, although
we realize that their definition best suits a statesman.[11] The following
synopsis of definitions illustrates, moreover, the consistency of understanding in ancient rhetoric.

10. For example, Fitzmyer, *The Gospel according to Luke I–IX*, p. 801; when
he commented on Lk. 16.8, he translated it as cleverness and shrewdness; Francois
Bovon, *A Commentary on the Gospel of Luke 9:51–19:27* (Minneapolis, MN:
Fortress Press, 1981), p. 801; he rendered it as 'acting intelligently'. Thus, it is much
more than informational knowledge.

11. The list that follows comes from rhetoricians' praise of public figures in the
Greco-Roman world, who are mostly elites, members of ruling bodies, and probably
literate. They make excellent sense in Plutarch's *Lives of Nobel Greeks and Romans*,
Suetonius's *The Lives of the Caesars*, and Josephus's portraits of Israelite Kings in
his *Antiquities*. One might well ask how these criteria would play out in the peasant
world of Jesus. When translated into Luke's vernacular, one would expect some
cross-cultural adaptation. The world of urban elites has little to do with the culture of
illiterate, agricultural peasants (see Acts 4.13-14).

Aristotle	Rhet. Herr.
It belongs to wisdom to take counsel, to judge the goods and evils and all things that are desirable and to be avoided, to use all the available goods finely, to behave rightly in society, to observe due occasions, to employ both speech and action with sagacity... Memory and experience and acuteness are each of them either a consequence or a concomitant of wisdom; or some of them are as it were subsidiary causes of wisdom, as for instance experience and memory, others as it were parts of it, for example good counsel and acuteness (*Virt. Vit.* 4.1-2).	We will be using the topics of Wisdom if we compare advantages and disadvantages, counseling the pursuit of the one and the avoidance of the other; if we urge a course in a field in which we have a technical knowledge of the ways and means whereby each detail should be carried out; or if we recommend some policy in a matter whose history we can recall either from direct experience or hearsay—in this instance we can easily persuade our hearers to the course we wish by adducing the precedent (3.3.4).

We have, then, two different definitions from two different rhetorical authors, and from different times; but they have much in common. Given the consistency of rhetoric in antiquity, we would expect them to share many common items, such as practical wisdom (*phronēsis*), which was often considered the mother of the other virtues, the most essential for the rest of them. It would be recognized if it counseled:

1. Judgment of what is good or evil, what is desirable and to be chosen or to be avoided, what is advantageous or disadvantageous.
2. A practical and expert knowledge of what is useful, even technical knowledge of the ways and means to achieve something.
3. Sagacity about what to say and do... Right behavior in society, in accord with conventional values, such as honor and shame.
4. Ability to recommend a policy, based on history and experience.
5. Memory and experience and acuteness to give good counsel; ability to persuade by adducing precedents
6. Foresight, capacity for clear decisions about present needs; ability to judge the whole sense of something from its beginning to its end.

Often ancients distinguished practical from theoretical wisdom,[12] a distinction needed to appreciate the practical character of the six items listed above. As is often noted, this wisdom functions to point out which

---

12. Aristotle makes this distinction in *Nich. Eth.* 4.5-6 (1140a-1141a).

course of action is to be taken in specific situations. Practical 'wisdom' for the ancients, moreover, needs to be considered in terms of the values of that culture, in particular, the premier value of honor and shame; hence it means being savvy about how to succeed in a very aggressive world— their world, not ours.

The six common criteria for 'wisdom' are rather abstract, since they come from those who theorize about rhetoric and philosophize about virtue. We can, however, tailor that list to let it reflect the ways of ordinary people, and so make it more manageable for considering how Jesus might be portrayed as 'wise' in Luke's gospel. If ancient rhetoricians delighted in distinguishing and dividing, we counter with an attempt to consolidate. Therefore, we propose to study 'wisdom' in terms of the following classifications: (1) telling good from evil; (2) identifying sources of wisdom; and (3) considering it in terms of perspicacity or foresight. The most important among these three is the first, 'telling good from evil', and so we begin there.

Luke's Account of Jesus' Virtue of 'Wisdom'

Our hypothesis remains that Luke began his training by studying progymnastic rhetoric and learning what constituted the virtue of wisdom. He portrays Jesus as being exceptionally wise and savvy, especially in his ability to tell good from evil. Let us take each description of practical wisdom just mentioned as the template to bring to the surface illustrative materials in Luke's narrative.

We note, first of all, that Luke distinguishes practical wisdom (*phronēsis*) from *sophia*. For him *phronēsis* indicates cleverness and shrewdness, that is, savvy ways of acting (12.42 and 16.8); but in contrast, *sophia* seems to refer to knowledge of norms and customs that one learns (2.40, 52) or to sapiential wisdom (11.31, 49), namely, part of one's socialization. As we shall see, a savvy servant is one put in charge of the household to perform certain assigned tasks well (12.42), and the dishonest steward acts with cleverness in accommodating his master's debtors to his own advantage (16.8). Jesus, however, learned *sophia* at home (2.40, 52), which implies that he learned the norms and customs for an obedient boy and the correct behavior of a well-trained youth. But *sophia* also refers to knowledge of history and tradition, as in the case of the Queen of the South (11.31) or wisdom sayings (11.49). All of Luke's usage of these two terms may be seen below in contrast.

Practical Wisdom (*phronēsis*)	Wisdom Learned (*sophia*)
'With the spirit and power of Elijah he will go before him, to turn the hearts of parents to their children, and *the disobedient to the wisdom of the righteous*, to make ready a people prepared for the Lord' (1.17).	'The child grew and became strong, *filled with wisdom*; and the favor of God was upon him' (2.40).
'And the Lord said, "Who then is the faithful and *prudent manager* whom his master will put in charge of his slaves, to give them their allowance of food at the proper time?"' (12.42).	'And Jesus *increased in wisdom* and in years, and in divine and human favor' (2.52). 'The queen of the South...came from the ends of the earth *to listen to the wisdom of Solomon...*' (11.31).
'And his master commended the dishonest manager because he had *acted shrewdly*' (16.8).	'The Wisdom of God said, "I will send them prophets and apostles, some of whom they will kill and persecute"' (11.49). '...for I will give you *words and a wisdom* that none of your opponents will be able to withstand or contradict' (21.15).

Luke distinguishes wisdom-as-cleverness in many and various ways. The following are my suggestions about the face and sound of 'wisdom' in which Luke provides a narrative expression of this first virtue. The net is cast widely on purpose, because it is our judgment that wisdom was expressed in a wide variety of ways. All of these refer either to the words or actions of Jesus; that is, they describe Jesus' behavior, not abstract remarks by Luke himself about characters in his narrative (e.g., Lk. 1.6).

Jesus Can Tell Good from Evil
Practical wisdom does not concern itself with philosophical discussions of what is good or evil. Instead, it refers to the ability of a man with discerning judgment to distinguish good actions from base ones, honorable people from dishonorable ones, or what is advantageous from its opposite. Luke narrates a lengthy list of events which illustrate that Jesus was constantly distinguishing good (people, actions) from evil. We begin with mention of this fact which illustrates the type of wisdom characteristic of Jesus.

> No good tree bears bad fruit, nor again does a bad tree bear good fruit; for each tree is known by its own fruit. Figs are not gathered from thorns, nor are grapes picked from a bramble bush. The good person out of the good treasure of the heart produces good, and the evil person out of evil treasure produces evil; for it is out of the abundance of the heart that the mouth speaks (6.43-45).

In principle, there are good and bad trees, which are known by their respective fruit. Moreover, good fruit (figs, grapes) cannot be harvested from bad bushes (thorns, brambles). Both of these truisms serve as metaphors for good and bad persons: 'The good person out of the good treasure of the heart produces good, and the evil person out of evil treasure produces evil'. Both metaphor and application are clear and distinct, which is nothing particularly novel. But the final remark serves as the test of good/bad fruit or person. Without outward expression, one cannot know what is 'within' a heart or a treasure, until the person manifests goodness or badness in *speech*: 'It is out of the abundance of the heart that *the mouth speaks*'. Therefore, Jesus declares that there are good/bad persons, who are known by their speech.[13] Since the principle is clear, let us look at some specific examples.

Several times Jesus distinguishes two kinds of people on the basis of speech: some people only talk the talk, but others also walk the walk. 'Why do you call me "Lord, Lord", and do not do what I tell you?' (6.46; see 11.27-28).[14] Only at the end of the story does Jesus distinguish the non-action of his Pharisaic host from the courteous actions of the 'sinful woman'. Whereas Simon extended no etiquette to Jesus and so shamed him, the woman provided all that was absent and more (7.44-46). A verbal invitation to dinner differs from actual etiquette shown.

---

13. If this remark is intended to be thematic, then it applies to the endless verbal question–answer battles between Jesus and the Pharisees.

14. 'Lip service' was a common phenomenon in the ancient culture where honorable speech satisfied the public expectation of showing respect. The classic example is the contrast between two sons in Mt. 21.29-31. The second son did not embarrass his father in public, but gave lip-service to his command; the other son shamed his father by saying in public 'I will not', but honored him afterwards by doing the will of the father. Similarly, Mark chastises some Pharisees for lip-service of the commandment to 'Honor Father and Mother': 'Isaiah prophesied rightly about you hypocrites, as it is written, "This people honours me with their lips, but their hearts are far from me; in vain do they worship me, teaching human precepts as doctrines"' (Mk 7.4-6).

Discerning Advantageous from Disadvantageous

Wisdom manifests itself in a person who can distinguish what is advantageous from what is disadvantageous; thus a wise man can urge the proper choice. Sometimes Jesus only states that a certain action has a reward (*misthos*, 6.35), and observes that other actions come with credit or reward: 'What credit is that to you?' (credit = *charis*, 6.32, 33, 34). In fact, 'Your reward will be great, and you will be children of the Most High' (6.35). At other times, a simple gesture will earn a return greatly out of proportion to it: 'Give, and it will be given to you. A good measure, pressed down, shaken together, running over, will be put into your lap; for the measure you give will be the measure you get back' (6.38). But how to calculate what is advantageous (see 9.27)?

In one section of his gospel Luke has gathered together various statements by Jesus about sufficiency (advantageous) and insufficiency (disadvantageous). After talking about a rich person blessed with an unimaginable harvest (super sufficiency), Jesus says that he is 'not rich towards God' (12.20-21), and so suffers insufficiency. Jesus exhorts a husband and wife about their insufficiency. Jesus advises the landless male not to worry about food and his woolless wife not to worry about clothing. In his calculus, 'Life is more than food, and the body more than clothing' (12.23). The landless husband observes ravens, who 'neither sow nor reap, they have neither storehouse nor barn', but have sufficiency: '...yet God feeds them'. The woolless wife considers 'the lilies, how they grow: they neither toil nor spin'. But sufficiency: 'In fact, even Solomon in all his glory was not clothed like one of these'. Thus, 'Do not keep striving for what you are to eat and what you are to drink, and do not keep worrying'. Where is advantage here? 'Instead, strive for his kingdom, and these things will be given to you as well'. Obviously Jesus' appreciation of 'advantage' (mere sufficiency) is clearly not that of the itinerant husband and wife. He insists, however, 'Seek the Kingdom of God', where they will find sufficiency, '...and these things will be given to you as well'.

Advantage is regularly observed when rewards and punishments are juxtaposed. An honorable acknowledgment of Jesus is reciprocated with an honorable acknowledgment of that person, whereas a shameful rejection warrants a shameful return—and all of this taking place in the most honorable of public spaces, '...before the angels of God' (12.8-9). Later, two servants' behavior is contrasted, each with its own reward or punishment. The first servant awaits the master returning from a wedding feast and opens the door as soon as he arrives. The master responds to this honorable behavior with his own honoring of the servant, which is surprisingly hyperbolic: 'He (the master) will fasten his belt and have them sit down to eat, and he will come and serve them' (12.37). This is a world turned upside down (Acts 17.6), where the master serves the servants. But how advantageous! In contrast, the haughty servant flouts any authority over him, calculating that since 'My master is delayed in coming', there is no future accountability, and so he loses all control: '[He] begins to beat the other slaves, men and women, and to eat and drink and get drunk' (12.45). This slave lacks all 'wisdom', and so is completely shamed when the master surprisingly returns: 'The master of that slave…and will cut him in pieces, and put him with the unfaithful' (12.46). 'Wisdom' is greatly rewarded (advantage), but folly brings destruction (disadvantage).

Finally, Jesus recommends an unusual behavior by an appeal to advantage.[15] Where to sit as an invited guest? People in love with honor seek the first and best seats, but Jesus advises disciples to take the last and lowest ones.[16] The calculus which makes this advantageous is the hope that 'The host comes and says to you, "Friend, move up higher"; then you will be honored in the presence of all who sit at the table with you' (14.10). Only the promise of advantage warrants the savvy judgment: 'All who exalt themselves will be humbled, and those who humble themselves will be exalted' (14.11).

Similarly, whom should one invite to a meal? The savvy answer is to invite those who can reciprocate, but this does not accord with the wisdom of Jesus. He counsels against inviting 'your friends or your brothers or your relatives or rich neighbors' (14.12), based on an argument from advantage: 'They may invite you in return, and you would be repaid'. Inviting those who can invite in return is wise in the eyes of all attending, because it is advantageous (balanced reciprocity). But in Jesus' calculus of wisdom, one should 'invite the poor, the crippled, the lame, and the blind', who are socially stigmatized and undeserving of this honor. Why? Because it is advantageous: 'Because *they cannot repay you*, you will *be repaid at the resurrection of the righteous*' (14.14). As was the case with 12.8-9, the recompense for this 'foolishness' will occur in the most honorable place in the cosmos, namely, in the presence of God. Thus

---

15. K.J. Dover, *Greek Popular Morality in the Time of Plato and Aristotle* (Berkeley, CA: University of California Press, 1974), pp. 180-87; he discusses 'advantage' in terms of justice and reciprocity. This observation by no means cancels out consideration of 'advantage' in terms of practical wisdom to know what is advantageous or not.

16. Fitzmyer (*The Gospel according to Luke X–XXIV*, p. 1045) spotted the cultural value of honor in play: 'He lets it be known that real honor will come not from one's self-seeking choices, but from what is bestowed on one by another'.

Jesus regularly argues an un-wise series of actions which, while disadvantageous on earth, prove most advantageous in God's kingdom and according to God's calculus.

'Reading People': Knowing their Minds and Hearts

Jesus is not the only character in Luke who reads hearts or knows what others are thinking or what they are plotting. The angel Gabriel read the heart of Zechariah and knew his failure (1.20). John read the hearts of 'You brood of vipers' (3.7),[17] which is what prophets generally do. John, however, does not read Jesus well. In 3.15-17, he only alerts the crowds that 'One who is more powerful than I is coming'. As news about Jesus later travels, however, John sends messengers to Jesus with the question: 'Are you the one who is to come, or are we to wait for another?' (7.18-20). Jesus responds clearly, expecting that John will read him correctly (7.22), although not everyone who has seen or heard Jesus has a change of heart.[18] 'And blessed is anyone who takes no offence at me' (7.23, see 7.12). Jesus himself teaches the crowd how to read John correctly: 'What then did you go out to see? A prophet? Yes, I tell you, and more than a prophet. This is the one about whom it is written, "See, I am sending my messenger ahead of you"' (7.26-27).

But we focus on how Jesus and the Pharisees read each other, successfully and unsuccessfully. Because we consider it an important aspect of 'wisdom', it is worth recognizing how Jesus continually reads hearts, knows what people are thinking, and perceives their questionings and plottings.

> When Jesus perceived their questionings... (5.22).

> Even though 'he knew what they were thinking, he said to the man who had the withered hand, "Come and stand here"' (6.8).

> When Jesus perceived their questionings... (9.46).

> But he knew what they were thinking and said to them, 'Every kingdom divided against itself becomes a desert, and house falls on house...' (11.17; see 24.25, 38).

17. Bruce J. Malina and Richard L. Rohrbaugh, *Social Science Commentary on the Synoptic Gospels* (Minneapolis, MN: Fortress Press, 1992), p. 302.

18. The Pharisees did not read John correctly: 'By refusing to be baptized by him, the Pharisees and the lawyers rejected God's purpose for themselves' (7.30), and 'For John the Baptist has come eating no bread and drinking no wine, and you say, "He has a demon"' (7.33).

Luke expresses this wise ability of Jesus in another way, when he narrates how Jesus could see 'faith' in someone, namely, that a person accepted him as uniquely connected with God, and so took his healings as his credentials. Although we count seven of these instances, a sample will suffice. After the display of respect by a Roman military officer, Jesus read his heart: 'I tell you, not even in Israel have I found such faith' (7.9). After a woman touched him in public, seeking healing, Jesus said, 'Daughter, your faith has made you well' (7.50; see also 8.48; 17.19; 18.42).

We focus now on how Jesus, who can tell good from bad, reads his major critics, the Pharisees. Encounter after encounter with Pharisaic critics resulted in Jesus publicly reading them, not as having authority to make custom and law, but as 'hypocrites'—hypocrites, that is 'pretenders', who act and speak as though they had special abilities or authorization. They only masquerade as righteous. Their costume portrayed them outwardly as one thing, but the person wearing it was inwardly corrupt. They looked honorable to their public, but were hiding their true selves. The Pharisees, self-appointed guardians of the law, read Jesus as a non-observant person, who taught 'the Kingdom of God', but did not act as they thought one should act who was obedient to God's Law. In short, they read him as a hypocrite and worse. And Jesus returns the favor by calling them hypocrites.

Some cultural information may help here to assess how both Jesus and the Pharisees are reading each other. First of all, recent studies have shown that deception, ambiguity, and disguise were endemic in antiquity.[19] How difficult it was for anyone to penetrate public disguise and deception. This, moreover, is not just a New Testament problem. Even the word 'hypocrite' derives from a play-actor on stage, so that attendees saw only a mask, but discerned character only with difficulty.[20]

The public role of the Pharisees was that of rule makers and enforcers of Israel's purity rules in Galilee, and so they naturally became the primary critics of Jesus.[21] According to their construal of purity concerns, Jesus did not appropriately keep sabbath, nor fast, nor maintain distance

19. John J. Pilch, 'Lying and Deceit in the Letters to the Seven Churches: Perspectives from Cultural Anthropology', *BTB* 22 (1992), pp. 126-34; Jerome H. Neyrey, 'Deception, Ambiguity, and Revelation: Matthew's Judgment Sciences in Social-Science Perspectives', in Alan Avery-Peck, Daniel Harrington, and Jacob Neusner (eds.), *When Judaism and Christianity Began* (Leiden: Brill, 2004), pp. 199-230.

20. See Richard A. Batey, 'Jesus and the Theatre', *NTS* 30 (1986), pp. 563-74; Augustine Stock, 'Jesus, Hypocrites, and Herodians', *BTB* 16 (1986), pp. 3-7.

21. Anthony J. Saldarini, *Pharisees, Scribes, and Sadducees in Palestinian Society: A Sociological Approach* (Wilmington, DE: Michael Glazier, 1988), pp. 50-75, 174-98.

from 'sinners and tax collectors', nor practice washing rituals. In anthropological terms, they perceive Jesus as a deviant, in fact, a 'witch',[22] who is best dealt with in terms of their exposure of his hidden poison and their attempted exclusion of him from the group.

In such a context, the dynamics of labeling and deviance theory indicate conventional strategies for coping with such pernicious labels. The one of interest to us is called 'condemning the condemners'.[23] Basically it consists in a 'shift from the behavior of the alleged deviant actor to the motives and behaviors of those who disapprove of his or her violations. The condemners, it can be claimed, are themselves deviants in disguise; they are impelled by personal spite'.[24] This abstract description is realized in the accusation of hypocrisy against the condemners.

These opponents were feuding over significant matters. It was generally accepted that in principle the Pharisees protected the core of the law by outwardly building consecutive fences around it, thus making much of defending even the outermost fence. This became a strategy of intolerance, since they perceived that the least infraction was a plague which would eventually corrupt the core. Hence, they are known as those concerned with what is outside or on the surface. One can see this clearly in the following challenge–riposte exchange.

> A Pharisee invited him to dine with him; so he went in and took his place at the table. The Pharisee was amazed to see that he did not first wash before dinner. Then the Lord said to him, 'Now you Pharisees clean the outside of the cup and of the dish, but inside you are full of greed and wickedness. You fools! Did not the one who made the outside make the inside also?' (11.39-41).

The ritual of purification of hands before eating symbolized the guarding of the orifice of the mouth, a primary entrance to the inside of the body. Purified hands meant that clean foods would properly be put in the mouth; disregard of hand washing signaled unconcern for boundaries and for potential contamination. Jesus condemns his condemners by observing

---

22. 'Witch' is anthropological shorthand for a person whose exterior appears correct, but whose interior is corrupt, polluted, and aggressive. See Bruce J. Malina and Jerome H. Neyrey, *Calling Jesus Names: The Social Value of Labels in Matthew* (Sonoma, CA: Polebridge Press, 1988), pp. 25-30. See Jerome H. Neyrey, 'Bewitched in Galatia: Paul in Social Science Perspective', *CBQ* 50 (1988), pp. 72-100; Neyrey, 'Witchcraft Accusations in 2 Cor 10–13: Paul in Social Science Perspective', *Listening* 21 (1986), pp. 160-70.

23. Malina and Neyrey, *Calling Jesus Names*, pp. 63-65.

24. Malina and Neyrey, *Calling Jesus Names*, p. 64.

how Pharisees are concerned to 'clean the outside of the cup and dish', but neglect what is already inside them, 'inside you are full of greed and wickedness'. If they condemn Jesus for unconcern for things outside, he condemns them for ignoring what is already corrupt inside, that is, what is genuine, not potential evil. 'You fools!' God is concerned with both, the inside and outside.

The next figure gathers most of this mutual labeling recorded in Luke. Because Jesus' reading of the Pharisees results from their prior labeling of him as a disguised evil, we benefit from observing the labeling–deviance choreography in the narrative.

Pharisees Labeling Jesus	Jesus Labeling Pharisees
– 'He casts out demons by Beelzebul, the ruler of the demons' (11.15).	– 'Beware of the yeast of the Pharisees, that is, their hypocrisy' (12.1).[25]
– 'Who is this who is speaking blasphemies?' (5.21).	– hypocrisy for concern about tithes but 'neglect (of) justice and the love of God' (11.42)
– 'Look, a glutton and a drunkard, a friend of tax-collectors and sinners!' (7.34).	– 'For you love to have the seat of honour in the synagogues and to be greeted with respect in the market-places' (11.43).
– 'If this man were a prophet, he would have known who and what kind of woman this is who is touching him— that she is a sinner' (7.39).	– 'You are like unmarked graves' (11.44),
– 'The Pharisees and the scribes were grumbling and saying, "This fellow welcomes sinners and eats with them!"' (15.2).	– 'The Pharisees, who were lovers of money' (16.14).
Their Actions to Remove Jesus	**Actions Which Will Ruin Them**
– 'They were filled with fury and discussed with one another what they might do to Jesus' (6.11).	– 'Nothing is covered up that will not be uncovered, and nothing secret that will not become known' (12.2).
– watching, spying on Jesus (6.7; 7.39; 14.1).	

It is not enough to label one's opponents as hypocrites, they must be subjected to a public ritual of condemnation, which is the purpose of the 'woes' in Lk. 11.42-44.

Therefore, in many and various ways Luke presents Jesus as having astute practical wisdom. Fundamentally Jesus can tell what is good from

25. The ruler of the synagogue in 13.15 should be considered a Pharisee, because his criticism of Jesus is identical to theirs.

what is evil, what is desirable from what is undesirable, and what is advantageous from what is disadvantageous. Luke's audience may well ask by what criteria Jesus discriminates and distinguishes.

How Jesus Calculates his Judgments

Implied in Jesus' wise determinations is a calculus which in the world's eyes is folly and brings only shame. In its eyes, scales should be balanced: invitees should invite in return. By what calculus would anyone voluntarily choose shame and social diminishment? At a very minimum, the *lex talionis* should prevail: hurt is responded to with hurt, injury with injury, insult with insult. Shame is never an option and must never be considered.

But before the drama of Jesus' preaching tour begins, Luke has established a calculus which describes how God sees things. 'He has brought down the powerful from their thrones, and lifted up the lowly; he has filled the hungry with good things, and sent the rich away empty' (1.52-53). Thus Luke articulates a calculus in the very beginning of his narrative, which should be considered a topic statement of the way God sees the world, and so Jesus also. This calculus is publicly stated in Acts 17.6. Therefore, what is shameful in men's eyes may be honorable in God's eyes; and what is honorable in men's eyes might be shameful in God's eyes. Jesus, according to Luke, knows this calculus, which legitimates many of his 'wise' judgments.

We will examine Lk. 6.20-24 in this light later on in this book. But examples of this calculus of honor and shame function in many other of Jesus' remarks. For example, Jesus has two judgments to render about John the Baptizer. On the one hand, 'among those born of women no one is greater than John'; but 'the least in the kingdom of God is greater than he' (7.28). 'Greatest' and 'least' contrast John, who was 'proclaiming a baptism of repentance for the forgiveness of sins' (3.3), with the one who 'will baptize you with the Holy Spirit and fire' (3.16). John only prophesied the Kingdom, but Jesus began it. The calculus honors John, but honors Jesus more (see 3.15; 7.18-30).

In the eyes of men, it appears natural for the disciples to argue about who 'among them was the greatest' (9.46). But after Jesus articulated his calculus about honor and shame in 9.22, 23-27, such a competition becomes shameful. Wise man that he is ('aware of their inner thoughts'), Jesus corrects them by positioning a child—totally bereft of all honor—as the paradigm of honor (see 18.15-17). Jesus says two things. First, by this he declares where honor lies: 'Whoever welcomes this child in my name welcomes me, and whoever welcomes me welcomes the one who sent me' (9.48), which establishes a trajectory for true honor. And, second, it establishes a pattern, a reversal of where true honor resides, '...for the least among all of you is the greatest' (9.48b). The calculus is about honor and shame: who has it and why? Jesus, however, inverts the poles of great and least; in his eyes, being without conventional honor constitutes greatness, and vice versa (see 13.30; 14.11).

One more illustration may help. Jesus honors God, 'Father, Lord of heaven and earth', for God's calculus: 'You have hidden these things from the wise and the intelligent and have revealed them to infants; yes, Father, for such was your gracious will' (10.21). In Jesus' calculus, last is first and least is greatest; shame is honor, and honor, shame. Here, the 'infants' are declared wiser than the 'intelligent', because 'such was your gracious will'. Furthermore, a secret is told, and like all secrets, only a select few know, which is a mark of honor.[26] Luke also records a contrast between 'many' vs. 'few' (13.23-24).

Thus, in addition to knowing that Jesus judges, counsels and evaluated in terms of what is good or bad, advantageous or disadvantageous, Luke informs his audience of the calculus whereby Jesus makes these determinations. The calculus, moreover, extends throughout the entire gospel, from the Magnificat in 1.51-52, through the report on the words and deeds of Jesus, and especially into the values expressed in Jesus' shame-by-men, but vindication-by-God (9.22).

'How does this man have such learning?' (John 7.15)

'Where did this man get all this? What is this wisdom that has been given to him?' (Mk 6.2). The witness to the clever, savvy wisdom of Jesus lies in Jesus' socialization, his engagement with his culture, 'He went to the synagogue on the sabbath day, as was his custom' (Lk. 4.16). The synagogue was his school. Knowledge of the Scriptures and especially ability to employ just the right passage to the right problem was also part of experience in the synagogue. By surviving in a combative environment where the only game is challenge and riposte, Jesus became adept at an early age (see Lk. 2.46-47). None of these materials speak to encyclopedic information, but rather to the ability to wield the stuff at hand for attack and defense. They speak more to his training in controversy than to his informational education.

26. Jerome H. Neyrey, 'The Sociology of Secrecy and the Fourth Gospel', in F. Segovia (ed.), *What Is John?* II. *Literary and Social Readings of the Fourth Gospel* (Atlanta, GA: Scholars Press, 1998), pp. 79-109; John J. Pilch, 'Secrecy in the Mediterranean World: An Anthropological Perspective', *BTB* 24 (1994), pp. 151-57.

Inasmuch as the 'wisdom' described in the encomium is practical, not encyclopedic, how did a savvy man come by this wisdom? In the rhetorical definitions of 'wisdom', the sources of practical wisdom are: 'Memory and experience and acuteness' (Aristotle, *Virt. Vit.* 4.2); ancient audiences did not look at school education so much as at training. 'Memory, experience, and acuteness' are the results of proper socialization, which are learned in ways quite different from Paul's education: '... brought up in this city at the feet of Gamaliel, educated strictly according to our ancestral law' (Acts 22.3). In fact, Mk 6.2 and Mt. 13.54, as well as Jn 7.15, express the opinion of Jesus' peers that he had no such education. How can a lowly artisan, a 'carpenter, the son of Mary and brother of James and Joses and Judas and Simon' have wisdom to be so successful a teacher? 'How does this man have such learning, when he has never been taught?' (Jn 7.15). These remarks invite several considerations. (1) If not schooled, then of what did Jesus' socialization consist for him to have such knowledge and the skill to employ it? (2) What genres of expressing 'wisdom' were available to Jesus, an illiterate peasant?

Socialization

We have noted previously how Luke emphasized that Jesus made pilgrimage annually to Jerusalem to celebrate Passover. Moreover, Luke also remarks that Jesus attended synagogue weekly, 'He went to the synagogue on the sabbath day, as was his custom' (4.16). These two attest that Jesus was indeed socialized. Of whatever a synagogue service consisted (readings, psalms, prayers), Jesus had remembrance of these. This last point gives plausibility in Luke's view that Jesus knew the Scriptures well, which undergirds his ability to argue 'proof from prophecy'. Moreover, this memory of Scripture was indeed 'practical', in that Jesus is given credit for the ability to select passages and phrases from the Scripture to function as ripostes to challenges.

Rhetorical Genres for Expressing 'Wisdom'

We suggest the following genres as available ways for Luke to illustrate Jesus' wisdom: use of *exempla* and precedents,[27] metaphors and similes, and finally, maxims/proverbs.

---

27. Earlier we quoted Herrenius speaking about practical wisdom: 'We can easily persuade our hearers to the course we wish by adducing the precedent' (3.3.4).

Exempla *and Precedents*

Luke frequently mentions Jesus using *exempla* and precedents from the past in his argumentation. Jesus compared himself to Elijah and Elisha in two ways: they were rejected prophets and they brought God's favors to non-Israelites (4.25-27). He cites the example of David who 'entered the house of God and took and ate the bread of the Presence, which it is not lawful for any but the priests to eat' (6.3-4) to justify his disciples gleaning grain on the sabbath. Later in the story, Jesus cites Nineveh and the Queen of Sheba as examples of wise listeners who heard the word of God and acted on it (11.30-32), in contrast with 'this evil generation... who asks for a sign' (11.29). Speaking of the mysteriousness of the time of the Kingdom, Jesus compares his age to that of 'the days of Noah and of Lot' where people went blindly about their business with no heed to imminent danger (17.26-29). Although no precise example is given of Scriptural precedents for 'suffering and entering into glory', they are claimed (24.26-27).

Metaphors and Similes

In addition to *exempla* and precedents from the Scriptures, Luke reports that Jesus regularly employed similes and metaphors to make his point. Questions attacking Jesus, such as, 'John's disciples, like the disciples of the Pharisees, frequently fast and pray, but your disciples eat and drink' (5.33) are resolved by appeal to 'common sense' by means of similes, such as this two-pronged answer: first, a wedding feast takes precedence over a day of fasting; and second, new cloth is discontinuous as a patch on an old garment, just as new wine belongs in new skins (5.36-38)—commonsense, savvy replies. In addition to Jesus' use of Scriptural *exempla*, common-sense examples of human living count for much. Similarly, in response to the indignant criticism of the woman bent for eighteen years who came for healing on the sabbath, Jesus counters with a homely metaphor: 'You hypocrites! Does not each of you on the sabbath untie his ox or his donkey from the manger, and lead it away to give it water?' (13.15). Again, in answer to the shameful treatment of Jesus at Simon's supper, Jesus tells a story of two debtors, 'one owed five hundred denarii, and the other fifty'. The creditor 'cancelled the debts of both of them', itself a hyperbolic action, which served as the answer to the question, 'Which of them will love him more?' (7.42). What could be cleverer than to have the Pharisee himself answer this question: '"I suppose the one for whom he cancelled the greater debt". And Jesus said to him, "You have judged rightly"' (7.43). In conclusion, these similes and metaphors function as clever ripostes to challenges. Their ordinariness might be taken for granted, but they are savvy responses from a wise man to immediate criticisms.

Maxims, Proverbs, and Wisdom Sayings

As we begin consideration of Luke's report on Jesus' clever use of wisdom sayings, we suggest that what scholarship labels a 'wisdom saying' was taught in the progymnastic handbooks as a 'maxim'.[28]

Hermogenes	Aphthonius	Nicholas
Maxim (*gnōmē*) is a summary statement, in universal terms, dissuading or exhorting in regard to something, either making clear what a particular thing is (*Preliminary Exercises* 8-9 [Kennedy, pp. 77-78]).	Maxim (*gnōmē*) is a short summary statement, in declarative sentences, urging or dissuading something. Some maxims are protreptic, some apotreptic, some declarative; and some are simple, some compound, some credible, some true, some hyperbolic (*Preliminary Exercises* 25 [Kennedy, p. 99]).	Maxim (*gnōmē*) is a general statement, giving some counsel and advice for something useful in life…a maxim consists in a number of words, for while furnishing an enthymematic demonstration of the subject, at the same time it provides general advice (*Preliminary Exercises* 25 [Kennedy, p. 99]).

A 'maxim' is a short and general remark. It persuades or dissuades, and is useful in life. In short, it has no particular locus, only where it makes a point; it contains its own warrant and seems independent of a source. Nicholas notes that it has probative power, 'an enthymematic demonstration of the subject' (see Quintilian, *Inst. Orat.* 8.5.3). What makes it 'wise' or savvy? Does it tell good from bad? Maxims, proverbs, and savvy wisdom sayings are general and elastic and can be used anywhere. Their wisdom lies in their apt use to refute a criticism. Do these say anything about the savvy wisdom of Jesus?

Below is a list of maxims from Luke's gospel;[29] but, to read them as clever, savvy wisdom sayings, we must begin with another proverb which

28. Progymnastic definitions are necessarily concise, but Quintilian provides a fuller treatment of this (*Inst. Orat.* 8.5.1-35). At one point he notes that the Latin *sententia* is the equivalent of the Greek maxim: 'Although all the different forms are included under the same name, the oldest type of *sententia*, and that in which the term is most correctly applied, is the aphorism, called *gnōmē* by the Greeks' (*Inst. Orat.* 8.5.3).

29. Of particular usefulness in this regard is the work of John Dominic Crossan, *In Fragments: The Aphorisms of Jesus* (San Francisco, CA: Harper & Row, 1983). For a discussion of maxims in Paul's letters, see Rollin A. Ramsaran, 'Living and Dying, Living Is Dying (Philippians 1:21): Paul's Maxim and Exemplary Argumentation in Philippians', in Anders Eriksson, Thomas Olbricht, and Walter Übelacker (eds.), *Rhetorical Argumentation in Biblical Texts: Essays from the Lund 2000 Conference*

urges clever, savvy reading of cryptic things, such as parables. How common is the urging of Jesus, 'Let anyone with ears to hear, listen!' Jesus commands this again and again (Mt. 11.15; 13.9, 43; Mk 4.8, 23; Lk. 8.8; 14.35; Rev. 2.7; 13.9). We suggest that this proverb or maxim[30] calls for 'wisdom' (*phronēsis*) to search for the clever, savvy, and hidden meaning—hidden from the many, but accessible to the few. This proverb/ maxim implies that there are opposed understandings, not physical ears of differing capacities. Thus the proverb itself needs clever interpretation. Most of the time it concludes a parable, urging the clever and the wise to be alert. In Revelation, it urges the church at Ephesus to read the letter with sagacity: 'Let anyone who has an ear listen to what the Spirit is saying to the churches' (2.7); it also interrupts the presentation of the vision of the beast (13.9). Obviously, then, it urges a special kind of hearing or wisdom, which we consider practical wisdom. It is, then, the proverb to interpret all of the proverbs (Mk 4.13). And, it satisfies the rhetorical definition of a maxim by Hermogenes, as 'a summary statement, in universal terms, dissuading or exhorting in regard to something'.

Moreover, Luke records another proverb/maxim which explicitly urges clever and practical wisdom. After the parable about the steward, Jesus gives suggestions on how to make practical use of the story. The master of the steward praised the shrewd (*phronimōs*) behavior of the steward, thus labeling it 'wise' and contrasting it with un-shrewd judgments: '...for the sons of this world are shrewder in dealing with their own than are the sons of light' (16.8). Thus, two kinds of people are contrasted: those shrewd, like the steward, opposed to un-shrewd people. The difference lies in the possession of cleverness, wisdom, or *phronēsis*, for which there is praise and non-praise.

Although those who have eyes to see may offer more proverbs than those listed below, these are sufficient to make an argument here.

1. 'Truly I tell you, no prophet is accepted in the prophet's home town' (4.24).
2. 'Those who are well have no need of a physician, but those who are sick' (5.31).
3. 'They are like children sitting in the market-place and calling to one another, "We played the flute for you, and you did not dance. We wailed, and you did not weep"' (7.32).

(Harrisburg, PA: Trinity Press International, 2002), pp. 325-39. Curiously, however, although Parsons and Martin (*Ancient Rhetoric*) carefully discuss seven of the genres found in an encomium, they have very, very little to say about 'maxim'.

30. Commentators consider it so self-evident that they skip commenting on it as a proverb or maxim.

4. 'When you see a cloud rising in the west, you immediately say, "It is going to rain"; and so it happens. And when you see the south wind blowing, you say, "There will be scorching heat"; and it happens' (12.54-55).
5. 'The children of this age are more shrewd in dealing with their own generation than are the children of light' (16.8).

Since we have already commented on 8.8 and 16.8, let us examine the remaining three for common structure and purpose.

'Truly I tell you, no prophet is accepted in the prophet's home town' (4.24)
Although it is found in diverse places and serves diverse purposes, several classical usages are pertinent to how Luke employs it. We note three functions, all defensive: (1) 'to avoid humiliation'; (2) 'to reject a rejection'; and (3) 'to turn criticism back on its giver'. After Jesus spoke in the synagogue at Nazareth, attendees there reject what he said, effectively rejecting his right to speak. Jesus defends his honor by reminding them of this typical—and bad—behavior by Israel; he rejects their rejection and implies at the same time that he is an authorized 'prophet'. Finally, he challenges his challengers. His wise perception of the situation facilitates his clever adaptation of a defensive weapon, giving a riposte to their challenge. The wisdom here: wear armor, be prepared for battle.

'Those who are well have no need of a physician, but those who are sick' (5.31)[31]
This also is a common, widely known proverb, which illustrates the three functions mentioned above. The episode begins with a challenge to Jesus: 'Then they said to him, "John's disciples, like the disciples of the Pharisees, frequently fast and pray, but your disciples eat and drink"' (5.33). Jesus' riposte has two edges. How obvious (i.e., wise, savvy) for people to honor a wedding feast in preference to a fast day. Moreover, Jesus argues on the wise principle that he and his teaching should be discontinuous with past practice; no (wise) person sews new cloth on old, nor puts new wine in old skins. The proverb in 5.31 serves to seal Jesus' argument. Thus, it functions in a challenge–riposte exchange in which opposites are contrasted, one preferable to the other. In his exchange, Jesus avoids the humiliation of criticism, as he rejects others' rejection of his right to act the way he does; and he effectively condemns his condemners.

31. John Nolland, 'Classical, and Rabbinic Parallels to "Physician, Heal Yourself" (LK. IV 23)', *NovT* 21 (1999), pp. 193-209.

'They are like children sitting in the market-place and calling to one another, 'We played the flute for you, and you did not dance. We wailed, and you did not weep' (7.32)

After answering the question sent by John the Baptizer, Jesus gratuitously honors John, confirming the honor already given him by the crowds: 'And all the people who heard this, including the tax-collectors, acknowledged the justice of God, because they had been baptized with John's baptism' (7.29). In a sense, it belongs to Jesus' wisdom to declare John wise. But others judged differently: 'By refusing to be baptized by him, the Pharisees and the lawyers rejected God's purpose for themselves' (7.30). So, who is wise? Who judges wisely? Luke's audience already knows how to judge wisely. On the one hand, 'All the people who heard this...acknowledged the justice of God, because they had been baptized with John's baptism'. On the other hand, all know that 'by refusing to be baptized by him, the Pharisees and the lawyers rejected God's purpose for themselves' (7.29-30, italics added). Luke's audience knows now what wise judgment looks like.

How, then, do we understand the proverb in 7.33-34? As we shall see in a later discussion on the virtue of self-control, there has been no little controversy over the interpretation of the episode narrated in 7.31-35. The proverb under consideration sits in the middle of a story, and its meaning must surely relate to *all* of the characters there. First, the Pharisees, who were just judged, because 'By refusing to be baptized by him (John)... (they) rejected God's purpose for themselves' (7.30) are likely the referent of 'the people of this generation', to whom the proverb is addressed. Second, the main character, John, receives Jesus' lavish praise (7.24-28), balancing his rejection by the Pharisees (7.30). And, of course, Jesus. Wendy Cotter's excellent interpretation of this[32] argues that the proverb, spoken by Jesus, functions as an attack on the attackers of both John and Jesus. The central issue is their unreasonable rejection of John and Jesus on the basis of slanders about their eating habits. The proverb attacks Jesus' attackers (Pharisees?), because of their unreasonable rejection. Moreover, another proverb supports Jesus as it says, 'Nevertheless, wisdom is vindicated by all her children', that is, by John and Jesus. This proverb, then, typically exhibits the usual elements: (1) it is defensive in nature; (2) it functions to avoid humiliation because of scurrilous accusations; and (3) it condemns the condemners by contrasting the adult wisdom of Jesus with the minds of his critics, who are likened to children.

---

32. Wendy J. Cotter, C.S.J., 'The Parable of the Children in the Market-Place, Q (Lk) 7:31-35: An Examination of the Parable's Image and Significance', *NovT* 29 (1987), pp. 289-304.

The force of wisdom 'justified' cannot be underestimated, because it contrasts wisdom's children with the children of folly.

Therefore, let us gather together what we have come to know about proverbs/maxims in Luke. First of all, we expect that readers will consider biblical proverbs as examples of rhetorical maxims, whose description is found in the *progymnasmata*.[33] Maxims = proverbs = wisdom saying, at least on a popular level. Second, Luke makes general statements, which may function in any number of various settings, apropos particular contexts, thus giving them specific content and distinctive functions. Third, in Luke proverbs/maxims all occur in situations of challenge and riposte, such that the proverb constitutes the riposte to the challenge, a defensive function. Fourth, many parables operate on the basis of opposites, that is, contrasts between good vs. evil and wise vs. foolish. Therefore, the criteria noted above prove to be very useful in assessing just how a proverb functions: (1) to avoid humiliation; (2) to reject a rejection; and (3) to challenge a challenger. Moreover, Jesus' opponents totally reject his right to speak and teach, which issues in his rejection of their rejection. Therefore, the proverbs are excellent testimony to the cleverness, practical wisdom, and *phronēsis* of Jesus. He is a champion in the contest; he is the wisest player in the game.

Foresight: Seeing the Big Picture from Start to Finish

By this we mean that the savvy wise man is able to assess an action from beginning to conclusion, to take the long view, and to appreciate how cause and effect operate in events. According to the classical definitions of a maxim seen earlier, the wise and savvy man is credited with skills for perceiving how: (1) to judge the whole sense of something from how it begins to how it ends; (2) to recommend a policy in a matter whose history he can recall; and (3) to urge clear decisions about present needs. But, does this mean that a wise man can predict the future? How does a person in antiquity 'tell time?'

As we modern urbanites begin this inquiry, we should realize that we do not tell time as did the peasants of Galilee. We are all aware of the distinction between the way the Swiss reckon time and how the Mediterranean world does. Therefore, we must be culturally careful about what 'foresight' means for Luke, Jesus, and his agricultural audience. How did Jesus and contemporaries tell time? What terms for time are

---

33. Although Luke was trained in the theory of rhetoric, he did not himself write a rhetorical treatise. It is doubtful, moreover, that either Luke or his audience knew the many distinctions into which rhetoricians would divide the genus maxim/*gnōmē*.

we likely to hear in the gospels: 'So do not worry about tomorrow, for tomorrow will bring worries of its own. Today's trouble is enough for today' (Mt. 6.34). Jesus' preferred time word in Luke is 'Today' (4.21; 19.5, 9; 22.34; 23.43).[34] Jesus also speaks about 'today and tomorrow', but not in any sense that 'tomorrow' is future: 'If God so clothes the grass of the field, which is alive today and tomorrow...' (12.28) and 'Yet today, tomorrow, and the next day I must be on my way' (13.33).

In contrast, our modern culture prizes watches, clocks, timetables, schedules, date books, computers and smart phones which tell us instantly the 'correct time' and date. This greatly matters to people who commute to work and juggle complex schedules every day. Moreover, it is often said that modern folk are virtually ignorant of the past, of history, and of precedent. Everything is new every day, but with an eye on tomorrow's obligations. Furthermore, our culture virtually mandates that we live looking ahead, keeping before us the mortgages on our houses, the notes on our cars, the pensions for our retirement, etc. How totally foreign was the life of a peasant farmer from that of an office or factory worker. So we should expect that when we consider how Jesus and his peasant audience 'told time', we ourselves need some time travel to another cultural world.

This matter has been carefully studied, so that all is needed here is clarity on how ancient peasants told time. The emphatic mention above of 'today' as a cultural orientation contrasts with our calibration according to the future. Bruce Malina's presidential address to the Catholic Biblical Association forced scholarly attention to the problem of 'telling time' across cultures.[35] He was building on the work of anthropologists who were developing a cross-cultural model of how peoples in different cultures assessed 'time',[36] which has become accessible to biblical scholars, who in turn have employed it with profit to understand documents such as the

34. Hans Conzelmann, *The Theology of Luke* (New York: Harper & Brothers, 1960); he interpreted 'today' in terms of salvation history; here the term is more modestly considered in light of the anthropology of time.

35. Bruce J. Malina, 'Christ and Time: Swiss or Mediterranean?', in his *The Social World of Jesus and the Gospels* (London: Routledge, 1996), pp. 179-214; this is a reprint of his presidential address to the Catholic Biblical Association, 'Christ and Time: Swiss or Mediterranean?', *CBQ* 51 (1989), pp. 1-31.

36. Florence Kluckhohn and Fred Strodbeck, *Variations in Value Orientations* (Evanston, IL: Row & Peterson, 1961); Nancy D. Munn, 'The Cultural Anthropology of Time: A Critical Essay', *Annual Review of Anthropology* 21 (1992), pp. 93-123; Pierre Bourdieu, 'The Attitude of the Algerian Peasant toward Time', in *Mediterranean Countrymen: Essays in Social Anthropology of the Mediterranean* (ed. Julian Pitt-Rivers; Paris: Mouton, 1963), pp. 55-72.

gospels.[37] Thus 'telling time' is an aspect of one's cultural world, a part of how individuals operate successfully in their cultural context. As Malina's article warned us, it matters whether we tell time like the Swiss or like the people of the Mediterranean, especially agricultural peasants in Jesus' world. It has been observed that present-oriented people, i.e., Jesus and his peasant world, 'pay little attention to what has happened in the Past and regard Future as both vague and unpredictable'.[38]

It has often proved valuable for modern readers to compare and contrast their values and thought processes with those of antiquity in a chart which makes the differences salient. The following figure contrasts the outlooks of those who are present-oriented (i.e., New Testament world) with those who are future-oriented (i.e., USA today). We suggest that peasant time is 'present' and USA time is 'future'.

Present and Forthcoming Time Orientation	Future Orientation
1. Localization of objects and goals in the present.	1. Localization of objects and goals in the extended or distant future.
2. Activity occurs in the present to achieve proximate goals.	2. Activity occurs in the present to achieve remote goals.
3. Temporal integration makes the proximate forthcoming continuous with the present, yet with no personal control over the realization of outcomes.	3. Temporal integration makes the distant future continuous with the present, with cause–effect cognition that enables personal control in achieving outcomes.
4. The forthcoming derives from continued survival or existence; since survival is precarious, focus is on maintaining positive outcomes in the present in order to assure what is forthcoming; hence the assessment of the forthcoming is the same as the assessment of the present.	4. Future follows from the successful attainment of proximate goals relating to the future; survival in the present is taken for granted; hence the assessment of future goals directs present behavior.
5. The present drives and propels what is forthcoming.	5. The future drives and propels what is present.[39]

37. John J. Pilch and Bruce J. Malina, *Handbook of Biblical Social Values* (Eugene, OR: Cascade Books, 2012), pp. xxvi-xxxvii; John J. Pilch, *Healing in the New Testament* (Minneapolis, MN: Fortress Press, 2000), pp. 1-17; and Jerome H. Neyrey and Eric Rowe, 'Telling Time in the Fourth Gospel', *HvTSt* 64 (2008), pp. 291-322.

38. Pilch, *Healing in the New Testament*, pp. 14-15.

39. This chart depends on Malina, 'Christ and Time: Swiss or Mediterranean?', p. 186.

Where, then, do we locate 'forthcoming' or 'foresight'? These words
do not refer to anything 'future'. After all, trying to know the future
was fundamentally evil (Deut. 18.9-11); those attempting to know it
were shaming God for trying to access what belongs to God alone.
Furthermore, peasants did not consider the summer harvest as *future*
because of earlier sowing and plowing in the spring, neither the birth
of a child after a pregnancy. The end (harvest, birth) is already in the
beginning, and its fruition is continuous with it. Growing grain, while
a long process, is nevertheless a continuous one;[40] conception ending in
birth is a single process. One hopes that sowing will end in harvesting
and one desires that pregnancy will terminate in birth; but these are both
unsure, only forthcoming—if all works out well. Thus, we are advised to
consider time for ancient peasants as 'present-forthcoming', not future.
As we begin considering 'foresight', we repeat the classical definition of
wisdom as the ability to assess an action from start to finish, to take the
long view, and to appreciate cause and effect operative in an action, that
is, to have 'foresight'.

'Foresight' is not 'prophecy', nor is it related to 'prophecy-fulfilment'.
Prophets might indeed be given to speak about the future, an event discontinuous with what is currently happening. Thus in present time people are
told that something is awaiting them in a time and place discontinuous
with their present experience (i.e., the Messiah, the Kingdom of God);
they do not and cannot know what is discontinuous, especially when it
will occur. Present time they know, but future events are known only
to God (Mk 13.32), and to those to whom God reveals them. However,
when foresight is the perspective of a maxim or of savvy wisdom, the
wise man who uses it is credited with an astute present reading of present
time. The wise man understands that an action which is immediately
begun contains the seeds of its completion. The conclusion of an action
is already contained in the action itself, although many un-wise people
do not see this. 'Foresight', then, refers to a wise man's ability to see the
whole of an action.

Jesus appears particularly adept at seeing the large picture and thus
recommending a policy that will have a positive outcome. Unlike the
precariousness of agriculture and pregnancy, the outcomes he describes
are sure and reliable, not unlike death and taxes. Jesus can see that 'as
you sow, so shall you reap', but he often exhorts to behavior which is
not part of the regular ways of the world. Hence, the outcome is hardly
what disciples would experience as forthcoming, but he says that it is.

40. Nils A. Dahl, 'The Parables of Growth', *ST* 5 (1951), pp. 140-47.

After exhorting disciples to act out of the ordinary ('Love your enemies, do good to those who hate you, bless those who curse you', 6.27-28), they are told that such behavior is a 'credit' to them, with a result that is unimaginable: 'Your reward will be great, and you will be children of the Most High' (6.35). This reward, we argue, will be realized in the life of the person who so acts. A landless peasant and his wife are told to ignore immediate necessities like food and clothing, a bizarre strategy. Instead, 'Your Father knows that you need them. Instead, *strive for his kingdom*, and these things will be given to you as well. Do not be afraid, little flock, for it is your Father's good pleasure *to give you the kingdom*' (12.30-32). To a peasant such exhortation seems like folly, but Jesus is certain that the outcome is forthcoming. This seeking and receiving will occur in the lives of the man and the woman.

The wise always have justice before their eyes. But Jesus proposes actions which are foolish in traditional eyes, because they step apart from all recompense or *talio*. Where is the wisdom in 'Love your enemies, do good to those who hate you...if anyone strikes you on the cheek, offer the other also' (6.27-29)? On the other hand, if one gives, then 'It will be given to you...the measure you give will be the measure you get back' (6.38). But Jesus envisions, 'A good measure, pressed down, shaken together, running over, will be put into your lap' (6.38). Balanced reciprocity, the universal norm of 'today', is challenged by altruistic reciprocity, something not part of a peasant's dealing with people or kin.[41]

This 'wise' Jesus also urges calculation: will this beginning bring a favorable outcome? The classic illustration is Jesus' exhortation in 14.26-33. The context is discipleship; but, because Jesus considers discipleship costly, he is concerned about whether a would-be disciple knows what he is getting into. He begins this exhortation with a frightful warning: 'Whoever comes to me and does not hate father and mother, wife and children, brothers and sisters, yes, and even life itself, cannot be my disciple' (14.26-27). Think twice! In support of this he tells an illustrative story about wise calculation:

> For which of you, intending to build a tower, does not first sit down and estimate the cost, to see whether he has enough to complete it? Otherwise, when he has laid a foundation and is not able to finish, all who see it will

---

41. The appropriate cultural background to this is the anthropological model known as 'reciprocity'. Marshall Sahlins introduced this to students of antiquity: *Stone Age Economics* (Chicago: Aldine-Atherton, 1972); for New Testament usage, see Bruce J. Malina, *Christian Origins and Cultural Anthropology* (Atlanta, GA: John Knox Press, 1986), pp. 98-111.

begin to ridicule him, saying, 'This fellow began to build and was not able to finish'. Or what king, going out to wage war against another king, will not sit down first and consider whether he is able with ten thousand to oppose the one who comes against him with twenty thousand? If he cannot, then, while the other is still far away, he sends a delegation and asks for the terms of peace (14.28-32).

Jesus foresees that some will calculate correctly to become wise disciples of Jesus, and others won't calculate at all, for whom he foresees 'ridicule and mocking'. He is hardly predicting the future, only stating that there are two types of people, the wise and the foolish, whose success or failure is already contained in the actions they begin. Wise and prudent people can make a proper calculation; not so, un-wise or foolish people.

In a comparable situation, Luke presents another episode about discipleship (9.57-62). But as we approach the story, readers savvy about cultural differences will know that volunteering is very bad behavior in Jesus' world. So the teeth of audiences are already set on edge as 'fools' come to Jesus, because none of them seem to have done a proper calculus for discipleship. The first person states, 'I will follow you wherever you go' (9.57), but has no idea of the cost of this discipleship until Jesus responds, 'Foxes have holes, and birds of the air have nests; but the Son of Man has nowhere to lay his head' (9.58). Jesus equivalently tells him that hereafter he will have no home, no family, and no support, the same as his Master. Jesus invites the second man, but he has an immediate impediment. He puts family before Jesus: 'Lord, first let me go and bury my father'. Moreover, he did not calculate that Jesus would respond thus, 'Let the dead bury their own dead; but as for you, go and proclaim the kingdom of God' (9.60). A third person volunteers, but conditionally, '…but let me first say farewell to those at my home' (9.61). Jesus' response suggest that he did not calculate wisely first: 'No one who puts a hand to the plough and looks back is fit for the kingdom of God' (9.62). All three either volunteer to follow or are exhorted to follow Jesus. All three, however, are immediately told that family, household, and kinship must be sacrificed as the cost of following Jesus, a very steep price— folly in the eyes of their families. Jesus, the wise figure with foresight, sees these actions from start to finish and knows the price each must pay successfully to complete them. The volunteers do not. Wise man vs. foolish men; foresight vs. lack of calculus.

In Jesus' foresight, certain actions will be rewarded, some positively and others at great loss. While this would seem obvious, the Scriptures are filled with references to 'fools', who do not consider the consequences of their actions. For example, there are wise and foolish servants in the master's employ. Some are on alert: '...dressed for action with lamps lit; like those who are waiting for their master to return...so that they may open the door for him as soon as he comes and knocks' (12.35-36). These savvy servants are twice declared honorable in the story: '*Blessed* are those slaves whom the master finds alert when he comes...If he comes during the middle of the night, and finds them so, *blessed* are those slaves' (12.37-38). But shameful are the servants who calculate no recompense for their evil deeds:

> But if that slave says to himself, 'My master is delayed in coming', and if he begins to beat the other slaves, men and women, and to eat and drink and get drunk, the master of that slave will come on a day when he does not expect him and at an hour that he does not know, and will cut him in pieces, and put him with the unfaithful (12.45-46).

Clever and savvy servants are honored and profit greatly ('He will fasten his belt and have them sit down to eat, and he will come and serve them', 12.37). The foolish servant will fare miserably at the hands of his master, who 'will cut him in pieces'. Wise servants calculate how their honorable behavior will fare, but foolish ones live in a foolish world. Jesus, however, knows the fate of the wise and the foolish, how present actions will end.

Jesus concludes his sermon on the plain with a contrast between two kinds of trees, a good tree which bears good fruit and a bad one, producing bad fruit. This generalization is applied to two types of people hearing his words. Talk is cheap; actions speak louder than words; don't just talk the talk, but walk the walk. His remarks in 6.46-49 conclude his sermon on the plain with a contrasting description of success and failure, namely, how did each beginning fare? What results follow? First, he addresses those who only talk: 'Why do you call me "Lord, Lord", and do not do what I tell you?' (6.46; see 13.26). He then contrasts their conclusion with that of a person who 'hears my words and does them'. Both build a house, a necessary security, but one foolishly, the other wisely.

> I will show you what someone is like who comes to me, hears my words, and acts on them. That one is like a man building a house, who dug deeply and laid the foundation on rock; when a flood arose, the river burst against that house but could not shake it, because it had been well built. But the one who hears and does not act is like a man who built a house on the ground without a foundation. When the river burst against it, immediately it fell, and great was the ruin of that house (6.47-49).

The wise Jesus knows that the ways of the righteous and the unrighteous end differently. So, he can foresee the fates of those who build on rock or on sand. Fools, obviously, either don't know the end of their foolish way or don't care. Jesus, the wise teacher, does know.

When challenged to answer an aggressive question, 'Lord, will only a few be saved?', he side-steps this by challenging all in his audience to act wisely: 'Strive to enter through the narrow door; for many, I tell you, will try to enter and will not be able' (13.23). The prudent, who strive to enter, will in fact enter. But for fools, the door will be shut in their faces. Jesus warns the fools that talk is cheap, but what is needed is wise action: 'When once the owner of the house has got up and shut the door, and you begin to stand outside and to knock at the door, saying, "Lord, open to us", then in reply he will say to you, "I do not know where you come from"' (13.25). Familiarity doesn't count: 'We ate and drank with you, and you taught in our streets'. But that is not enough: 'Go away from me, all you evildoers' (13.26-27). The ways of the prudent and the foolish end differently.

Summary and Conclusions

1. We are now introduced to the encomiastic category of 'accomplishments' and its expression in the canonical four virtues, in particular, 'wisdom' or *phronēsis*. We know, moreover, that we are considering practical wisdom which is adept at cleverly assessing situations and at acting with savvy actions.

2. When all of the distinctions made by rhetoricians are digested, practical wisdom consists primarily of knowing how to discern contrasting things and persons: good from evil and the wise from the foolish. A person with this practical wisdom can distinguish the genuine from the fake, the true from the hypocrite. Because of this, the wise man can tell the advantageous from the disadvantageous, and so can urge wise persons to choose one and avoid the other. The wise man is adept at reading people, distinguishing a friend from a foe. He knows when others lie in wait for him to trap him. And he proposes actions to distinguish those who can complete a task from those who foolishly begin without calculating what it takes to finish it.

3. This information allows us to observe Luke constantly presenting Jesus as a very savvy, clever person. Luke has not gathered all instances of this in one place and prefaced them with terms suggesting this type of wisdom. Parables and healing stories are gathered according to genre, but not wisdom sayings. Rather, Jesus manifests this practical wisdom

throughout the narrative, but only when appropriate, itself a mark of practical wisdom. Furthermore, since all in Luke's world knew about this kind of wisdom (if only from Israel's proverbs) they were able to appreciate its various manifestations.

4. When we consider this, we ask on the basis of what values or customs did Jesus calculate his practical wisdom. What constituted wisdom or foolishness in his eyes? In the eyes of others? This question invited us to consider how unconventional Jesus' judgments were, unconventional in the eyes of many, but not so in God's eyes. Moreover, this depends on knowledge of cultural values, such as honor, to observe this calculation.

5. Whence comes this wisdom? Because it is less a matter of formal learning and more of experience, we argue that Jesus was socialized to know the slipperiness of practical decisions vis-à-vis the attempts of others to make rules and enforce them. Like most wise people, Jesus appreciates precedents found in Israel's Scriptures, which allow latitude in regard to the formal norms proposed by others—that is, when appropriate. For example, the hungry David! Moreover, Jesus has been socialized with the commonplace wisdom found in traditional maxims, proverbs and wisdom sayings—the stuff one learns at home, in a village, or in a synagogue. Because they are conventional, widespread, and convincing, Jesus' use of them indicates a clever way of defending himself and of proposing savvy solutions. Another aspect of practical wisdom is found in his ability to grasp matters from beginning to end, and to estimate how a particular beginning will end. In short, his foreknowledge expresses his ability to separate wheat from chaff, and the wise from the foolish. Alas, too few people seem able to make these judgments.

6. If practical wisdom is everywhere, then is it too loose an idea for audiences to spot and appreciate? Perhaps the correct response is, 'Let those who have ears to hear, hear'.

Chapter 5

ENCOMIUM:
ACCOMPLISHMENTS AND VIRTUES: JUSTICE

> First among the claims of justice are our duties to the gods, then our duties
> to the spirits, then those to country and parents. (Aristotle, *Virt. Vit.* 5.2)

As we continue examining the rules in the progymnastic encomium for
describing 'accomplishments', we do not presume to know the cultural
meaning of each of these virtues, especially what the ancients thought
about the virtue of justice. We must, then, become familiar with the
meaning of justice as discussed in Aristotle and in rhetoric close to the
time of Luke. A synopsis of rhetorical definitions of justice look like this:

Aristotle	Rhet. Herr.
To justice it belongs to be ready to distribute according to desert, and to preserve ancestral customs and institutions and the established laws, and to tell the truth when interest is at stake, and to keep agreements. First among the claims of righteousness are our duties to the gods, then our duties to the spirits, then those to country and parents, then those to the departed...' (*Virt. Vit.* 5.2-3).	We will be using the topics of justice if we show that it is proper to repay the well-deserving with gratitude; if we explain that we ought to punish the guilty; if we urge that faith ought zealously to be kept; if we say that the laws and customs of the state ought especially to be preserved; if we contend that alliances and friendships should scrupulously be honored; it we make it clear that the duty imposed by nature toward parents, gods, and fatherland must be religiously observed... (3.3.4).

Among the common items we find are: (1) distribution should be made
according to desert; (2) duties to fatherland, gods and family be kept;
(3) laws and customs be observed; and (4) loyalty (alliances, friendships,
and agreements) be honored. Why do this? While commentators notice
mention of 'justice' in Lk. 11.42 ('...you neglect justice and the love of

God'), they do not recognize it as one of the four canonical virtues, nor appreciate what it means in the Greco-Roman cultural world. Thus, when we consider the actions of Jesus in the light of the fulsome understanding of 'justice' stated above, we uncover materials simply passed over.

Jesus' Justice and his Duties

Although Paul exhorts the Romans, 'Owe no one anything, except to love one another' (13.8), normal human beings had many and various duties and debts. As noted above, in classical treatments of justice, we learn the commonplace that all mortals have duties, 'duties to the gods, to country and parents'. But in considering these three objects of duties, we should also make the common distinction which the ancients made between the two basic institutions in their world, namely, the institutions of politics and kinship,[1] for this effects how we consider the three objects of duties. While we accept that duties are owed to the gods, the *polis* and the family, we understand that duties to God belong to the political institution, as do those to the *polis*, whereas duties to parents reflect the kinship institution.[2] Thus when we examine Luke's treatment of justice vis-à-vis the behavior of Jesus, we find it necessary to make the same kind of institutional distinctions. At this point, we understand that Jesus' duties to God are expressed by various ways in which 'obedience' is expressed.

Duties to God

Luke expresses Jesus' debt of obedience to God most clearly in his use of the word *dei*.[3] Its frequency is a well-known fact that does not need to be repeated. But what matters is in what ways Jesus expressed that he had a debt to God.

---

1. In his *Politics*, Aristotle distinguished the state (political institution) from the household (kinship institution). For understanding Luke's distinction between the two institutions, see John H. Elliott, 'Temple versus Household in Luke–Acts: A Contrast in Social Institutions', in *The Social World of Luke–Acts: Models for Interpretation* (ed. Jerome H. Neyrey; Peabody, MA: Hendrickson, 1991), pp. 211-40.

2. Readers are reminded of the distinction made in the previous chapter concerning Lk. 2.41-52. 'Duties' there were owed to God ('my Father's business') and to family; moreover, inasmuch as Jesus is located in the political shrine, the Jerusalem temple, once again two institutions are contrasted, politics (temple) and kinship (family residence in Nazareth).

3. Charles H. Cosgrove, 'The Divine *DEI* in Luke–Acts', *NovT* 26 (1984), pp. 168-90; R.L. Mowrey, 'The Divine Hand and the Divine Plan in the Lukan Passion', *SBLSP* (1991), pp. 558-75.

2.49 Did you not know that I must be in my Father's house?[4]

4.43 I must proclaim the good news of the kingdom of God to the other cities also; for I was sent[5] for this purpose.

9.22 The Son of Man must undergo great suffering, and be rejected (17.25; 24.7)

12.50 I have a baptism with which to be baptized, and what stress I am under until it is completed!

22.37 This scripture must be fulfilled in me (see 24.44)

This term for Jesus' debt to his father extends from his earliest years (2.49), through his teaching (4.43), and unto his death and vindication (22.37; 24.26). We should also include here all of the times that Jesus prays (6.12; 11.1-4), his praise of God (10.21) and when he prays psalms (23.46 = Ps. 31.5).[6] We know that Jesus had duties to God and that he fulfilled them.

Duties to Israel

I am grouping here all of Jesus' observances which attest to his socialization as an observant Israelite. Indeed, 'Israel' is a political institution, and all acts of public piety are debts paid to this institution. Jesus was circumcised, dedicated on the fortieth day, and made annual pilgrimages to Jerusalem for Passover, all actions confirming that he was an orthodox member of the House of Israel.[7] Fasting is also a political action;[8] likewise

---

4. Commentators debate whether 2.49 should be translated as 'my Father's *house*' or 'my Father's *business*'. See the discussion of Nolland, *Luke 1–9:20*, pp. 131-32. Either way, duties to God are evident.

5. Many narrative characters in Luke send or are sent on tasks, which implies duties both imposed and received. But there is a special usage whereby persons of high rank (God) send agents (angels) on tasks, which are concerned with matters of great importance. Often Jesus acknowledges that he 'was sent' by God (4.43; 10.16; 11.49) or God's spirit 'sent' him (4.18). God's angels were sent to announce important births, such as that of John (1.19; 7.27) and Jesus (1.26). On the one hand, these commissions create a debt to God, who sends the messenger, and on the other hand, the person receiving the commission is likewise indebted to God (see also 14.32). All of these 'sendings' should be considered as occurring in the political institution of Israel.

6. For the sake of completeness, we should add the times when Jesus keeps Passover and his custom of attending sabbath synagogue. In these he is fulfilling his debt to God.

7. When Joseph obeys the command to register for the imperial census at Bethlehem, he fulfils a political duty (2.1-7).

8. Malina, *Christian Origins and Cultural Anthropology*, pp. 185-204.

attendance at synagogue. Jesus even instructed the cleansed leper to offer the appropriate sacrifice for his purification (5.12-17). Duties owed Israel are fulfilled in public, in the political institution.

Duties to Parents/Kin

The unique expression of this occurs when Jesus is twelve years old and remains in Jerusalem after Passover. On the one hand, he expresses his duty to God-who-is-Father, but not to his own parents: 'Did you not know that I must be in my Father's house?' (2.49); however, 'He went down with them and came to Nazareth, and was obedient to them' (2.51). However long a process his growing into adulthood took, he fulfilled his duties to his parents.

But, one must consider other remarks by Jesus which seem to be anti-family. It is an omission, to be sure, but Luke does not know the dispute about 'Honor your father and mother' found in Mk 7.9-13. But he has three collected sayings in which a potential disciple is told to prefer discipleship with him to kin and family, a radical change of duty (Lk. 9.57-62). Jesus has no house or kinship dwelling, and so a true disciple will be like his master, homeless and kinless. Even the hallowed task of burying a father is rejected in favor of discipleship; nor is a disciple allowed 'first to say farewell to those at my house'. The exhortation states that the duties of discipleship (duties to Jesus and to Him who sent him) are superior to kinship duties.[9] If, as many do, we take the syncrisis between his God-who-is-Father (2.49) and Jesus' human father (2.51) as a programmatic topic statement, then the anti-family materials in 6.20-24 and 9.57-62 exemplify once more that contrast.

Other Duties of Justice

Luke reports Jesus honors the fact that servants fulfil their duty as servants to their masters, that is, duties in the kinship institution: 'Do you thank the slave for doing what was commanded? So you also, when you have done all that you were ordered to do, say, "We are worthless slaves; we have done only what we ought to have done!"' (17.9-10).[10] Luke, moreover, is

9. For a social science treatment of this topic, see Jerome H. Neyrey, 'Loss of Wealth, Loss of Family and Loss of Honor: A Cultural Interpretation of the Original Four Makarisms', in Esler (ed.), *Modelling Early Christianity*, pp. 139-58.

10. The concluding maxim in 17.10 is hard to translate: 'So you also, when you have done all that you were ordered to do, say, "We are *worthless* slaves; we have done only what we ought to have done!"' Are they 'worthless' or 'unprofitable'? They state that they have acted out of duty to their master, and so they are worthwhile in two ways: first, '...when you have done all that you were ordered to do' means that they truly fulfilled 'all' their duties to their master; and second, '...we have done only

remarkable for the frequency of his references to 'debts'; his treatment of human debts, however, shocks many hearers, because one creditor cancels debts (7.42) and another greatly reduces them (16.5-6).

Justice and the Sermon on the Plain (Luke 6.20-49)

From the beginning of his gospel to the end of Acts, Luke paints a picture of a world structured by a general principle that persons get what they deserve. For example, Zechariah is struck mute because he did not believe the angel's words: 'Because you did not believe my words...you will become mute, unable to speak, until the day these things occur' (1.20). One thief silences the other one with a statement of retributive justice: 'We have been condemned justly, for we are getting what we deserve for our deeds' (23.41). This continues in Acts where Ananias and Sapphira are both struck dead for lying (5.1-11). For his blasphemy, Herod was devoured by worms: 'Because he had not given the glory to God, an angel of the Lord struck him down, and he was eaten by worms and died' (12.20-23). Although Paul escaped shipwreck, onlookers thought it only just that he be bitten by a viper: 'This man must be a murderer; though he has escaped from the sea, justice has not allowed him to live' (28.4). All of these episodes exemplify the classic definition of justice: 'as you sow, so shall you reap'. This was stated by Aristotle, 'to distribute according to desert', and in *Rhet. Herr.*, 'we ought to punish the guilty'.

To appreciate this properly, we must put it in its cultural context. In the world of honor and shame, the person shamed is obligated to seek redress for the offense he has suffered. His honor and that of his family and clan are at stake, and it is simply socially unacceptable to be shamed and not seek redress. Moreover, in the world of Aristotle and all ancients, it was considered virtuous, even 'noble', to seek revenge.

> To take vengeance on one's enemies is nobler than to come to terms with them; for to retaliate is just, and that which is just is noble; and further, a courageous man ought not to allow himself to be beaten. Victory and honor are noble; for both are desirable even when they are fruitless, and are manifestations of superior virtue (*Rhet.* 1.9.24-25).

The extensive literature on 'revenge' in ancient Greece indicates that Aristotle inherited a noble tradition and that subsequent writers basically

what we ought to have done!'—they are dutiful slaves. If one takes this maxim as an example of litotes, that is, understatement, they are hardly 'worthless', because they are dutiful slaves, who deserve approval.

repeated the discourse.[11] Nor is Luke the only evangelist to deal with it.[12] Thus, it was axiomatic for the ancients to think that 'to retaliate is just (and noble)'. Nor is Luke the only evangelist to deal with it.

We are considering the sermon on the plain (6.20-49) in terms of the virtue of justice (*talio* and retribution). Because it is always unwise to cherry-pick one piece of the narrative not only from its immediate context, but from the whole document, we think it wise to see to what extent Luke's narrative expresses the form of justice known as giving to someone what is deserved. Upon reflection, Luke's narrative contains many instances of various aspects of justice, that is, *lex talionis*, *quid-pro-quo*, and reciprocity.[13] The following figure is intended to classify the extensive data in Luke into types of reciprocity.

Justice and *Talio*/Reciprocity	Things apart from Justice
1. As you sow so shall you reap – Do this and you will live (10.25-28) – Everyone who acknowledges me… whoever denies me before others will be denied before the angels of God (12.8-9) – From everyone to whom much has been given, much will be required… (12.48) – Blessed are those slaves whom the master finds alert when he comes… (12.39) – What must I do to inherit eternal life? (18.18-21)	**1. Good requited with evil** a) John (3.18-20; 7.18; 9.9) b) Gerasenes tell Jesus to go away (8.26-28) c) all challenge–riposte: the Good Jesus is attacked d) evil is not requited (9.51-56)
	2. Requital juxtaposed to forgiveness – millstone as punishment (17.1-2) vs. forgiveness of wrongs (17.3-4)

11. See Fiona McHardy, *The Ideology of Revenge in Ancient Greek Culture: A Study of Ancient Athenian Revenge Ethics* (1999), published at https://www.academia.edu/28361076.

12. For Matthew's treatment of this material, see Neyrey, *Honor and Shame*, pp. 182-83, 191-95, 203-10.

13. On this topic, see Christopher Gill, Norman Postlewaithe, and Richard Seaford (eds.), *Reciprocity in Ancient Greece* (Oxford: Oxford University Press, 1998); among the many significant articles in this collection are those by Hans van Wees, 'The Law of Gratitude: Reciprocity in Anthropological Theory' (pp. 13-49); and by Robert Parker, 'Pleasing Thighs: Reciprocity in Greek Religion' (pp. 105-26).

2. Crime and punishment	3. Kindness to non-kin
– Zechariah: 'Because you did not believe my words...you will become mute, unable to speak' (1.20) – (ruin of Jerusalem)...because you did not recognize the time of your visitation from God (19.41) – enter narrow door vs. door shut (13.24-25) – (Jerusalem)...your house is abandoned (13.35) – We have been condemned justly... we are getting what we deserve (23.41).	– Samaritan to Israelite; who is neighbor? (10.29-37)
3. Justice and duty – 'Render to Caesar...render to God' (20.19-26) – duty fulfilled + reward (12.35-38, 41-44; 17.7-10) – duty unfulfilled + requital (11.42; 12.39-40, 45-47)	**4. Favor shown, which is not reciprocity** – you have hidden these things...and revealed them to infants;...such was your gracious will (10.21-22) – Blessed are your eyes (10.23-24) – Foolish Samaritan (10.29-37)

Readers need to keep in mind the amount of Lukan material that deals with justice as *talio*: 'as you sow, so shall you reap'. These data are present from the start of the narrative to its closing, and occur widely within it. This is the major melodic theme, which appears frequently in variations. There is other music, but it is modest in length and restricted in location. Readers, then, should have no doubt about the clear and extensive articulation of justice-as-*talio*. Every segment of the sermon on the plain, therefore, must be interpreted vis-à-vis this major melody.

6.20-26

The sermon begins with contrasting 'blessings' and 'woes'.[14] Those addressed are publicly acknowledged as 'blessed',[15] and positioned first in the sermon, a most honorable place.[16] We argue that both 'blessings'

14. No two interpreters of 6.20-26 will agree, and many interpretations are not argued sufficiently. My interpretation may be found in detail in Neyrey, 'Loss of Wealth, Loss of Family and Loss of Honor', pp. 139-58.

15. We understand 'blessed' in terms of its honor and shame culture, as argued by K.C. Hanson, '"How Honorable! How Shameful!" A Cultural Analysis of Matthew's Makarisms and Reproaches', *Semeia* 68 (1996), pp. 81-112.

16. Although the person in 6.20-23 is not designated as 'first', he occupies that position. This term is easily supplied in a high-context culture, because it is so

and 'woes' are expressed in terms of justice, that is, a *talio* or retribution. Starting with 6.20-23, we can discern a pattern: first, someone has been unjustly harmed, but that injustice will be redressed (not by the person harmed).

A Person is Harmed	But Harm is Redressed
Blessed are you who are poor,	for yours is the kingdom of God.
Blessed are you who are hungry now,	for you will be filled.
Blessed are you who weep now,	for you will laugh.
Blessed are you when people hate you, and when they exclude you,	Rejoice on that day and leap for joy for surely your reward is great in heaven
revile you, and defame you	for that is what their ancestors did to the prophets.

These harms are happening to *one* person; they result, moreover, because this person has made a choice, '*on account of the Son of Man*'. The first three statements result *because of the fourth* one, which is the *cause* of the wretched conditions of the person who has been made 'poor', 'hungry', and 'weeping'. This person has been most unjustly treated: '...people hate you, exclude you, revile you, and defame you'. In the perspective of Jesus the speaker, this person was been expelled, cast out, cut off from the very group who should support, feed, console and honor him. This person, moreover, is a disciple of Jesus, because all this happens 'on account of the Son of Man'. This disciple has been very unjustly treated—according to Jesus' judgment. But the injury is balanced with justice according to a *talio*, with a benefit accruing to him which greatly exceeds the harm done him. The man reduced to begging will be recompensed with a 'kingdom'; his hunger, with food; and his weeping, with laughter. The cause of these injustices will be surpassed by 'your reward is great in heaven', which implies that the person injured and treated unjustly on earth will enjoy a most honorable heavenly patronage. The issue is honor: dishonored on earth (by earthly father), honored in heaven (by heavenly Father). And the agent of this new honor is the Author of all honor.

Is this a matter of justice? The just person is unjustly injured; he himself cannot exact revenge on those who hurt him. But in a kingdom of justice, there is a figure who has power to reverse earthly injustices, nay, to greatly redress them. The dishonored man, then, is considerably better off in the end. Two aspects of justice are in view: first, harm is balanced

obvious. It distinguishes 'important' from 'unimportant', and denotes 'superior in value' (Lk. 15.22) and 'that nothing surpasses'. BDAG 893-94 explains it as: 'pertinent to prominence, first, foremost, most important, most prominent'.

with blessing, a *talio*, and second, justice-as-loyalty is displayed ('on account of the Son of Man'). Readers are reminded of the manifestations of justice mentioned earlier: 'We will be using the topics of justice if we say that faith ought zealously to be kept…if we contend that alliances and friendships should scrupulously be honored' (*Rhet. Herr.* 3.3.4). The man so harmed, we repeat, because of loyalty to Jesus; he has kept faith with Jesus, and Jesus keeps faith with him. 'Your reward is great in heaven' means that God, too, is keeping faith; thus 'alliances and friendships are scrupulously honored'. The man who is harmed keeps justice with God; and God acts with justice toward him.[17] Thus, Jesus speaks justice to the man done harm, which is expressed as retributive justice.

6.27-31

Much is made of the way 6.27-31 begins. Obviously there is specificity mentioned, 'But I say *to you* that hear…' (6.27). To some this suggests that 6.27-49 is addressed to a different audience than 6.20-26.[18] Luke, however, states that Jesus addresses a broad group, who are all his disciples: 'He looked up at his disciples and said…' (6.20). At the beginning, in the hearing of all, Jesus first declares honorable certain disciples, that is those who have already suffered unjustly 'on…account of the Son of Man'. And their loyalty is confirmed by the restoration of their honor, according to a *talio* which is out of proportion to the injustice done them. Thus, while Jesus has his eyes on his disciples, when he begins speaking, he speaks first to those who have proven their loyalty. But all disciples are hearing this. Those spoken to in 6.27-31 belong to the broad group to whom Jesus began speaking in 6.20; they have heard what he said to genuine disciples. The remaining audience, too, appears to have suffered unjustly; but since their loyalty remains to be tested, retribution for injustice shown them awaits. They are not yet 'honorable'. Thus, Jesus first speaks directly to tested, loyal disciples, and then he speaks more broadly to other would-be disciples. Those who heard the prior praise now hear Jesus addressing them.

Second, while there are differences between the hostility experienced by disciples in 6.20-23 and 27-36, they seem slight. The honored disciples experience 'hate…exclude…revile…defame' (6.23), and the persons next addressed suffer from 'enemies…hate…curse…abuse' (6.27). Both

---

17. The same is conversely true of 6.24-26, where the person causing injury will be repaid proportionately. Indeed those who have will become have-nots, as was stated in Lk. 1.51-53.

18. See Fitzmyer, *The Gospel according to Luke I–IX*, p. 637; Nolland, *Luke 1–9:20*, pp. 294-95.

experience undeserved verbal shaming, which in both cases results with a severe loss of public honor and respect. Thus, the unjust experiences of both are basically the same, except that restoration of honor is declared only to those first addressed.

Third, the victims in 6.20-23 gain some retaliation, but not by their own actions, but from a person of high rank and status. As a result, these vindicated disciples are told 'Rejoice on that day and leap for joy, for surely your reward is great in heaven' (6.23). Nothing is said about any retaliation for those in 6.27-36 who also have enemies and who experience only 'hate...curse...abuse' (6.27). While the shame of the disciple in 6.20-23 will be reversed, nothing is said about the reversal of shame for the victims in 6.27-36. Their loyalty is still being tested.

Fourth, who is doing these unjust things? Why are they acting so? We argued above that the disciples in 6.20-23 are the victims/disciples of Jesus whose family and kinship network disown and expel him. This occurs because the disciple walks with Jesus, and for no other reason. The reason why those in 6.27-31 are hated, cursed and abused is not stated, except that they are 'disciples'. There is no evidence in Luke that they are victims of social injustice; so, we are not certain who has hurt them and why.

The narrative of Luke, however, contains many acts of hostility to the disciples of Jesus: (1) they are attacked as surrogates for their master (5.30, 33; 6.1-2—'on account of the Son of Man'); (2) they are maltreated in families split over allegiance to Jesus (6.20-23; 12.49-53; 14.25-27); and (3) because they are the ones who 'who acknowledge me before others', they will be brought '...before the synagogues, the rulers, and the authorities' (12.11). There are no other remarks about others suffering shame and injustice in Luke's narrative. We insist that these are all disciples, not general people in Jesus' peasant audience. They are maltreated by their families and kinship groups, but are not victims of aggression or attacks on their honor. In the light of this, we find no reason to conclude that the audience in 6.27-36 is in fact different from that of 6.20-23.[19]

Finally, if justice and honor are restored to the unjustly treated disciple, is there any sense of justice or *talio* in 6.27-36? The actions urged to the one who has enemies, who is hated, cursed and reviled, are bizarre and

---

19. Many commentators argue for an interpretation in which there is no trace of justice or *talio*. For example, Nolland (*Luke 1–9:20*, p. 294) says: 'Identified in vv 20-26 as people of great good fortune through their poverty and identification with the Son of Man, the disciples are in vv 27-38 are directed to that love of enemy and nonjudgmental generosity by means of which they may come along with the plan of God in this time when fulfillment of God's eschatological purposes begins'.

foolish to those in that cultural world. As we noted above, throughout Luke's narrative a full, clear, and traditional appreciation of justice-as-*talio* is articulated. People are requited according to their deeds. Someone (God) returns evil for evil, and good for good. But now disciples should return good for evil. How to understand this?

One the one hand, all the deeds urged ('love', 'do good', 'bless', 'pray for') might be considered acts of justice, i.e., patronal benevolence, if our understanding of justice is wide enough. Menander Rhetor included in his definition of justice how benefitting another is indeed an aspect of justice.

> Under justice, you should include humanity to subjects, gentleness of character and approachability, integrity and incorruptibility in matters of justice, freedom from partiality and from prejudice in giving judicial decisions, equal treatment of rich and poor, encouragement of city development (*Treatise* 1.416.5-10).

But Menander described a patron bestowing benefaction on a client, which creates an honorable debt in the client; and justice requires that the client fulfil his debt, which is honorable to both patron and client.[20] Here, however, the disciple is not bestowing goods on a client and seemingly not in expectation of some return; he gives to 'enemies', 'those who hate you', 'those who curse you', and 'those who abuse you'. He is, then, not their patron honorably bestowing benefaction. He owes his enemy nothing and he has no debt to repay; his 'enemies' are his unjust oppressors. There is no justice envisioned here; no balance is achieved, no *talio*.

On the other hand, how does this look in terms of the cultural values of honor and shame? We argue that Jesus proposes a strategy which eventually will redress the dishonor shown the disciple; that means, injustice will be redressed by justice and shame by honor—eventually. But this is a *calculated strategy*, a series of actions, which in some cause-and-effect relationship eventually turn the tables. Shame will be turned into honor.

We find throughout Luke a *heavenly principle* whereby the mighty are brought low and the lowly are lifted up. God is claimed to do this, as Mary said: 'He has scattered the proud...and brought down the powerful from their thrones, and lifted up the lowly; he has filled the hungry with

---

20. See van Wees, 'Reciprocity in Anthropological Theory', pp. 45-47; also relevant are the articles in the same collection by Sitta von Reden, 'The Commodification of Symbols: Reciprocity and its Perversions in Mendander', pp. 255-61, and David Konstan, 'Reciprocity and Friendship', pp. 279-301.

good things, and sent the rich away empty' (1.51-53). Jesus, too, articulates this strategy: 'For all who exalt themselves will be humbled, and those who humble[21] themselves will be exalted' (14.10; 18.14). 'Exalt' speaks to the value of 'honor' (high status) and 'humble' to 'shame' (low status). The clearest example of this is found in the contrast between the Pharisee and the Publican in 18.10-14. The Pharisee exalted himself as the prime example of someone who 'trusted in themselves that they were righteous and regarded others with contempt' (18.9); he prays in an exalted manner, even making honor claims before God. The Publican, however, made himself small, both in stature and location, thus forsaking status and public respect. The result: 'This man went down to his home *justified* rather than the other'. The maxim cited in 14.10 and 18.14 proves true. This implies, moreover, that there is advantage to making oneself small, humble, or honor less. A balance of sorts will eventually arrive.

Although it will be discussed in the next chapter, Jesus himself knows and accepts this strategy and calculus.[22] He knows that he faces utter and complete 'shame' ('mocked, insulted, spat upon...flogged, killed', 18.32), but also that God will exceedingly honor him, by raising him (18.33).[23] The vindicated Jesus will eventually articulate this calculus: 'Was it not necessary that the Messiah should suffer these things and then enter into his glory?' (24.26). The way to 'glory' (honor) is through 'suffering' (smallness). There is much advantage here, because God will exalt the lowly.

This calculus often appears in maxims, such as 'Some are last who will be first, and some are first who will be last' (13.30). In an honor–shame

21. 'Humble' (*tapeinos*) according to BDAG 990 has to do with status, prestige, and so, honor; a humble person abjures advance in honor and is content in his current status; he is not seeking greater honor. It is possible that someone be 'humbled', which means one is shamed, lowered in status or social importance. What difference is there between being humbled and humbling oneself? In 2 Cor. 12.21, God humbles Paul, and so reduces his honor and status in the eyes of the community, which is what God is said to do in Lk. 1.52. Therefore, a person humbled is a victim. But if someone 'humbles himself', one is publicly admitting that he 'is powerless to defend his status. See Bruce J. Malina, 'Humility', in Pilch and Malina (eds.), *Handbook of Biblical Social Values*, pp. 99-100.

22. It is also the case that the disciples who would follow Jesus have to reckon with this calculus and act in a way which eschews pursuit of honor (9.23-27).

23. In the last chapter, we will observe how the statement, 'You shamed him on earth, but God honored him in heaven', attests to Jesus' posthumous honors. Nevertheless, it is a clear articulation of the calculus discussed here.

world, 'first' equates with high status and honor, but 'last' with low status and low honor. There assuredly will be a reversal, when last is first and least is greatest. Furthermore, the calculus informs the controversy about 'who is the greatest' (9.46). In contrast to disciples competing for honor, Jesus 'took a little child and put it by his side'. 'Child' must be interpreted in terms of honor and shame to serve as the corrective to 'who is the greatest' (9.46). A child takes orders, but does not give them (Lk. 2.51); a child has no recognized status (yet); a child has yet to compete for prestige. A child, then, has no honor at all, nothing to claim or defend. Thus, in Jesus' world, 'The least among all of you is the greatest' (9.48).

The disciple who loves his enemy would seem to be making himself low, nay, lower than before. His enemy who hates him would correspondingly be making himself large. Thus, the strategy to reverse this unjust and shameful imbalance is to lower oneself further. For, 'All who exalt themselves will be humbled, and those who humble themselves will be exalted' (14.10; 18.14), just as the way to enter into honorable glory is to accept dishonorable diminishment.

6.31—'The Golden Rule'

This is a maxim, a generalization which is made specific by an author's positioning. If considered as the conclusion to 6.27-30, it stands in opposition to the comments in 6.27-30, where a disciple is urged to self-lowering. Moreover, in 6.27-30 nothing is said about retaliation or retribution, except for the devious strategy of becoming small as the way to becoming great. Yet 6.31 describes a strategy which is basically a calculated act of justice, a *talio*. 'Do to others as you would have them do to you' (6.31). One does not act out of altruism (give, don't get) but out of reciprocity (give and get). If this is the norm, then 'loving one's enemy, etc.' is a strategy to have the enemy love you in return. Furthermore, its clear articulation of reciprocity also stands in considerable opposition to 6.32-36, where a disciple is urged to do more than the basic or ordinary: 'what credit is that to you...even sinners do the same'. 'The Golden Rule' proposes a balance, an evident *talio*, which is not at all what is urged in 6.32-35. Moreover, the ancient world operated on a different axiom: help your friends and harm your enemies.[24] It may be a 'golden' rule, but it is in conversation with what went before or comes after it.

24. Mary Whitlock Blundell, *Helping Friends and Harming Enemies: A Study in Sophocles and Greek Ethics* (New York: Cambridge University Press, 1989). See also Elizabeth Belfiore, 'Harming Friends: Problematic Reciprocity in Greek Tragedy', in Gill, Postlewaithe, and Seaford (eds.), *Reciprocity in Ancient Greece*, pp. 139-51.

6.32-36

Because of the repetition of 'love' in 6.32, many have assumed that what follows is a continuation of the previous remarks. Jesus, however, is not proclaiming the 'love commandment' here (see Lk. 10.27, 37; Jn 15.12-13). If one wants to know what 'love' means here, it basically means doing the opposite of the way one is treated. 'Love' is counseled as the proper response to those who decidedly do not love you: 'Love your enemies, do good to those who hate you, bless those who curse you, pray for those who abuse you' (6.27-28).[25] In regard to the dishonoring of one's own body, the abused offers more opportunity for shame: 'turn the other cheek'. He also accepts the humiliation of being stripped naked[26] with loss of basic clothing, a shirt and coat. Only a fool would 'give' or lend with no expectation of return.[27] If altruism expresses giving what is good with no expectation of return, these sayings celebrate negative reciprocity. Here one who receives bad returns good, with no expectation of any balancing or *talio*. Furthermore, Luke speaks in terms of honor and shame, not in terms of the virtue of love. Thus far in the Sermon on the plain, the issue has been justice and retaliation, not 'love'. The ancients, moreover, never classified 'love' as a virtue.[28]

But, the maltreated disciples in 6.32-35 have 'enemies', as do the persons in 6.27-30. Although the severity of the situation described in 6.27-30 is elaborated in detail '(enemies...hated...cursed...abused'), the second disciples merely have 'enemies'. The first disciples expect no reciprocity and no reward. If they act as commanded, they have no advantage and no reward for their behavior. Neither is any balance restored, nor is retributive justice envisioned. But the second disciples are expected to show some reciprocity ('love those who love you'), but more. It is to their advantage, so they will receive 'a great reward'. While disciples in 6.27-30 act without any advantage, and receive *no* recompense and

25. For a social science reading of 'love and hate', see Malina and Rohrbaugh, *Social Science Commentary on the Synoptic Gospels*, pp. 57-58.

26. Loss of clothing is more than theft, because being stripped naked means terrible shame; see Jerome H. Neyrey, 'Nudity', in Pilch and Malina (eds.), *Handbook of Biblical Social Values*, pp. 118-22.

27. See P. Millett, *Lending and Borrowing in Ancient Athens* (Cambridge: Cambridge University Press, 1991).

28. We argue that 'love' be more carefully discussed, especially in terms of cultural understandings of it; first of all, what Greek word is being considered (*eros, philia, agapē*)? Does 'love' argue anything more than the 'golden rule' (6.31)? Ought this discussion be in conversation with the maxim 'Help your friends, harm your enemies'? See Blundell, *Helping Friends and Harming Enemies*, pp. 38-50.

no reward, great advantage is put before the disciples in 6.32-35. Same actions, but different outcomes.

We need to read 6.32-35 more closely, substituting for 'the love command' the cultural value of 'justice', which we have been examining. Let us read 6.32-35 in terms of reciprocity, and so, of balance and justice.

balanced reciprocity	**honorable?** expected of a good person	but **evil persons** do this too; so, **how honorable?**	**unbalanced reciprocity**	advantage
If you love those who love you...	what credit is that to you?	For even sinners...do the same	But love your enemies	Your reward will be great,
If you do good to those who do good to you...	what credit is that to you?	For even sinners...do the same	do good,	and you will be called children of the Most High
If you lend to those from whom you hope to receive...	what credit is that to you?	For even sinners...do the same	and lend, expecting nothing in return	

'Reciprocity', evident from start to finish, is argued in the following points.

1. Both disciples and 'sinners' practice balanced reciprocity: 'love those who love you, etc.' Is there any advantage to this? Since both good and bad people do it, it appears to be acceptable behavior; at least, both get 'credit' for acting according to cultural norms.
2. The actions appear good and proper: 'love, do good, lend to those who repay'. In this respect, both disciples and sinners do virtuous actions. This balance is presumed to be very satisfying to both actor and receiver.
3. But something is added which creates an imbalance. 'What "credit?"' speaks to an imbalance. 'Credit' translates *charis* which has nothing to do with money, loans, and economic reciprocity.[29]

---

29. No study of *charis* can be complete without taking into account the article of Parker, 'Pleasing Thighs'. He argues that *charis* creates a reciprocal benefit, but not one of commercial exchange.

'Credit' (i.e., *charis*), belongs in the world of honor and shame, not that of economics. It has to do with 'favor', having favor—a good reputation and respect—or finding favor in someone's eyes (BDAG 1079). Having *charis* means enjoying respect, praise and honor, worth more than gold. To paraphrase it, 'In whose eyes will you look favorably?'

4. Something not found in 6.27-30 occurs in 6.32-35 when 'lending' replaces 'bless, pray for'. 'Lending' means a loan which will not be collected: 'Lend, expecting nothing in return'. Inasmuch as all 'lending' is based on some form of balanced reciprocity, this lender negatively disadvantages himself (and family and kin). A loan which will not be repaid is a debt not satisfied, and so it is an unjust thing. 'Lending', moreover, relates to 'what *credit* is that to you?'

5. Whereas no advantage accrues to the actions urged in 6.27-30, there is great advantage in 6.32-35. 'Credit' or advantage comes in the form of a significant rise in honor—maybe not in the eyes of all, especially those who hate you. But an advantageous reward is credited to those who love their enemies. They are greatly rewarded by being 'called children of the Most High'. Except for the posthumous honor of Jesus (see the final chapter of the present volume), this elevation of statue is about as high as mortals may expect. Thus, virtue pays; it is rewarded; it receives 'credit' of the highest order.

6. Thus, as in 6.27-30, we observe a *strategy* to acquire greater honor by volunteering to experience greater shame. We saw earlier how this strategy operated on the principle of 'All who exalt themselves will be humbled, and those who humble themselves will be exalted' (14.10; 18.14). Once again, the strategy for a disciple to be 'exalted' (i.e., honored) is to make himself less and smaller, in this case, to do good to one who does him evil.

7. Let us look more closely still. They will be honorable in Jesus' eyes, of course, and more importantly, in God's eyes. By receiving a new birth status, they will be chips off the old block; like Father, like son. But in what respect? 'He is kind to the ungrateful and the wicked'. Now we must walk delicately, because Luke is using unusual language here. God is 'kind', which says too little: 'kind' (*chrēstos*) implies that someone is showing benefaction. If God is acting as benefactor, what benefaction does God bestow? To whom? And why?

8. The translation of 'kind' (*chrēstos*) as 'forgiving' is an infelici-
    tous rendering, and more consideration of 6.35 argues against this
    interpretation.[30] The word 'kind' is *chrestos*, not *eleos*; and its
    social dynamic is entirely different.[31] If *chrestos* does not mean
    'merciful', where does it belong? I see an adequate understanding
    of it in Rom. 2.4, 'Do you presume upon the riches of his kindness
    and forbearance and patience?' God's benefaction is to give sinners
    the time/opportunity to repent and thus receive forgiveness of sins.

This finds support when we look more carefully at what Luke repeatedly
says about 'repentance' and 'forgiveness'. First of all, we remember that
the frequent and dominant articulation that God's justice is that of *talio*,
as you sow, so shall you reap. We have seen this already. Second, a survey
of what 'forgiveness' means in Luke yields the following data. Clearly in
1.77 and 3.3, John preaches conditional forgiveness of sin: 'a baptism of
repentance for the forgiveness of sins'. Repentance, then forgiveness. This
is the same dynamic in 17.3-4 where the disciples are told that when a
sinner 'repents', then they forgive the sinner. Repentance, then forgiveness
(see also 24.47; Acts 2.38; 3.19 etc.). It is worth noting that in 11.4, the
benefaction of 'forgiveness of sins' must be balanced with 'forgiving
everyone indebted to us'. Some action is required for 'forgiveness'.
Therefore, Luke is consistent that 'forgiveness' follows 'repentance'.
But in 6.36, there is no repentance in sight, and so 'forgiveness' is not an
adequate rendering of being 'kind' (*chrestos*). Rather, God would be seen
as a benefactor who allows time and opportunity for 'ungrateful and evil'
persons to repent, and then receive forgiveness.

To whom is God extending this benefaction? To 'ungrateful' and evil'
persons. In our culture ingratitude may be a social faux pas, but hardly
a bad or evil thing.[32] The same cannot be said of Luke's cultural world.
If debts must be repaid, then 'gifts' given must be reciprocated in some

30. On this point, see Fitzmyer, *The Gospel according to Luke I–IX*, pp. 223-24.

31. Most translations of 6.36 render *oiktirmos* as 'merciful', which does not
distinguish it sufficiently from other Lukan terms, such as (1) concern and kindness
toward others, such as God's faithfulness to Israel (*eleos*, 1.50, 54, 58, 72, 78) and
Jesus to petitioners (17.13; 18.38, 39); (2) compassion, pity: *oiktirmos* (only in
6.35); (3) to feel for (*splagchnizomai*, 7.13; 10.33; 15.20); (4) to be merciful/expiate
(*hilaskomai*, 18.13); and (5) to forgive (*aphiemi*) sins.

32. Robert A. Emmons, *Is Gratitude Queen of the Virtues and Ingratitude
King of the Vices?* (2017). Published as https://scottbarrykaufman.com/wp-content/
uploads/2017/09/Emmons-paper-for-Gratitude-Complaint-consultation-September-
2017.pdf.

way, if only by honoring the giver. Our preferred lexicon speaks about 'ingratitude' as 'a cardinal sociocultural crime in the Gr-Rom world' (BGAD 159), a judgment based on many classical sources. If, then, the unjustly treated disciples are to be like God, then they are so because they do not seek vengeance; but they do not 'love' or 'forgive' their enemies without qualifications, but allow time for them to repent. With repentance, it is possible that the offenders will act justly and balance the scale and restore the injured to their honorable place.

6.36

How to treat this? Is it the thematic conclusion of 6.32-35, and so determines its meaning? Is it simply an axiom, which is an add-on, but not a rhetorical conclusion? Moreover, when 6.35 and 36 are compared, they appear to be talking about different things:

> You will be children of the Most High
> He is kind (*chrestos*) to the ungrateful and to the wicked (6.35).
>
> Be merciful (*oiktirmones*) as your father is merciful (*oiktirmon*) (6.36).

First of all, 'kind' (*chrestos*) is not the same as 'merciful' (*oiktirmon*). *Chrestos* belongs in the field of benefaction, a benefit given with the expectation of change of behavior on the part of the 'ungrateful and evil'. *Oiktirmos* means 'display of concern over another's misfortune' (BGAD 700), seemingly with no return. Second, who are the persons to whom one is *oiktirmon*? Fellow disciples? 'Sinners?' 'Ungrateful and evil?' Different behaviors of God, but toward different persons, and with different outcomes.

Third, inasmuch as there are three types of reciprocity, what kind is expressed in 6.35 and in 6.36. Being 'kind' (6.35) serves a purpose: a benefaction of time for repentance. But it is a benefaction to which one must respond; a debt is incurred. Moreover, because this is a strategy to achieve a positive end, i.e. to restore an imbalance, it expresses balanced reciprocity (give and get). But being *oiktirmos* means concern for others in their need, which expresses altruistic reciprocity, where one gives and does not expect a return. Two types of reciprocity are juxtaposed.

Fourth, translating *oiktirmos* as 'merciful' pares the word of its denotations. Luke uses many words which translators render as 'mercy', suggesting forgiveness of sins, implying some form of reciprocity. But *oiktirmos* expresses altruistic reciprocity. For example, God shows altruistic 'mercy' (*eleos*) to Israel by keeping his promise of salvation (Lk. 1.50, 54, 58, 70, 78); petitioners ask from Jesus this kind of 'mercy'

(Lk. 17.13; 18.38-39); and it applies to what a true neighbor gives to a stranger in need (10.37). And these are all altruistic benefactions of God. Even a person canceling debts is showing 'mercy', and thus altruism. 'Mercy' as forgiveness of sins embodies balanced reciprocity, for this 'mercy' comes only after repentance, and so some balance is restored. The 'kindness' in 6.35 answers the question 'what credit is that to you', in that it expects some sort of repentance and so expresses retributive justice. The 'mercy' (*oiktirmos*) functioning in 6.36 seems to expect nothing in return

Fifth, contrary to 6.35 where a 'great reward' follows certain behavior, nothing comes with being *oiktirmon*? What advantage, then, is there? Is it a strategy of some sort? Sixth, retribution and *talio* are the stuff of 6.32-35, but what is the advantage in 6.36? Why do it? Will it restore justice? Seventh, if imitating God-who-is-kind produced a significant rise in status and honor, presumably for someone brought very low, what does *oiktirmon* do for a disciple? The 'Most High' serves as guarantor of the 'great reward'; but what role, if any, does 'your father' play in regard to your low status and honor? At least God could be said to be just in 6.35; but something is absent in 6.36.

Finally, when we compare Lk. 6.36 with Mt. 5.48 on this point, we cannot help noticing how different they are:

> You, therefore, must be *perfect* as your heavenly Father is *perfect* (Mt. 5.48).

> Be *merciful*, as your Father is *merciful* (Lk. 6.36).

Matthew's remark concludes 5.43-47 ('therefore...'), which treated the same material found in Lk. 6.32-36. But 'perfect' (*teleios*) is worlds removed from 'merciful' (*oiktirmos*). Finally, 6.36 is immediately followed by a statement about retribution and *talio*: 'Do not judge, and you will not be judged; do not condemn, and you will not be condemned' (6.37). Matthew 5.48 definitively ends the antitheses declared in Mt. 5.21-48.

6.37-38
Immediately, Luke calls attention to issues of justice and reciprocity/*talio*.

avoid conflict = avoid retaliation (negative: do not...)	as you sow, so shall you reap (positive: give and get)
Do not judge, and you will not be judged; do not condemn, and you will not be condemned	Forgive and you will be forgiven; give, and it will be given to you.

While parallel statements, they are hardly repetitive. The first ones advise against a bad action (judge, condemn); why? to avoid retaliation/ *talio*. The second pair urges positive action (forgive, give); why? advantage and benefit: 'you will be forgiven…it will be given to you'. Balance must be maintained; balanced must be restored; but 'balance' is in view. Whom does a disciple *not* judge? Presumably someone deserving of challenge and criticism. Is this person confronting the disciple? Minimally, it urges the disciple to avoid provocative action against someone, *so as to avoid* retaliation/*talio*. The advantage belongs to the one who does *not* start a conflict. But whom does the disciple forgive? Presumably, someone who has caused hurt to the disciple addressed. If the first remarks are negative (avoid harming another), then the second ones are positive (act to gain an advantage).

Second, 'kind' (*chrestos*) and 'merciful' (*oiktirmos*) simply do not cross over into 6.37-38. In 6.35 and 36, they describe actions toward wicked people offending disciples, which is not the case here. In fact, who acts benevolently to the disciple? Someone must be acting in this way, and it does not seem that one's opponent is doing this.

Third, there is advantage for all actors: they who do not harm others are not harmed; and if the one who is harmed forgives the harm, then he has a deposit on reserve. He has indebted someone, who owes him and must satisfy a debt. Advantage all around.

Fourth, the advantage of 'giving' greatly exceeds the loan.[33] Quid-pro-quo is general market practice; but this giver/lender will get back significantly more than his gift or loan: 'a good measure, pressed down, shaken together, running over,[34] will be put into your lap'. The giver is better off at the end than at the beginning.

---

33. Unless 'give' refers to alms, it is a request which puts a person asking in a challenging situation. 'Giving' is honorable, as in 'alms' or patronage or duty to one's family and kin. But the unqualified 'give' is also an honor challenge because one does not give to just anyone, but to those who can reciprocate; otherwise, it is foolish to hand over a family's assets to people who can return nothing; all of these figures are subsistent peasant family. In contrast to avoiding injustice, a command is given in 6.38 that, at first sight, is foolish, i.e., 'giving' with no consideration of return, which upsets common notions of justice, based on reciprocity.

34. Nolland (*Luke 1–9:20*, p. 301) is unusual for observing some kind of reciprocity here: 'One is not only to forgo the right to recompense but beyond that to extend openhanded generosity to the other person (cf. Acts 20.35). And he who extends such generosity may do so in the confident expectation that he will be the beneficiary of God's superabundant generosity (cf. Lk. 18:29-30)'. See B. Couroyer, 'De la mesure vous mesurez il vous sera mesuré', *RB* 77 (1970), pp. 366-70.

Fifth, 'The measure you give will be the measure you get back' is a very clear statement of just behavior; while it may not be altruistic, it is balanced reciprocity, which means that justice is maintained or restored.

Sixth, both the actions deferred and urged are *strategies*, that is, they are different ways to achieve some 'credit', some benefit.

Now we come to another maxim, 6.38b, which is popularly labeled 'the golden rule': 'For the measure you give will be the measure you get back'. As we consider it, many things need to be kept in view. First, in its rhetorical place, it concludes 6.37-38; its 'measure' is linked with the 'good measure' one gives. This maxim, then, does not appear to be an add-on. Second, it is a flat out statement of retributive justice: as you sow, so shall you reap or 'the measure you give will be the measure you get back'. Third, the advantage of acting in this way ('give') is that it creates a debt in the receiver which in justice must be repaid. And debts owed are a form of currency. Fourth, it clearly relates to v. 38a, where a gift is given and returned—a *talio*, and to v. 37, where no injustice to another will not warrant compensatory retaliation. Fifth, what happened to the 'enemies', the 'sinners', the 'ungracious and evil'? Are they still the recipients of the disciples' behavior? Therefore, the overall perspective of 6.37-38 in that of the virtue of justice. It remains, moreover, a *strategy* for achieving balance and justice. There is much advantage here.

It should be noted that acting out of the motive of advantage results in a dramatic elevation of status: 'Your reward will be great, and you will be children of the Most High' (6.35). And yet the disciple will shortly be told 'A disciple is not above the teacher, but everyone who is fully qualified will be like the teacher' (6.40). The first reward speaks to the advantage of the most precious commodity in antiquity: honor, expressed as status of children of God. The second reflects perhaps a *talio*, because the best a disciple might attain is to be honored as on the par with his teacher.

6.39-42

This 'parable'[35] not only follows 6.37-38 sequentially, but expands it by illustrating what 'judge not' might look like. We accept that the audiences in vv. 37-38 and vv. 39-42 are the same, namely, disciples. But now the disciples are not victims of another's injustice, but verge on being

---

35. Luke labels it a 'parable', but it is rhetorically a maxim or proverb, because its generality gives it lift to float and appear when helpful (see Mt. 15.14 and *G. Thom.* #34). Disciples and teachers commonly appear together in proverbs. Together they argue the case against the 'hypocrite'. For the phenomenon of parables often 'stacked', see Ramsaran, 'Living and Dying'.

perpetrators of harm to others.[36] The face of justice, then, will necessarily be different. Justice—if found—will eventually be given, 'a good measure', on the principle that 'the measure you give will be the measure you get back'.

Justice according to vv. 39-42, however, will occur when both unjust people ('blind leading the blind') fall into a pit. The 'end' in 6.37-38 will be beneficial, but not so in 6.39-42. Moreover, the protagonist in vv. 39-42 is both 'blind' and 'a hypocrite', not good character references; yet he is a disciple, who is actually called 'a brother' (not a *neighbor*). He responds, not to an enemy outside the circle of disciples, but to a 'brother', which implies reciprocal duties between them. But a disciple correcting a disciple? The correcting disciple seems to be assuming two new roles.[37] He is, to be sure, only a disciple, not a teacher; and since 'a disciple is not above the teacher, but everyone who is fully qualified will be like the teacher' (6.40), he encroaches on the domain of the teacher, *unless authorized to do so*.[38] But Jesus labels this 'blind disciple' who presumes to correct another a 'hypocrite', exposing unjust behavior happening.[39]

36. Many years ago it became popular to interpret 6.39-40 as referring to false teachers. But nothing in the texts warrants or supports that. The common phenomena of challenge and the quest for honor are sufficient to accord for the behavior of an over-reaching disciple.

37. No discussion of this would be complete without conversation with J. Duncan M. Derrett, 'Christ and Reproof (Matthew 7,1-5/Luke 6,37-42)', *NTS* 34 (1988), pp. 271-81.

38. Although disciples should not judge (6.37), there are later remarks in 17.1-4 which qualify this. The situations in both are quite different. The first warning against judging occurs in a detailed discussion of justice, balance, and *talio*; the second, however, is an independent and terse comment on general 'stumbling' among the disciples (a church matter?). The prohibition against 'judging' in 6.37-42 functioned to avoid all injustice among the disciples, which would otherwise occasion 'blindness and hypocrisy', requiring some sort of correction or balancing/*talio*. But judging in 17.1-4 describes a ritual regularly practiced for ensuring justice within a group. The verbs in 17.3-4 describe a formal process ('sin...rebuke...repent...forgive') to be repeated ('...sins against you seven time in a day and seven times turns back to you to say, "I am sorry"').

39. The hyperbole of 'splinter' vs. 'timber', while distinguishing small from large evils, implies that both of the 'blind persons' are liable for unjust actions. What is communicated by calling the criticizing disciple 'blind'? Jesus cures physical blindness (Lk. 4.18; 7.21-22), but here it denotes an evil which Jesus calls hypocrisy. This 'blindness', moreover, causes ruin to the pretender as well as to the one being led. A bad tree produces bad fruit. Justice will eventually occur, perhaps when the blind disciple repents, i.e. recognizes hypocrisy, and so returns to sighted status. Who will occasion this? Only the blind disciple.

This rebuke itself serves the purposes of justice, as it restores a balance, a quid-pro-quo.

6.43-45

We argue that a continuous communication is made which started in 6.20 and ends in 6.49, but it comes to us in sections, which may or may not relate to each other. 'Location' (what went before, what comes after) necessarily influences our reading. Previously, disciples were exhorted to act toward enemies in strange ways, which nevertheless produced advantage. Whereas in 6.27-36, the disciples had enemies, to whom they were urged to do good, in 6.39-41, the exhortation shifts to a disciple who is judging another disciple, whom Jesus warns of the evil of hypocrisy. But in 6.43-45, who is addressed? All previous actors are in the wings, as a generalized statement is made which covers both good and bad? Whereas victims with enemies were in view in 6.27-36, and only 'hypocrites' (not victims, but perpetrators) in 6.39-42, in 6.43-45 we see good vs. bad, for whom we need clues on how to distinguish them. The focus, then, shifts from specificity to generality.

And in regards to 6.46-49, the generality of 6.43-45 becomes specified by the contrast between 'say only' and 'say and do'. What was metaphorically stated about fruits and trees, good and bad, is balanced by the simile ('I will show you what he is like') about builders and houses. Although the 'badness' of fruit and tree was never requited, the failure expressed by 'say, but not do' is declared, as is the success of 'say and do' which is rewarded. It is hard to see justice operative in 6.43-45, but easy to observe in 6.46-49. As one sows, so one reaps. Thus, 6.43-45 is located between two clear statements about reciprocity/*talio*.

Many have observed that 6.43-45 contains many proverbs, which we call maxims. As all know, proverbs/maxims speak to generalities, which become specific when put into a specific context. But they are inherently generalizations, and appreciating them requires the kind of wisdom observed earlier which distinguishes good from bad and advantageous from disadvantageous. It is a truism that 'No good tree bears bad fruit, nor again does a bad tree bear good fruit' and that 'each tree is known by its own fruit'. Even when this metaphor is applied to persons, it is still a generality: 'The good person...produces good, and the evil person... produces evil'. Still more, 'out of the abundance of the heart that the mouth speaks'.

The communication is made by means of contrast/syncrisis, which, however, does not make anything more specific.

Good tree	vs.	bad tree	good man	vs.	evil man
good fruit	vs.	bad fruit	good treasure	vs.	evil treasure
figs	vs.	thorns	produces good	vs.	produces evil
grapes	vs.	thistles			

This generalized perspective is absolute, admitting no shading of meanings: either…or. Is there any aspect of justice here? Are the good rewarded and evil requited? What advantage is there to being good rather than evil. What constitutes 'good' or 'evil'? And who determines this and what does the determiner want to do about it? It appears, at first, that no aspect of justice that we have studied applies here. Wisdom, yes; but justice?

Yet let us examine 6.43-45 more closely. The contrasting words for good and bad trees and fruits are 'good' (*kalos*) vs. 'bad' (*sapros*), whereas persons (and treasures) are contrasted as 'good' (*agathos*) vs. 'evil' (*poneros*). This word, 'evil' (*poneros*) most recently identified a person given a benefaction from God: 'He is kind to the ungrateful and the evil' (*ponerous*, 6.35). It would be erroneous to conclude that God judges the good and the bad in such a way that the reward of the good is the same as that of the evil. Closer consideration of 'treasure' may help: a 'treasure', while basically a storehouse, metaphorically refers to a kind of debt owed an agent who has done well (BDAG 456). Disciples may 'store up treasure up for yourselves in heaven' (Mt. 6.20; cf. 1 Tim. 6.19). Luke records Jesus exhorting a rich man to 'sell all and you will have treasure in heaven' (18.22); therefore, God guarantees it or God will repay it. 'Treasure' here equates with 'reward' (*misthos*), just used in 6.23, 35. Thus, some sort of reciprocity is accurately presumed; 'good' and 'bad' people may be presumed to be awarded according to their deeds. Justice may be wearing agricultural clothing, but its claim is the same: 'For he will repay according to each one's deeds' (Rom. 2.6). Occasionally some commentators look more to the hearts and thoughts of the contrasted pair; but this is generally not the case.[40] Both 'produce', which should be considered as actions rather than thoughts.

6.46-49

The audience specified in 6.46-49 is immediately challenged with an aggressive question: 'Why do you call me "Lord, Lord", and do not do

---

40. Fitzmyer (*The Gospel according to Luke I–IX*, p. 643) compares 'fruit' here with good deeds (Hos. 10.13; Isa. 3.10; Jer. 17.10; 21.14); and Nolland (*Luke 1–9:20*, p. 308) says, 'V 45ab makes the obvious connection to the deeds of people: a good person does good; a bad person does bad'.

what I tell you?' (6.46). The generalized contrasts in 6.43-45 are replaced in specificity and in tone. Those addressed might be the common audience hearing 6.20-45, but not addressed in this manner. This final section has one and only one rhetorical aim: 'I will show you what someone is like who comes to me, hears my words, and acts on them'. The mode of argument resembles that of the previous section: there, metaphor (6.43-45), but here, simile. As was the case earlier, the argument consists of contrast/syncrisis: 'say and do' vs. 'only say', with their predictable outcomes, salvation vs. destruction.

The argument here is more than 'good is rewarded and evil requited' (6.43-45), but specifies what counts as goodness or badness, namely, how one reacts to Jesus. All are hearing, but not all are acting in just and productive ways. By speaking this long sermon, Jesus has benefitted many, that is, his benefaction was a gift that requires a response; some reciprocity is needed because all have incurred a debt because of Jesus' words and actions. Jesus' beneficial action requires a proper response. And there are good and bad responses; the good one is rewarded with salvation (from the flood), while the bad one is reciprocated with disaster. By the end of 6.46-49 the value of justice is restated. The reactions to Jesus' words warrant some reciprocity, the good one with salvation and the evil one with disaster. As one sows, so one reaps; and Jesus articulates this norm of justice and acts as God's spokesman about it.[41]

Its location, then, becomes rhetorically significant. If it were only giving specificity to the generalities of 6.43-45, it would serve well the argument of the sermon in this part. But it also functions as an ending to the whole of Jesus' remarks, a most significant rhetorical place. In that case, it may serve as a recapitulation and conclusion[42] in which the audience is asked to remember what has been argued. Cicero tell us all the rhetoric about a conclusion that we need to know.

> As a general principle for *summing up*, it is laid down that since the whole of any argument cannot be given a second time, the most important point of each be selected, and that every argument be touched on as briefly as possible, so that it may appear to be a refreshing of the memory of the audience, rather than a repetition of the speech' (*Inv.* 1.52.98, italics added).

---

41. Jesus must be credited now with authority to be called 'Lord, Lord', and so he has authority to declare who is wheat and who is chaff, and what will happen respectively to each. He acts with justice to establish justice. Recall that in 6.40 he was spoken of as 'teacher'.

42. Jerome H. Neyrey, 'In Conclusion...John 12 as a Rhetorical *Peroratio*', *BTB* 37 (2007), pp. 101-13.

We suggest that the rhetorical question, 'Why do you call me "Lord, Lord", and do not do what I tell you?' (6.46), has the rhetorical force of 'in conclusion'. It urges the audience addressed from 6.20 to 6.45 to sum up what Jesus, teacher and speaker, has been saying throughout. As expected, he does not argue the argument 'for a second time', but 'touches on it' as briefly as possible. He 'refreshes their memory' with signature contrasts between good vs. evil or just vs. unjust. As he has said throughout 6.20-49, disciples are declared just or unjust by their actions. Just actions are rewarded, but evil ones requited. The location of 6.46-49 at the terminus of the address states once more that justice is expressed in retaliation and *talio*. As one sows, so one reaps.

Therefore, in 6.20-49 Jesus articulates a principle whereby people are considered just or unjust, with corresponding retribution. Although he does not dramatize justice by means of a just action, he is credited with being an authentic teacher of justice ('Lord, Lord'). His audience, moreover, is actual or invited disciples to whom he declares how he assesses justice, which actions lead to success/salvation, or failure/ destruction (cf. 14.28-33). Justice here has two faces: first, retributive justice according to one's deeds, as in 'As you sow, so you reap'; and second, by accepting more injustice, a disciple treated unjustly eventually has justice restored, according to the principle, 'All who exalt themselves will be humbled, but all who humble themselves will be exalted' (18.14). Thus justice as recompense or *talio* operates throughout 6.20-49.

Justice and Keeping Ancestral Customs, Institutions, and Established Laws

Inasmuch as the initial mention of this aspect of justice derives from Greek classical sources, it would apply to matters of the *polis* or the insti- tution of politics. Moreover, how did they distinguish or define each of the terms 'customs', 'institutions', and 'law'? Aristotle states: 'To justice it belongs to be ready...to preserve ancestral customs and institutions, and the established laws' (*Virt. Vit.* 5.2). The same is repeated in *Rhet. Herr*: 'We shall be using the topics of justice if we say that...the laws and customs of the state ought especially to be preserved' (3.3.4). Athens and Rome are separated not only by language, but by legal systems and especially by cultural differences. Thus, it is not possible to equate Aristotle's 'customs' with Cicero's 'rules of conduct', or Greek institu- tions with Roman *consuetudo*, or the 'established laws' of Athens with Roman 'principles'. Still more difficult is it to bring this triad together in an attempt to understand Luke. What is needed is some mediation, which Bruce Malina provided.

Malina follows the distinctions made in the social sciences concerning these matters, and so he uses the terminology *norms, customs, and laws*.[43]

Norms	Customs	Laws
Human relationships are patterned and controlled by more or less obvious rules of behavior in the *kinship/family institution*.	Bodies or sets or collections of norms are given sanctions; that is, someone puts teeth into the norms when they are not followed or enforces the norms; thus custom is sanctioned by the *same social institutions* that norms themselves create.	Customs from other institutions were given sanctions, but law doubly institutionalizes customs by having government power enforce and sanction what was previously custom. Law generally refers to the *political institution*.

Families develop 'oughts' or norms (domestic roles come with duties), about which all in the villages and towns agree: 'this is the way we do it'. In time, these become a formalized set of norms, called customs, which now *must* be performed, the performance of which is enforced by some institution, but the difference being that some body or institution claims: 'We can *force* you to do this (fines, shunning, abuse, etc.)'. It is likely, moreover, that in time these customs will be considered 'the law of the land', and can be enforced by an institution with power.[44]

Looking toward Luke's appropriation of this triad, we know that norms most likely originate in the institution of kinship, which are regularized for all in the geographical area, and which all accept. Malina appreciates how these norms-becoming-customs are enforced by administrators, which in the case of the gospels means the actions of Scribes and Pharisees.[45] They enforce their understanding of these norms-become-customs by verbal censure, which threatens loss of honor. They neither fine nor chastise, but only verbally label people as 'observant'

43. Malina, *New Testament World*, pp. 154-59.

44. These distinctions, although articulated by modern anthropology, are rooted in classical discussions of the same. See Sally Humphreys, 'Law, Custom and Culture in Herodotus', *Arethusa* 20 (1987), pp. 211-20; John Gould, 'Law, Custom and Myth: Aspects of the Social Position of Women in Classical Athens', *JHS* 100 (1980), pp. 38-59; Robin Osborne, 'Law in Action in Classical Athens', *JHS* 105 (1985), pp. 40-58; and Michael Herzfeld, '"Law" and "Custom": Ethnography *of* and *in* Greek National Identity', *Journal of Modern Greek Studies* 3 (1985), pp. 167-85.

45. This is the homeland of 'labeling and deviance theory'; see Malina and Neyrey, *Calling Jesus Names*, pp. 36-67.

or 'non-observant (sinners)'.[46] Using the social currency of honor, they strive to enforce their interpretation of the proper and only way of observing customs. On occasion, the leaders of the House of Israel did execute flagrant violators for what they considered violations of 'the Law'. Some thoughtful consideration, then, needs be given to how Luke considers the behavior of Jesus, whether he practiced justice in keeping the norms, customs, and laws.

Luke used a variety of terms which have to do with this triple classification: (1) customary manner of behavior (*ethē*), (2) traditions (*eiōtha*), (3) an order for a specific action (*entolē*), and (4) established procedure (*nomos*). He is not, of course, following the definitions in our lexica, because he has already sorted and classified them into his pattern. I suggest the following fit with the triple group mentioned above. As I understand Luke's pattern, certain things may be 'customary', but without an evident means of enforcement. Luke's Jesus would reduce them to 'norms' or accepted behavior or traditions. We can, however, be quite certain what Luke means by *nomos*. He reports that Jesus most sacredly observes the first of the commandments, worshiping God alone (4.1-11); he voices the 'Great Commandment' in 10.25-28; he supports the Ten Words (18.20), and acknowledges the Sabbath commandment. Although Luke does not report Jesus' endorsement of the command to 'Honor Father and Mother' (as does Mk 7.9-13), it is included in the Ten Words in 18.20. Luke reports Jesus himself speaking about these 'laws', implying that he both knows them and endorses them.

But what about other matters considered at least customary if not traditions, the transgression or omission of which the Scribes and Pharisees would quickly condemn? We list the following as controversial whether they are merely norms or customs:

1. persons with whom one eats (5.27-32; 15.1-3)
2. washing rituals (11.38-41)
3. fasting (5.33-35)
4. taxes to Caesar (20.20-26)

These are not matters of 'law', and there is no explicit command in Scripture to observe them, nor is there any mechanism to enforce non-compliance. Some may consider them 'customs', but the only people in Luke's narrative who are concerned about them as 'customs' are their

46. John R. Donahue, 'Tax Collectors and Sinners: An Attempt at Identification', *CBQ* 33 (1971), pp. 39-61.

makers and enforcers, namely, the Scribes and Pharisees. One wonders whether the population of Galilee considered them 'customs' to be observed, which were accompanied with a sanction.

Nowhere is Jesus ever said to contest that 'Keep holy the Sabbath' is a law, one of the Ten Words. But controversy swirls around his practical observance of it.

Jesus' 'customary' behavior	Pharisaic Criticism: 'It is not permitted'
'He went to the synagogue on the sabbath day, as was his custom' (4.16).	
'He was teaching them on the sabbath' (4.31).	----------
'One sabbath while Jesus was going through the cornfields, his disciples plucked some heads of grain, rubbed them in their hands, and ate them' (6.1).	'But some of the Pharisees said, "Why are you doing what is not lawful on the sabbath?"' (6.2).
'On another sabbath he entered the synagogue and taught, and there was a man there whose right hand was withered' (6.6).	'The scribes and the Pharisees watched him to see whether he would cure on the sabbath, so that they might find an accusation against him' (6.7).
'Now he was teaching in one of the synagogues on the sabbath...Jesus called her over and said, "Woman, you are set free from your ailment"' (13.10-12).	'The leader of the synagogue, indignant because Jesus had cured on the sabbath, kept saying, "There are six days on which work ought to be done; come on those days and be cured, and not on the sabbath day"' (13.14).
'On one occasion when Jesus was going to the house of a leader of the Pharisees to eat a meal on the sabbath...there was a man who had dropsy. And Jesus asked the lawyers and Pharisees, "Is it lawful to cure people on the sabbath, or not?"' (14.1-3)	'But they were silent' (14.4).
'If one of you has a child or an ox that has fallen into a well, will you not immediately pull it out on a sabbath day?' (14.5).	'And they could not reply to this' (14.6).

Several conclusions are possible: (1) while it is permissible for Jesus to 'teach' on the sabbath day, healing is 'unlawful'; (2) Jesus uses arguments against this censure, one an *exemplum* from Scripture (1 Sam. 21.1-6), another a common-sense reason, namely, farmers watering their flocks on the sabbath (13.15; 14.5). Both his teaching and his (justifiable) healing do *not* violate his understanding of how to keep the commandment. (3) Reactions matter: the crowds applaud, but the critics are reduced to silence. Certain 'customs', then, are not agreed upon. This expresses a conflict about the status of sabbath observance, not that it should be ignored, but how it should be kept. In observing it, Jesus differs from the Pharisees' interpretation of it as a genuine 'custom-law'; he reduces certain observances of it to the level of norms, which observers applaud.

Moreover, Luke often qualifies the Law as something given *by Moses*, reducing its absoluteness and thus its sanction. For example, Jesus' 'purification' is done 'according to the law of Moses' (2.22); the healed leper are commanded to act 'as Moses commanded' (5.14); and the Levirate marriage should be followed because 'Moses wrote for us...' (20.28). This contrasts sharply with his citation from the Scriptures, '...This was to fulfil what was written', by God.

Luke's treatment of 'law', 'custom', and 'norm' may seem at first not sufficiently clear, but if Acts is allowed to reflect the direction of Luke's thinking, then this matter can be clarified. For example, in Acts Luke refines a conflict into an engagement between Israelite 'customs and law' and the practices of Jesus' disciples. For example, Stephen and others are accused of 'speaking against Moses' (6.11) and saying that Jesus will 'change the customs that Moses handed down' (6.14). In the latter remark, Luke uses a technical term, 'customs', and states that they are *Moses'* norms. Even circumcision is labeled 'the custom of Moses' (15.1). Luke affirms an attempt to force proselyte compliance: 'It is necessary to circumcise them, and to charge them to keep the law of Moses' (15.5). The conflict could not be clearer: 'Some believers who belonged to the party of the Pharisees affirmed that circumcision and other things in the law *must* be kept', thus elevating them above the level of 'customs' to that of 'law'. This evaluation is challenged by Peter who demotes them as a 'yolk...that neither our fathers nor we have been able to bear' (15.10). James continues this argument: 'It is my judgment that we should not trouble those of the Gentiles who turn to God' (15.19); "It has seemed good to the Holy Spirit and to us to lay upon you no greater burden than these necessary things"' (15.28). Because the directives sent to the Gentiles have no censure backing them, we do not consider them 'customs', but 'norms'. Circumcision, a law to the Pharisees, is not a law to the Gentiles. Obviously the absoluteness and strictness of Pharisaic 'customs' is being reduced when the Gentiles are asked to follow norms which allow for a common table for all disciples. The Jerusalem church is definitely not reviving any 'dietary' concerns and turning them into 'laws' for which there are sanctions.

In summary, Luke reports that both Jesus and his disciples were aware of the distinction between 'norms', 'customs', and 'laws'. This is most evident in Acts, where the early disciples formally distinguished what must be observed from that which was considered 'norms', rules of behavior without censure and with necessary adaptability. The issue of the Ten Words is never challenged, although the practical observance of something like 'Keep holy the Sabbath' argues that its practice was being reformulated. Except for the threat of social shaming, there is no censure of it ever mentioned. In fact, observance of the sabbath is *not* an issue in Acts, but only in Luke's gospel. Inasmuch as consideration of this is conducted in the service of showing the virtue of justice, Jesus' public behavior must be attested as 'just', that is, he demonstrates that virtue. Jesus indeed keeps 'ancestral customs, institutions, and established laws', but not as Pharisees and Scribes assess them.

Justice: To Tell the Truth and to Keep Agreements

We mentioned above that Jesus fulfilled his duties to God, Israel, and family. Yet, this does not exhaust what Aristotle meant by 'keeping agreements'. Jesus himself declared that he was 'sent' to do a task and perform a role. He states this at the very beginning when he declares to his hometown synagogue: 'The Spirit of the Lord is upon me, because he has *anointed me* to bring good news to the poor. He has *sent me* to proclaim release to the captives...' (4.18-19/Isa. 61.1-2, italics added). He accepts this as his commission and duty, claiming that his behavior is fulfilling a Scripture: 'Today this scripture has been fulfilled in your hearing' (4.20). First, this is a programmatic or initial statement which covers all that Jesus will subsequently do and say. Second, the text of Isaiah and Jesus' appropriation of it imply that he acts in the role of a prophet. Moreover, the bestowal of this role was done by God's sending the Spirit on Jesus at the Jordan (3.22); hence it is true that 'The Spirit of the Lord is upon me, because he has anointed me' (4.18). However commentators label this (covenant, commissioning, agreement), Jesus acknowledges that God has assigned him a role and a task commensurate with it. It matters, then, that people acknowledge this, as they do in 9.48 and 10.16. Jesus was 'sent' by God, that is, set aside for a role and task. He is faithful and will keep this agreement.

Cleopas, at the end of Jesus' career, articulates what Luke intended his readers to understand by Jesus' prophetic role: 'The things about Jesus of Nazareth, who was a prophet mighty in deed and word before God and all the people' (24.19). Luke's audience can connect what Isaiah said about a prophetic role in 4.18-19 with what Cleopas claims had happened (24.19), as well as all prophetic acts in between. In regard to 'mighty in word', Luke has much to say (4.43; 8.1; 10.1). And after a mighty deed, the crowds are wont to acclaim: 'they glorified God, saying, "A great prophet has risen among us!" and "God has looked favorably on his people!"' (7.16). It comes as no surprise that when Jesus asks what the crowds think of him, the disciples respond, 'John the Baptist; but others, Elijah; and others, that one of the ancient prophets has arisen' (9.19). Therefore, Luke affirms that Jesus acts with justice when he keeps his agreement with God. He acts as he was commissioned.

One might flip this around and ask whether Jesus is accused of acting contrary to the will of God? He was charged with blasphemy, 'Who is this who is speaking blasphemies? Who can forgive sins but God alone?' (5.21). But that charge is refuted by the healing which Jesus subsequently performs 'Amazement seized all of them, and they glorified God' (5.26). Nor is he a 'false prophet'. Although adept at recognizing hypocrisy, he himself is never charged with the same.

Summary and Conclusions

1. More topics of the progymnastic encomium are in view. The search for virtuous behavior to be praised is found in the four canonical virtues, in this case, 'justice'. We know, moreover, how the ancients understood this virtue from their own definitions and comments. Although it is possible that modern scholarship might try to process 'justice' in terms commensurate with current usage, they risk ethnocentricity. We are showing respect for that cultural world by this kind of inquiry. Thus, to examine 'justice' in Luke, we are suitably equipped for the task.

2. Ancient understandings of virtue and justice are abundant, not only in rhetoric but in 'moralia',[47] as found in Plutarch. Emic reports, such as those of Aristotle, Herrenius, and Cicero, should always be preferred to etic ones. But so far, New Testament interest in 'justice' has been confined to theological examinations of Paul's letters. This current study, however, provides a broader, that is, a more rhetorical consideration of it which opens many doors for investigation. Something new and significant is now available for scholarship.

3. Lukan demonstrations of Jesus' exercise of justice are not gathered into one place, much less identified as such. This has not been a problem for several reasons. First, rhetoricians regularly tell writers and orators to skip the convenient label and narrate what a virtue

---

47. See Dover, *Greek Popular Morality*, pp. 180-83, 306-10.

looks like. Second, Luke knows his audience and so he can presume some knowledge of this virtue by them because of commonplaces and topoi on topics such as 'virtue' and 'justice'. His audience then can tag various items correctly because they are primed to know the commonplaces; the same cannot be said for modern readers.

4. Now that we identify 'duties' as an essential part of justice, we can correctly label as 'just' all of Jesus' actions which fulfil his duties to God, nation, and family. This correspondingly indicates his performance of duties to the two institutions of his world, politics and kinship. Knowing what fulfilment of duties meant then, we can understand when Jesus appears not to follow traditional obligations, but proposes new norms. Luke makes it clear that such behavior by Jesus does not indicate that Jesus rejects certain duties, but that he is differently defining them more in keeping with what he knows God wants.

5. Justice has been seen to be a Janus-figure and has two faces. The common fact expresses justice as 'as you sow so shall you reap'. We have seen how pervasive this understanding of justice is in the whole narrative. But justice has a second face which qualifies the first, when it suggests that God does not strictly follow this. Jesus' continued presence with 'tax collectors and sinners' suggests an offer of repentance extended, not a judgment of retribution. He himself sets a new paradigm on responding to evil, based on his understanding of how God acts. This is most conveniently found where acts of altruism are described. Moreover, disciples are instructed how to be like God.

6. In addition to Luke's use of 'must' (*dei*) to express Jesus' duty to God, he also declares the role and status of Jesus as ascribed to him. By the Spirit, God anointed Jesus as a prophet, mighty in word and deed. He justly fulfilled this role, which was regularly acknowledged by the crowds. It seems clear, then, to affirm that Jesus was honorable in his practice of the virtue of justice.

7. Finally, we have good grounds to confirm that Luke continues to tell the story of Jesus according to the categories of the progymnastic encomium.

Chapter 6

ENCOMIUM:
ACCOMPLISHMENTS AND VIRTUES: COURAGE

Courage makes men perform noble acts in the midst of dangers (Aristotle, *Rhet*. 1.9.8).

Bravery is a disposition of the soul obedient to the highest law in enduring vicissitudes (Cicero, *Tusc. Disp.* 4.53).

Bravery deals with acts of endurance...to bravery are subordinated perseverance, intrepidness, great-heartedness, stout-heartedness, and industriousness (Arius Didymus).[1]

We now know that the progymnastic handbooks give instructions for considering the 'accomplishments' of a person as their 'deeds of the soul'. Moreover, they specify as 'deeds of the soul' the four canonical virtues, wisdom, justice, courage, and self-control. After studying 'wisdom' and 'justice', we now turn to 'courage'. In keeping with the format of this book, our inquiry into Luke's presentation of Jesus in terms of 'courage' begins by asking what the ancients themselves thought about it. If Luke has a clear idea of this virtue, he most likely learned it from the rhetoricians he studied to become the accomplished author he was.

How Ancient Rhetoric Defines 'Courage'

We turn once more to ancient rhetoricians to tell us how they defined this virtue and in which social contexts they expect it to be displayed. Again, a synopsis of opinions is helpful.

---

1. Arius Didymus, *Epitome of Stoic Ethics* 5b2 (ed. Arthur J. Pomeroy; Atlanta, GA: Society of Biblical Literature, 1999), p. 15.

Aristotle	Herennius	Cicero
To courage it belongs to be undismayed by fears of death and confident in alarms and brave in face of dangers, and to prefer a fine death to base security... It belongs to courage to labor and endure and play a manly part. Courage is accompanied by confidence and bravery and daring, and also by perseverance and endurance (*Virt. Vit.* 4.4, and 2.3).	When we invoke as a motive for steadfastness in courage, we shall make it clear that men ought to follow and strive after noble and lofty actions...for an honorable act no peril or toil, however great, should divert us; death ought to be preferred to disgrace; for country, for parents, guest-friends, intimates, and for the things that justice commands us to respect, it behoves us to brave any peril and endure any toil (3.3.5).	Courage is the quality by which one undertakes dangerous tasks and endures hardships. Its parts are confidence, patience, perseverance... Confidence is the quality by which the spirit has placed great trust in itself with a resolute hope of success. Patience, a willing and sustained endurance of difficult and arduous tasks for a noble and useful end. Perseverance, a firm and abiding persistence in a well-considered plan of action' (*Inv.* 2.163).

All three share these common aspects: (1) bravery in the face of danger; (2) labor, endurance, and perseverance; (3) preference of a noble death to base security; and (4) its parts are 'confidence, patience, perseverance'. From other sources, we also find that courage can be expressed by boldness of public speech.[2] Rhetorical definitions are intentionally generic, broad, and meant to cover different times, persons, and issues. As commonplaces or stereotypes, they need some tailoring for our project.

First of all, we note that the ancients recognized two kinds of courage, one appropriate in aggressive combat such as war, and another in the context of enduring and persevering hardships. In classical times, courage is best displayed in a martial context, by soldiers and warriors, that is, when important matters are at stake. The courage needed to wrestle in the

---

2. Courage should be admired on the grounds of the governor's frankness (*parrhêsias*) to the emperors' (Menander Rhetor, *Treatise* II.416.23-28). Sometimes it refers to boldness in speech and public presence, independent of whether its context is attack or resistance: (1) public boldness (*parrēsia, parrēiazomai,* 1 Thess. 2.2); persons are exhorted to 'take courage' (*euthumeō,* Phil. 2.19; Acts 27.22); *epairō tēn kephalēn* (Lk. 21.28); and *tharreō/tharseō* (Jn 16.33; 2 Cor. 5.6); (2) resistance to challenge (*tolmaō,* Mk 12.34).

gymnasium pales in comparison with that needed for military battles. But another kind of courage befits persons engaged in the constant conflicts of daily life, the endless push-and-shove characteristic of an honor based society.[3] Thus, the ancient authors distinguished two types of courage: courage when a soldier attacks, and courage when someone stands his ground.

This distinction was clearly articulated by John Fitzgerald in his book on the hardships which a wise man must endure, *Cracks in an Earthen Vessel*. Apropos of a courageous attack, he says: 'As the *Iliad* amply attests and Aristotle affirms, it is preeminently in war that this quality is seen, with a man's battle scars being the token of his valour'.[4] But he makes an important distinction: 'But courage is not simply bold speech and staunch but passive endurance of hardships. Courage is also active, for it is "the thoroughly considered undertaking of perils"' (Cicero, *Tusc. Disp.* 4.54.163). Later he amplifies this with reference to Seneca's consideration of a good man: 'A good man will do what he thinks will be honorable for him to do, even if it involves toil; he will do it even if it involves harm to him; he will do it, even it involves peril' (*Ep.* 76.18). Courage, then, is both aggressive and defensive. This understanding can serve us well as we now consider how Luke narrates Jesus manifesting courage.

Jesus, Courage, and the Gospel of Luke

From our study of Luke, we suggest the following three areas where Jesus himself displays courage and where he exhorts his disciples to the same.

Courage as Defense and Endurance	1. Attacked by Evil Spirits (4.1-14)
	2. all challenges and ripostes
	3. facing traps, tricks, and ambushes
	4. endurance

---

3. Richard L. Rohrbaugh, 'Honor: Core Value in the Biblical World', in Dietmar Neufeld and Richard E. DeMaris (eds.), *Understanding the Social World of the New Testament* (London: Routledge, 2010), pp. 109-25; Rohrbaugh, 'Legitimating Sonship'.

4. John T. Fitzgerald, *Cracks in an Earthen Vessel: An Examination of the Catalogues of Hardships in the Corinthian Correspondence* (Atlanta, GA: Scholars Press, 1988), p. 88.

Courage as Challenge and Attack	1. attacking his attackers (11.42-52; 19.44-47; 20.1-5; 21.5-6) 2. bold public speech: – before Herod (9.7-9; 13.31-32) and Pilate (23.1-25), – concerning Rome and Caesar (20.21-27) 3. all healings[5] 4. Jesus' own challenges: – challenge to kinship institution (12.49-53) – challenges to honor and shame in families (6.20-24) – distancing his own family (8.19-20) 5. volunteers warned off (9.57-62)
Courage: Exhortation to Disciples	1. courage and boldness of speech by disciples (success, 21.12-15; failure, 22.54-62) 2. courage demanded of disciples (9.23-27; 10.17-20) 3. courage to forego vengeance (6.27-31)

Courage as Defense and Endurance

Who attacks Jesus? The list includes three: Satan (aka Beelzebul), and his minions; his Galilean critics, that is, Pharisees, Scribes, and Lawyers; and his elite opponents in Jerusalem.

Attacked by Evil Spirits (4.1-14)

It has been noted that readers of Luke do the gospel a disservice when they fragment a narrative so as to lose its rhetorical logic and emphasis. Thus it is all the more important for Luke's audience to hear the sequence of events beginning with the Spirit-investment of Jesus (3.21-22), then the genealogy of Jesus (3.23-38) and finally his testing (4.1-13).[6] Many commentators label 4.1-13 a 'temptation', a weak rendering of *peirazō*; it is not a seduction, but an outright assault on Jesus because of claims made earlier, that Jesus has been ascribed the role and status of 'Son of God'. Just as all CPAs, MDs, and LLBs, after completing their programs, take exams for public certification of their competence, so this 'testing' of Jesus will make evident that the claim on Jesus' behalf is correct and that he is able to live up to that claim. Richard Rohrbaugh is unique in explaining what claim is challenged in Lk. 4.1-13:

5. It is well argued that the cause of illnesses in Jesus' time was thought to be spirit aggression; see John J. Pilch, 'Sickness and Healing in Luke–Acts', in Jerome H. Neyrey (ed.), *The Social World of Luke–Acts: Models for Interpretation* (Peabody, MA: Hendrickson, 1991), pp. 200-209.

6. Fitzmyer, *The Gospel according to Luke (I–IX)*, pp. 186-94, because he operated from a cultural understanding of honor claims and conflicts, extends the series of linked episodes through 4.30.

A claim this outlandish, however, must be challenged. After all, the claim is being made that one born of the lowliest of peasant circumstances has been raised to Son of God. Virtually the entire social spectrum has been traversed. Luke's Jesus is thus a classical social anomaly who acts entirely out of keeping with his birth status and social authority. Hence Luke must explain himself quickly or risk losing his reading audience.[7]

Much fine work has been done explaining the episode, which we leave to those with more time to read elsewhere.[8] We focus on the story as the inaugural attack upon Jesus, in which Jesus defends himself with great courage and cleverness. Luke concludes the story by noting that Jesus' opponent left the field of battle: 'When the devil had finished every test, he departed from him until an opportune time' (4.13). It is generally conceded that the 'opportune time' is the passion narrative (see 22.3, 31 and 53).[9] Be that as it may, Luke records many other encounters between Jesus and demons and unclean spirits.

Attacking the Attackers
Are these challenges (4.33, 41; 8.28; 9.42; 11.14-23) attacks upon Jesus which call for defensive courage? Are they also his attacks on the attackers? They occur when Jesus demonstrates the powers given him by God's Spirit (4.18-19). In the first one, Jesus 'went down to Capernaum… and was teaching them on the sabbath' (4.31). Even as Jesus drew great praise for his teaching ('They were astounded at his teaching, because he spoke with authority', 4.32), another voice is heard from 'a man who had the spirit of an unclean demon', who countered the praise of Jesus with, 'Let us alone! What have you to do with us, Jesus of Nazareth? Have you come to destroy us? I know who you are, the Holy One of God' (4.34). Because of the counter quality of these remarks, we consider them an attack. Jesus, however, attacks his attacker: 'Jesus rebuked him, saying, "Be silent, and come out of him!"' Success: '[the demon] came out of him without having done him any harm'.[10] Courage here means both standing one's ground and taking up the attack.

7. Rohrbaugh, 'Legitimating Sonship', p. 188.

8. Birger Gerhardsson, *The Testing of God's Son* (Lund: Gleerup, 1966); Fearghus O'Fearghail, 'Rejection at Nazareth', *ZNW* 75 (1985), pp. 60-72.

9. Fitzmyer, *The Gospel according to Luke (I–IX)*, p. 518; Nolland, *Luke 1–9:20*, p. 182; Jerome H. Neyrey, *The Passion according to Luke: A Redaction Study of Luke's Soteriology* (Eugene, OR: Wipf & Stock, 1985), pp. 58-62, 177-79.

10. The vocabulary of the 'exorcism' stories is that of martial conflict; see Howard Clark Kee, 'The Terminology of Mark's Exorcism Stories', *NTS* 14 (1978), pp. 242-46.

Later that same day, Jesus rebuked the spirit harming Peter's mother-in-law; and when evening came, he laid hands on all those sick with various kinds of diseases, and cured them. Because we understand that in this culture 'illness' was caused by spirit aggression,[11] when Jesus 'heals' them, he is attacked by those spirits: '...they came out of many, shouting, "You are the Son of God!"' But he rebuked them, attacking his attackers, by silencing them, '...and would not allow them to speak'. At battle's end, the demons were subject to Jesus' power, and acknowledged his super role and status. The same pattern occurs when Jesus crossed the lake to 'the country of the Gerasenes', where a man with many, many demons confronted Jesus. The attacker is instantly attacked and defeated: 'He fell down before him... "What have you to do with me, Jesus, Son of the Most High God? I beg you, do not torment me"' (8.28). The demon had already yielded in his attack, because 'Jesus had commanded the unclean spirit to come out of the man' (8.29). In all these, Jesus attacks an attacker, a spirit who has attacked someone else and who now confronts Jesus (cf. 9.38-43). Thus, Jesus displays courage which wins the victory.

The issue of who was attacking whom comes to a head after Jesus '...cast out a demon that was mute' (11.14). This results in a serious attack on Jesus, namely, the accusation that his power comes from Jesus' very enemy: 'He casts out demons by Beelzebul, the ruler of the demons' (11.15). Jesus resolves the issue in two ways. First, Jesus, who masters demons, cannot be an ally of Beelzebul: 'Every kingdom divided against itself becomes a desert, and house falls on house. If Satan also is divided against himself, how will his kingdom stand?' (11.18). Allies do not war against each other. Second, in a simile, Jesus likens Beelzebul to 'a strong man, fully armed, guarding his castle, whose property is thus safe' (11.21). But, 'when one *stronger than* he attacks him and overpowers him, he takes away his armor in which he trusted and divides his plunder' (11.22). In this context, 'the strong man' guarding his castle is Beelzebul; and 'the stronger one' who attacks him,[12] overpowers him, despoils him, and plunders his castle is Jesus. Thus, Jesus argues that he attacks the attacker and defeats him. Therefore, in every combat with a demon, evil spirit, or Beelzebul himself, Jesus attacks the attacker and thoroughly triumphs.

---

11. See n. 5 above; other data would include: (1) spirit of blindness (Mt. 12.22); (2) spirit of dumbness (Lk. 11.14); (3) spirit of deafness and dumbness (Mk 9.17, 25); (4) spirit of casting down (Lk. 9.39, 42); (5) spirit of crippledness (Lk. 13.11); and (6) spirit of wind and storm (Mk 6.47-49).

12. John earlier identified Jesus as 'he who is coming' as 'stronger than I' (3.16); Jesus, of course, was this 'stronger one' alluded to in 3.16, but now formally identified as 'the stronger one' in 11.22. Power only predicted is now claimed.

The combat between the unclean spirits and demons seems to end in victory for Jesus, but the war continues. We are told much later that when 'Satan entered into Judas called Iscariot' to work Jesus' death (22.3), Jesus did not act to block this. In regard to Peter, however, Jesus defends him: 'Simon, Simon, listen! Satan has demanded to sift all of you like wheat... but I have prayed for you' (22.31-32). On the scorecard, Judas plays for the enemy, but Peter for Jesus and God; both, however, battle Jesus' premier opponent. When Jesus is arrested, there is no attack or defense against 'your hour, and the power of darkness' (22.53), because now it is the will of God that Jesus be submitted to the ultimate defeat, death (22.42).

Courage in Attacking the Institution of Kinship

How easy it is to stand by tradition and defend the social forms it expresses. Not much courage needed there. But to challenge in any way the foundational institution of common social life would be either foolish or courageous. We are not claiming that Jesus, like some modern anarchists, sought to destroy 'family' as such, but that he had many and strong criticisms of it, when it impeded the freedom of village sons to become his disciples.

We know nothing about Jesus' family life after 2.52. When he was 'about thirty years old', he no longer lived in Nazareth, which implies that he was no longer a member of his family. It requires much imagination to consider the circumstances of his leaving of the family home in Nazareth, perhaps the same struggles which awaited Jesus' own disciples. Presumably Joseph had died; and if Jesus left, who was going to support and protect his mother? When he moved his craft to the lake, what source of income supported his mother? Wasn't he supposed to 'honor his mother and father' by caring for them in their old age and burying them? Luke's next mention of Jesus' family is hardly felicitous. Jesus and his true disciples are 'inside', whereas his family is 'outside'. It is implied that if they acknowledged his prophetic role, they would be believers and so be inside, but they are not: 'His mother and his brothers came to him, but they could not reach him because of the crowd. And he was told, "Your mother and your brothers are standing outside, wanting to see you"' (8.19-20). His response is to distance himself from them: 'But he said to them, "My mother and my brothers are those who hear the word of God and do it"' (8.21).[13] Something ranks higher than the institution of family

13. When Jesus first appears in Nazareth (4.16-29), Luke says nothing about the composition of the synagogue, if any relatives are present. But quickly the whole assembly rejects him, even trying to kill him. Whether relatives or acquaintances, all reject him.

and kinship (cf. 2.48-49). Finally, Luke does *not* mention that Jesus' mother attended his crucifixion (23.55). If any kin were in Jerusalem for that Passover, they are *not* attending Jesus' execution.[14] All of this matters because it gives some background to Jesus' talk about disciples and their ties to their families.

Jesus begins his sermon on the plain[15] by declaring some behavior 'honorable' and some 'shameful'. We note immediately that Luke mentions only four makarisms, which are balanced by corresponding reproaches. We argued an interpretation of this in the previous chapter and need only repeat highlights of it here. Jesus addresses in 6.20-23 persons who succeeded in resisting the conservative restraints by their family/kinship groups. Those addressed are *not* four different people beset by four different crises.[16] They are disciples who suffered the same fate, a social catastrophe, namely, expulsion from their families. Hence, the fourth, climactic remark explains what caused the other three crises. This *one* person has experienced all of this: 'people *hate* you, and *exclude* you, *revile* you, and *defame* you' (6.22). This speaks to overpowering social shame, a catastrophic separation of a disciple of Jesus from his family. The restraints of the conservative families did not succeed, but ended in the separation of disciples from them.

These four powerful verbs declare that the person so treated is utterly shameful in the eyes of family and neighbors. We pause to assess their seriousness.

-   'hate' is the opposite of love, which has to do with group attachment.[17] Hate means formal rejection and denial of loyalty by family (see Lk. 1.71; 16.13; 19.14); sometimes it is considered virtuous to hate what is evil or disobedient.[18] But not here, for the person 'hated' is a disciple of Jesus and is hated for this very reason.

14. 'But all his acquaintances, including the women who had followed him from Galilee, stood at a distance, watching these things' (23.49). Inasmuch as Luke distinguished these 'acquaintances' from 'relatives' (2.44), there is no reason to include kin here. See Fitzmyer, *The Gospel according to Luke I–IX*, p. 1520.

15. Readers wanting a fulsome reading of this sermon should consult a work such as Hans Dieter Betz, *The Sermon on the Mount: A Commentary on the Sermon on the Mount, including the Sermon on the Plain (Matthew 5:3–7:27 and Luke 6:20-49* (Minneapolis, MN: Fortress Press, 1995).

16. For a fuller exposition of this, see Neyrey, 'Loss of Wealth'.

17. Bruce J. Malina, 'Love', in Pilch and Malina (eds.), *Handbook of Biblical Social Values*, pp. 106-108.

18. Neyrey, 'In Conclusion'.

- 'exclude' describes the process which regularly takes place between what is holy and what is unclean (Lev. 13.4 LXX); Ezra 10.8 suggests the meaning of 'falling under the ban'; in Luke it means 'separating' so as to judge or punish, and so has the sense of 'to outlaw' from a social group.
- 'revile' and reproach are acts of shaming someone (Mt. 11.20; 27.44; Rom. 15.3; 1 Pet. 4.14); the predominant sense is 'disgrace', 'shame', 'scandal', then 'abuse', and 'objurgation'.
- 'defame', literally means 'cast out your name as evil'. Although it has been argued that 'the name' here is '*Christianos*',[19] a man's personal name or reputation[20] is at stake; Luke speaks of someone speaking calumny, that is, of attacking the public reputation and honor of another.[21]

This composite fate speaks of disciples shamed by their families, with the result that they are completely shamed in the eyes of kin and neighbors. The material or economic effects of this are not hard to imagine, as the Tosefta describes the plight of someone thus banned: 'One does not sell to them or receive from them or take from them or give to them. One does not teach their sons a trade, and does not obtain healing from them' (*t. Hul.* 2.20). If he is an artisan, then public reproach will result in loss of employment and trade; if a peasant farmer, the loss of cooperation in planting and harvesting, a break in marriage contracts, an absence from the reciprocal feasts among villagers at weddings and the like. Why, however, does this happen. Jesus is particularly clear: '...on account of the Son of Man' (6.22). Thus the 'how honorable' label which Jesus ascribes to this person is due precisely because this person broke with his family institution to follow Jesus. If Jesus himself had some negative

19. Fitzmyer, *The Gospel according to Luke I–IX*, p. 635.

20. This is no minor matter; see 'Labeling Theory', in Malina and Neyrey, *Calling Jesus Names*, pp. 35-42, 81-85.

21. Sometime the term 'persecution' is thought to summarize this treatment. Indeed previous studies focused on the 'forms of persecution' which befell the early disciples of Jesus as formal judicial acts; D.R.A. Hare, *The Theme of Jewish Persecution of Christians in the Gospel according to St. Matthew* (Cambridge: Cambridge University Press, 1967); Göran Forkman, *The Limits of Religious Community* (Lund: C.W.K. Gleerup, 1972). They describe 'persecution' as a form of exclusion from the synagogue, not, however, the formal *niddui*, but rather 'an informal ban employed by every community...toward individuals it despises' (Hare, *The Theme of Jewish Persecution*, p. 53). The Fourth Gospel speaks of disciples 'cast out of the synagogue' (Jn 9.22; 12.42; 16.2) or simply 'expelled' (Jn 9.34).

experience with his own family such that he broke with it (or they put him out), then Jesus could well be honoring here those who have followed in the master's footsteps. Nevertheless, honorable courage is awarded by Jesus to those disciples. Therefore, Jesus' honoring of 'shameful' sons serves as a bold challenge to the traditional conservatism of the family.

Luke narrates other sayings of Jesus, which we judge speak to his courageous attack on family conservatism.[22] In Luke 12, we find two other statements about the family, one cryptic and the other quite explicit. In the first one (12.22-31), Jesus describes a scene in which a man and a woman lack the basic necessities of peasant living. The story begins with the exhortation: 'Do not worry about your life, what you will eat, or about your body, what you will wear. For life is more than food, and the body more than clothing' (12.22-23). To whom is this addressed? 'Disciples'. Why these? Jesus often speaks here about 'possessions' vs. 'treasure' (12.32-34), warning his disciples 'Be on your guard against all kinds of greed; for one's life does not consist in the abundance of possessions' (12.15). But 'family inheritance' or 'possessions' or 'treasure' are found only in families and among kin, where they function as magnets to hold members there.

But in 12.22 Jesus tells his disciples to forsake the security which a family provides: 'Do not worry about your life, what you will eat, or about your body, what you will wear'. As the story unfolds, two people are in view, a male and a female, but not just any male and any female. Most likely we are to take them as husband and wife, hence a family unit, which is *not* part of any household. Significantly they lack the basic resources found in every family: food, clothing, and shelter. Moreover, they lack the very stuff for growing food (land) and weaving cloth (sheep). Why? The man who has no land is told to 'Consider the ravens: they neither sow nor reap, they have neither storehouse nor barn, and yet God feeds them' (12.24); why not him also? The woman, who has no sheep and so no wool, is told to 'Consider the lilies, how they grow: they neither toil nor spin… But if God so clothes the grass of the field, how much more will he clothe you' (12.27-28). This exhortation is not addressed to all peoples: not *all* males and females lack certain things and not *all* things, but land and wool. They are *not* victims of some periodic famine. They lack a household which would naturally provide such basics.[23] From 6.20-23 we know that some persons are excluded from land and wool '…on account of the Son of Man'. This husband and wife are surely disciples, and likely

22. Neyrey, 'Loss of Wealth', pp. 149-53.

23. See J. Duncan M. Derrett, 'Birds of the Air and Lilies of the Field', *DR* 105 (1978), pp. 181-92.

the same people. Their families have banished them from their kinship groups because of loyalty to another group. They are exhorted to have courage, especially in the form of endurance of hardships for the sake of the kingdom.

> And do not keep striving for what you are to eat and what you are to drink, and do not keep worrying. For it is the nations of the world that strive after all these things, and your Father knows that you need them. Instead, strive for his kingdom, and these things will be given to you as well (12.29-31).[24]

Who was going to declare 'honorable' those whom their families label 'shameful'? In 6.20-23 Jesus is speaking for his Father, and he repeats that here: 'Your Father knows that you need them'. Moreover, 'strive for his kingdom, and these things will be given to you as well'. Their loss is '...on account of the Son of Man'; but resolution comes from 'your Father who knows that you have basic needs', in whose kingdom disciples will be given them.

If there is any doubt that Jesus provokes stress in the kinship institution, his subsequent words remove all doubt (12.49-53). Just as he himself passes through an ordeal (fire...baptism), some—not all—will also be put to the test. This is Jesus' active doing, not general family conflicts, which is evident when he states, 'Do you think that *I have come to bring peace to the earth*? No, I tell you, but *rather division*!' (12.51, italics added). And his division means a radical attack on family ties. We note, moreover, that all relations in a given household (six adults) are set at odds by Jesus: (1) father vs. son, who owes traditional obedience to his father; (2) mother vs. daughter; and (3) mother-in-law vs. daughter-in-law. The daughter-in-law is likely the wife of the son. This family knows no harmony, only division and conflict. To repeat, Jesus himself causes this 'division'; it would seem to have much to do with discipleship and the alienation of the sons from their restraining households.

Finally, in a section which deals with meals, food, and invitees, some disciples are warned off expecting sustenance from their families: 'Whoever comes to me and does not hate father and mother, wife and children, brothers and sisters, yes, and even life itself, cannot be my disciple' (14.26). This prefaces an exhortation to foresee the social death that a disciple must endure to be a disciple. Jesus supports this with

---

24. Wilhelm Wuellner, 'The Rhetorical Genre of Jesus' Sermon in Luke 12:1–13:9', in Duane F. Watson (ed.), *Persuasive Artistry: Studies in New Testament Rhetoric in Honor of George A. Kennedy* (JSNTSup, 50; Sheffield: Sheffield Academic Press, 1991), pp. 93-118.

parallel stories about beginnings which failed because the protagonist did not take foresight before his undertaking. Jesus is hardly concerned with 'building a tower' or 'waging a war'. But provident disciples are warned against 'wealth': 'None of you can become my disciple if you do not give up all your possessions' (14.33). But 'possessions' mean land, a family house, and kinship networks who are a person's only support.[25]

One final collection of exchanges focuses on family matters, and matters of no minor significance. In three successive exchanges, the controversial issue has to do with the relations of would-be disciples and their families and kinship groups. The rhetorical figure here is a chiasm:

A   Someone speaks to Jesus (9.57-58).

   B   Jesus speaks to someone (9.60).

A' Someone speaks to Jesus (9.61-62).

All three remarks, moreover, have to do with the institution of kinship. Jesus has neither house nor home, '...nowhere to lay his head'. If no house, then no household or family or land; if no household, then no land (food) or wool (sheep) or shelter. When Jesus says to another, 'Follow me', this presumes what was just said: no family, no household. But the man addressed cannot follow Jesus until he fulfils family duties: 'First let me go and bury my father'. Clearly this man does not '...hate father and mother, wife and children' (14.26). The third man volunteers to be a disciple, but again family ties hold him fast, because he must 'first say farewell to those at my home'. And put Jesus in second place? The conflict is radical: family/kinship vs. association with Jesus.

These remarks differ from the declarations of honorable behavior (6.20-23), which had to do with the loss a disciple could suffer for discipleship. There, a man's family cut him off. Here, would-be disciples fail the critical test of being able to cut themselves off from family ties. For this failure there is no honor. They are not 'fit for the kingdom of God'. In all of them, however, Jesus and his disciples must reject the bonds of kinship and accept distancing from the primary institution which supports them.

---

25. Mark reports Jesus telling Simon that those who have given up 'house or brothers or sisters or mother or father or children or fields, for my sake and for the sake of the good news' will receive 'a hundredfold now in this age—houses, brothers and sisters, mothers and children, and fields' (10.29). Luke, however, seems to urbanize Jesus' remark by pruning Mark to 'house or wife or brothers or parents or children' (18.29-30).

Courage in Defense of Self: Challenge and Riposte

Modern readers, who do not live in the agonistic culture of the ancient world, have difficulty in appreciating how thoroughly aggressive life was then. For example, Plutarch frequently remarks on this as a common phenomenon: 'The sensible man will guard against the hatred and anger which in the marketplace is imposed by rivalry, in the gymnasia and the palaestra by ambition, in politics and public munificence by eagerness for glory, at dinner and again in drinking by frivolity' (*Table Talk* 1.4). In addition to this general statement, Plutarch gives specific examples of it:

> The Aetolians and the Archaranians, neighboring Greek peoples, ruined one another by their aggressiveness, and the inhabitants of Chalcedon and Byzantium were led by their innate enmity to fight a battle in the Bosporus over a quarrel about a thole. And in the case of private neighbors... proximity sometimes provides the occasion for many affronts (*Commentary on Hesiod's Works and Days* 49).

Scholars of classical Greece have had much to say about this.[26] In such a cultural context we focus on the common form of agonism expressed in the challenge/riposte exchanges in the gospels and in Luke in particular. We note, moreover, that this challenge–riposte exchange is called in the *progymnasmata* a *chreia*, one of the genres Luke surely learned because he employed it frequently.

Almost all of the challenges to Jesus are cast in the form of a question. From studies of the rhetoric of questions, we know that the ancients rarely asked questions for information, but employed questions as weapons.[27] In this cultural context we should evaluate a common form of agonism expressed by challenging questions–responses in Luke's narrative.

The following catalogue of questions which challenge Jesus is lengthy, the frequency of which underscores their significance in Luke's narrative. While this does not represent a complete list, it is sufficient to describe what typically happened to Jesus in public, and how necessary was his defense.

> 'Why do you eat and drink with tax collectors and sinners?' (5.27-32)

> 'The disciples of John fast...so too the disciples of the Pharisees, but yours eat and drink?' (5.33-30)

---

26. Dover, *Greek Popular Morality*, pp. 229-34; David Cohen, *Law, Violence, and Community in Classical Athens* (Cambridge: Cambridge University Press, 1995), pp. 70-75, 90-101, 128.

27. Neyrey, 'Questions, Chreai, and Challenges to Honor'.

'Why are you doing what is not lawful on the sabbath?' (6.1-5)

'Is it lawful on the sabbath to do good or to do harm?' (6.6-11)

'Teacher, what must I do to inherit eternal live?' (10.25-28)

'Lord, do you not care that my sister has left me alone to serve?' (10.38-42)

'Are you telling this parable for us or for all?' (12.41-48)

'Is it lawful to heal on the sabbath or not?' (14.1-6)

'What shall I do to inherit eternal life?' (18.18-30)

'Tell us by what authority you do these things?' (20.1-8)

'Is it lawful to give tribute to Caesar, or not?' (20.20-26)

'In the resurrection, therefore, whose wife will the woman be?' (20.27-40)

In addition to recognizing the rhetorical function of questions as challenges, we can also identify them according to the genre of *chreia*, the rhetorical form taught in the *progymnasmata*. A *chreia* was the common form which dramatized an attack upon the wisdom of a wise man, which he always rebuffed, thus solidifying his reputation as a wise person. Although we considered this previously as a demonstration of savvy wisdom, the fact that Jesus faced these attacks constantly and stood his ground testifies to his courage. He lacked no courage to appear in public, where he manifested perseverance, itself a mark of courage.

Some general observations are useful as we begin this inventory. First of all, the questioner might be the rule maker and enforcer in the synagogue world; it matters when the Scribes and Pharisees question Jesus or his disciples about their failure to observe customs (5.27–6.5). Second, Luke tips off his reader to the hostility of the question by noting that it was a trap, a trick, or an ambush. 'Just then a lawyer stood up to test Jesus. "Teacher", he said, "what must I do to inherit eternal life?"' (10.25); this lawyer asks another aggressive question: 'Wanting to justify himself, he asked Jesus, "And who is my neighbor?"' (10.29). This pattern, moreover, is repeated in all of the *chreiai* and question challenges. Therefore, given the frequency of the challenges to Jesus and their evident hostility, the audience of Luke would have no difficulty in crediting Jesus with a persistent, high-level of courage to face these challenges day after day and week after week.

Courage as Boldness of Speech

Rhetorical definitions of courage include among its parts confidence and boldness. Menander Rhetor used a word in his definition of courage, which became significant in the New Testament: 'Courage should be admired on the grounds of the governor's boldness (*parrēsias*) to the emperors' (*Treatise* II.416.23-28). Paul, it was said, 'went into the synagogue and spoke boldly (with *parrēsia*)' (Acts 19.8). After Peter spoke, 'the rulers, elders, and scribes saw the boldness (*parrēsian*) of Peter and John and realized that they were uneducated and ordinary men' (Acts 4.13). Paul reminded the Thessalonians that 'though we had already suffered and been shamefully maltreated at Philippi, we had courage in our God to speak boldly to you the gospel of God' (1 Thess. 2.2). Thus, the virtue of courage was manifested by bold, confident speech, which was often expressed by New Testament authors by some form of *parrēsia*.

We observe here that Jesus displayed courage by his bold and confident public speech, in particular, when he made his own public challenges to his opponents. On occasion he berated 'the crowds' for persistent obtuseness: 'This generation is an evil generation; it asks for a sign, but no sign will be given to it except the sign of Jonah' (11.29). This, of course, is spoken in public, not to a select few, but to many. Subsequently, after a Pharisee challenged him (11.39), Jesus turns from a single Pharisee to Pharisees in general, calling all of them shameless: 'But woe to you Pharisees! For you tithe mint, rue, and herbs, and neglect justice and the love of God... Woe to you Pharisees! For you love the seat of honor in the synagogues and to be greeted with respect in the marketplaces' (11.42-44).

Who are these 'Pharisees'? What risk does Jesus take in calling them out? One particular description of the Pharisees casts them in sociological terms, which greatly helps to make evident what boldness Jesus displayed in his public challenge to them:

> From a sociological viewpoint, the Pharisees function as rich and powerful patrons of the peasants within the village society and as brokers for the peasants in their relations with the outside world. Luke's objection to them is that they do not care for the poor who depend on them and have a claim on their patronage, especially their generosity and reciprocal, just relations. The Pharisees' use of purity regulations to maintain social order leads to unjust relationships. In response Luke defines true uncleanness as a moral, not a ritual, deficiency.[28]

Pharisees also function as the rule makers and enforcers[29] in the countryside, which suggests that they are public figures with connections to the elite and powerful. They are, then, not just local critics of Jesus but they claim considerable authority to organize their world. Jesus' 'woe' is a confident,

28. Saldarini, *Pharisees, Scribes and Sadducees*, p. 176.
29. Malina and Neyrey, *Calling Jesus Names*.

bold public challenge to significant public people. It speaks the language of courage.

Immediately after, Jesus turns his bold public criticism on 'lawyers'. Earlier a lawyer had tested Jesus with a question, 'What must I do to inherit eternal life?' (10.25); Jesus in turn asked a counter-question: 'What is written in the law? What do you read there?' (10.26). This lawyer tried to recover by asking another question: 'But wanting to justify himself, he asked Jesus, "And who is my neighbor?"' (10.29). Jesus is only their latest target, for they earlier rejected John: 'By refusing to be baptized by him [John], the Pharisees and the lawyers rejected God's purpose for themselves' (7.30). So by the time Jesus speaks boldly against them, Luke's audience knows that they are opponents as well as people of some social standing, so formidable foes. Luke's audience, then, knows how to assess them, when Jesus publicly shames them: 'Woe also to you lawyers! For you load people with burdens hard to bear, and you yourselves do not lift a finger to ease them. Woe to you! For you build the tombs of the prophets whom your ancestors killed... Woe to you lawyers! For you have taken away the key of knowledge; you did not enter yourselves, and you hindered those who were entering' (11.46-52). According to Luke, while responding to one lawyer, Jesus spoke about all of them. And so, Jesus' challenging and public remarks illustrate his courage. The lawyer failed to respond immediately and in public, which made the reproach sting all the more. But the lawyers' riposte to this is not far off: 'When he went outside, the scribes and the Pharisees began to be very hostile towards him and to cross-examine him about many things, lying in wait for him, to catch him in something he might say' (11.53-54). It is a credit to Jesus' courage to take on such opponents.

Bold Political Speech: Attacking the Political Institution
It is one thing for Jesus to speak boldly in Galilee to people without the ability to arrest or capture him, but quite another to speak boldly in the political capital of Israel and in its chief shrine.[30] Luke narrates three events in Jerusalem which express Jesus' bold actions: his entry into the capital city, his judgment on the city, and his challenge to its political shrine. When seen together, they constitute an extended and significant challenge to the political institution of Israel. Enough offense had already been given Jerusalem with the entrance of Jesus, joy to some, but poison

---

30. On the Levitical police who functioned both in the temple and in the city in general, see Joachim Jeremias, *Jerusalem in the Time of Jesus* (Philadelphia, PA: Fortress Press, 1975), pp. 209-10.

to others (19.37-40). Jesus' next bold action consists of a woe oracle for the capital city: 'As he saw the city...wept over it, saying... "The days will come upon you, when your enemies will set up ramparts around you and surround you, and hem you in on every side. They will crush you to the ground, you and your children within you..."' (19.41-44).[31] His challenging speech and actions climax in his entrance to the temple (19.45-46).

Commentators universally label Jesus' actions in Lk. 19.45-46 as his 'cleansing' of the temple, a term not found in any gospel account and perhaps culturally erroneous. How should we label the event? 'Cleansing' does not take into account the fact that the temple was the center of the political institution of Israel,[32] where it functioned as a bank where the rich and powerful people stored their wealth.[33] Moreover, vast wealth, which was needed to support the staff, provide sacrificial animals, and conduct appropriate restoration, was also lodged in the temple treasury.[34] This last item was supplied by the annual temple tax. Moreover, we should remember how costly it was for a peasant even to enter the temple: those who would enter had to buy a particular coin[35]—buying money always

---

31. Prophetic speech against the capital city was always judged as treason. Josephus reports that a certain Jesus (not the man from Nazareth) said this against Jerusalem: 'A voice from the east, a voice from the west, a voice from the four winds; a voice against Jerusalem and the sanctuary, a voice against the bridegroom and the bride, a voice against all the people' (*War* 6.5.3).

32. The explanation of the temple as a political, not a religious, institution is well argued in K.C. Hanson and Douglas E. Oakman, *Palestine in the Time of Jesus: Social Structures and Social Conflicts* (Minneapolis, MN: Fortress Press, 1998), pp. 131-59.

33. One may question the accuracy of the account in 2 Macc. 3.4-6, 10-12, but it is supported by scholarly studies of who deposited what in the temple bank. For easy access to this discussion, see Niell Q. Hamilton, 'Temple Cleansing and Temple Bank', *JBL* 83 (1964), pp. 365-72.

34. Martin Goodman, 'The First Jewish Revolt: Social Conflict and the Problem of Debt', *JJS* 33 (1982), pp. 417-27.

35. 'The Tyrian shekel (drachma) was minted there 125–19 BCE, and became the only coin for paying the temple tax which each Jew had to pay into the sanctuary treasury; it was available only there. This explains the reference in Matt 21:12 to "moneychangers". The moneychanger functioned as both a banker and financier. He sat at the gate of the Temple and made his services available for a fee. For example, when Antiochian tetradrachmas were exchanged for local shekels, a premium of 4%–8% was exacted. The Temple tax of a half shekel to be paid by adult males was specified in rabbinic instruction to be paid in silver didrachmas (=½ shekel) of Tyre' (John W. Betlyon, 'Coinage', in *ABD*, I, p. 1086).

costs more than the coins are worth.[36] Moreover, should they wish to make
any offerings, of bread and wine, they would have to buy those provided
by the temple—to ensure that they were properly tithed, etc. Thus 'those
who sold' were blocking peasants from entry into Israel's shrine. Jesus
acted and spoke with boldness: 'He entered the temple and began to drive
out those who were selling things there; and he said, "It is written, 'My
house shall be a house of prayer'; but you have made it a den of robbers"'
(19.45-46). Whose interests are served here? God's, of course. But also
those of Jesus' peasant associates, for whom the temple had become 'a
den of robbers'. Those whose interests are not served are the Jerusalem
elite, in particular the priests and their associates.

Jesus' bold speech concerning the temple continued along two lines.
First, Luke narrates that 'Every day he was teaching in the temple'
(19.47), '...as he was teaching the people in the temple and telling the
good news...' (20.1), and 'Every day he was teaching in the temple...'
(21.37-38). Thus, Jesus remained a constant and public irritant to the
Jerusalem/Temple elite. Although we do not know the text of his teaching,
his opponents found it so offensive that they plotted his death: 'The chief
priests, the scribes, and the leaders of the people kept looking for a way
to kill him' (19.47). Their initial move, however, was to attack Jesus
verbally: 'The chief priests and the scribes came with the elders and said
to him, "Tell us, by what authority are you doing these things? Who is
it who gave you this authority?"' (20.1-2). His bold speech served as a
verbal challenge to which there was no present riposte.

Second, Jesus spoke about the temple in words which foresaw its
ruin, which the elites considered nothing short of treason and blasphemy.
'When some were speaking about the temple, how it was adorned with
beautiful stones and gifts dedicated to God, he said, "As for these things
that you see, the days will come when not one stone will be left upon
another; all will be thrown down"' (21.5-6). While prophetic judgments
were made against Jerusalem and its shrine, this prophecy speaks to an
unknowable time. It is future, known only to God (Mk 13.32). We note
how Jesus sidesteps all requests for timing: 'Teacher, when will this be,
and what will be the sign that this is about to take place?' (21.7). At Jesus'
trial before the sanhedrin, witnesses testified that Jesus said that he would
himself destroy the temple: 'We heard him say, "I will destroy this temple
that is made with hands, and in three days I will build another, not made
with hands"' (Mk 14.58; Mt. 26.61); and the charge became one of the

36. See Jacob Neusner, 'Money-changers in the Temple: The Mishnah's Explana
tion', *NTS* 35 (1999), pp. 287-90.

barbs with which Jesus was mocked (Mt. 27.40; Mk 15.29). Although Luke does not report any of this, its mention in Mark and Matthew attests to the seriousness of any speech against the temple.

Courage, the Disciples, and Bold Public Speech

Like master, like disciple. If the master spoke boldly to his adversaries, so also should his disciples. After Jesus talks about the eventual destruction of the temple (21.5-6), hearers ask him about the timing of this. He sidesteps the chronological timing ('But before all this occurs...') and addresses his disciples about what awaits them. Jesus tells them that they will experience the same crises that he is about to undergo. But their arrest, persecution, and imprisonment are but the platform for bold public speech: 'You will be brought before kings and governors because of my name. This will give you *an opportunity to testify*. So make up your minds not to prepare your defense in advance; for I will give you words and a wisdom that none of your opponents will be able to withstand or contradict' (21.12-15; cf. Acts 6.10). As well as courage is required for bold speech, it can be manifested by 'endurance' (21.19).

Not all succeed at first in courageously speaking about Jesus, as was the case with Peter (22.54-62), but later he indeed speaks with boldness to the same opponents of his Master: 'When they saw the boldness (*parrēsian*) of Peter and John and realized that they were uneducated and ordinary men, they recognized them as companions of Jesus' (Acts 4.13). These same disciples then petition their Sovereign Lord: 'Lord, look at their threats, and grant to your servants to speak your word with all boldness (*parrēsias*)' (4.29). Paul also received encouragement directly from Jesus to speak boldly to governors and kings: 'The Lord stood near him and said, "Keep up your courage (*tharsei*)! For just as you have testified for me in Jerusalem, so you must bear witness also in Rome"' (Acts 23.11). Therefore, the exhortation to bold public speech by Jesus in Lk. 21.12-15 is dramatically realized by his disciples in Acts.

Courage and the Actions of Disciples

Although words such as 'boldness' and even 'courage' appear elsewhere concerning Jesus' disciples, no such terms accompany other things Jesus commands them to do. One can only imagine the courage necessary to act in this way: 'If any want to become my followers, let them deny themselves and take up their cross daily and follow me. For those who want to save their life will lose it, and those who lose their life for my sake will save it' (9.23-25). Later, they require a different sort of courage to perform Jesus' commission: 'The Lord appointed seventy others and sent them on ahead of him...' (10.1). The task is one of labor, accompanied by great risks: 'See, I am sending you out like lambs into the midst of wolves' (10.3). Not only that, they go with no preparation ('Carry no purse, no bag, no sandals') and act in a bizarre manner ('Greet no one on the road', 10.4). Their reception, moreover, is unsure: 'Whatever house you enter, first say, "Peace to this house!" And if anyone is there who shares in peace, your peace will rest on that person...' (10.6). If their bold speech that 'the kingdom of God has come near' (10.9, 11) is rejected, they must perform an act of public judgment: 'Whenever they do not welcome you, go out into its streets and say, "Even the dust of your town that clings to our feet, we wipe off in protest against you"' (10.11). They will encounter Jesus' enemies, demons (10.17). Even to begin this commission, the disciples must summon up much courage.

Courage to Forego Vengeance
One distinctive characteristic of justice is to act according to the *lex talionis*. Aristotle phrased it as 'to distribute according to desert' (*Virt. Vit.* 5.2), which in *Herennius* meant 'we ought to punish the guilty' (3.3.3); Cicero named it clearly, '...revenge... Revenge is the act of defending or avenging ourselves' (*Inv.* 2.160-161). An attack on one's honor demands retaliation, which presumes courage to attack the attacker. Thus, in the agonistic world of Jesus, every insult, offense, and even physical attack demands a corresponding re-action. Only a coward would forego this. But what courage did Jesus demand when he forbade all retaliation and revenge? 'Love your enemies, do good to those who hate you, bless those who curse you, pray for those who abuse you. If anyone strikes you on the cheek,[37] offer the other also; and from anyone who takes away your coat do not withhold even your shirt...' (6.27-31).

Jesus requires that they play what in others' eyes is the coward, the fool, the person who cannot defend his honor, which culturally equates with surrendering one's manhood. We know, however, that what is foolish in men's eyes is honorable in God's (cf. 1 Cor. 1.24-25). But to act in such a way requires a generous quantity of the virtue of courage. With Jesus the case is different. Except during his arrest and execution, he always responds to honor challenges, as in the case of the *chreiai* described above. He never leaves the playing field as do some of his opponents.

---

37. There is, of course, the example of Paul in Acts 23.1-5.

Courage and Death

In a subsequent chapter we will compare Luke's narrative of the death of Jesus with the traditional topos on 'noble death' popular in the ancient world. In the progymnastic rules for the encomium, students are instructed to report on the death of the person being praised, as a source of honor. Hermogenes has this to say about a 'noble death':

> The manner of his death, (for example) how he died fighting for his country; and if there was anything unusual about it, as in the case of Callimachus, because his corpse remained standing. And you will praise him because of who killed him; for example, that Achilles died at the hands of the god Apollo. You will examine also events after death: if they held games in his honor, as for Patroclus; if there was an oracle about his bones, as with Orestes (*Preliminary Exercises* 16 [Kennedy, p. 82]).

Although exemplified particularly in a warrior culture, a 'fine' or 'noble' death was also within the reach of other worthy people.

Summary and Conclusions

1. At this point, we know two things. First, we appreciate that in a typical encomium honor and praise are to be found in the accomplishments of a worthy person, in particular, in his virtues. Second, we know from our canvas of the remarks of ancient rhetoricians the scope of their understanding of this virtue. It was necessary for soldiers going into combat, and for persons at home who defended house, family, and nation. In particular, it was the hallmark of a man willing to risk dying for them, choosing a life of glory to a base life of cowardice.

2. Conventional New Testament lexica and word studies rarely identify the canonical items we are studying as 'virtues', much less, as one of the canonical four.[38] Unfortunately, this means that Jesus' deeds are rarely ever put in any rhetorical context. Even so, most commentators seem unaware of the meaning of a virtue such as 'courage' and the actions illustrating it. But this monograph bridges that chasm, when it identifies each virtue as a virtue and defines it as the ancients did. Moreover, often commentators who treat Jesus' words and deeds have no insight into the way rhetoricians and progymnastic authors instruct that they be treated.

---

38. BDAG 987 identifies only 'self-mastery' as such.

3. However, not all courageous actions are performed in the face of death. We recognize now that 'courage' apart from war will be expressed by 'confidence, patience, and perseverance', and manifested by bold public speech. 'Courage', the genus, has many species, which should be recognized as parts of the primary virtue.

4. Appreciating the many faces of 'courage', we can study Luke's narrative with a view to different aspects of this manly virtue: courage as *defense* (and endurance, patience and perseverance) and *offense* (challenge and attack, boldness of speech). It belongs to 'courage' to defend oneself against attack, as well as to attack the attackers.

5. Because Jesus moves within two institutions (kinship and politics), we must adjust our focus to see *who* is attacking him over *what issue, and in what institution.* Manly courage will be manifested differently in each. Until Jesus voluntarily allows himself to be arrested, he is shown to be victorious in all attacks and challenges. In this he is defending the role and status which God ascribed to him, and so is defending the interests of God.

6. When readers investigate the virtue of courage in Luke, they become aware of how thoroughly agonistic life was in Jesus' cultural world. This significant cultural background is often overlooked, as well as the fact that the fighting is sparked by issues of honor and shame, and conducted in the context of a zero-sum game where all good, honor in particular, are in limited supply. This, then, is what the view is from the ground.

7. When 'courage' is accepted as one of the canonical virtues, then it becomes one more argument for the hypothesis that Luke is composing his narrative according to the rule of an encomium to find honor for someone in their 'accomplishments', that is, their virtues, namely, the canonical four.

Chapter 7

ENCOMIUM:
ACCOMPLISHMENTS AND VIRTUES:
SELF-CONTROL

Of these three types of lives, the first is luxurious and self-indulgent as regards bodily pleasures, the second is acquisitive and avaricious, while the third is more conspicuous and more disordered than the other two—I mean the one that loves honor and glory (Dio Chrysostom, *Or.* 4.83-84).[1]

Practice self-control in all the things by which it is shameful for the soul to be controlled—gain, anger, pleasure, and pain (Isocrates, *To Demonicus* 1.21).

Self-restraint is a knowledge of what things are worth choosing and what are worth avoiding...to self-restraint are subordinated orderliness, propriety, modesty, and self-control (Arius Didymus 5b1-2).

We have come to the last item in the encomium's 'deeds of the soul', the virtue of 'self-control'. If previous consideration of the other virtues has weight, then all the more should we expect Luke to employ contemporary notions of self-control in his narrative about Jesus. Although self-control traditionally has to do with mastery of emotions and passions, namely, their control by reason, it also regulates much more of a person's social life by restraining extremes of behavior. It might best be understood as 'moderation'.

When we begin to consider 'self-control' (*sōphrosunē*) among the canonical virtues, we are confronted with a major problem, because it was defined and understood in various ways in classical philosophy and rhetoric. Since its meaning varied considerably over time, we need to consider its development more closely, to assess how an author like

---

1. Arius Didymus (ed. Pomeroy), *Epitome of Stoic Ethics*, pp. 13, 15.

Luke might have come to understand it. Fortunately, Helen North[2] wrote a definitive history of *sōphrosunē* in the ancient world, from which we draw our water. Moreover, William V. Harris has made contributions to understanding it, which further aid in understanding restraint.[3] Readers who desire a history of the development of '*self-control*' are directed to North's definitive study. For our purposes, we need only harvest recurring aspects of it to understand how it was and continued to be understood.

Very early, *sōphrosunē* was considered as a 'political virtue' necessary for good civic life which promoted democratic government over the rule of tyrants. Obviously some control of passions was deemed necessary for a good *polis*,[4] to keep people from over-reaching behavior. Because it was considered very close to *aidōs*, fear of losing public respect, moderation was intrinsic to it, as is expressed in Solon's remark *mēte lian* ('not too much').[5] This moderation became inseparable from *mēden agan* ('seek the mean') and *gnōthi seauton* ('know your place in society'), which speak to moderate behavior guided by proper self-knowledge.[6] In time, however, this one virtue was divided into two by Aristotle:

2. Helen North, *Sophrosyne: Self-Knowledge and Self-Restraint in Greek Literature* (Ithaca, NY: Cornell University Press, 1966); North, *From Myth to Icon: Reflections of Greek Ethical Doctrine in Literature and Art* (Ithaca, NY: Cornell University Press, 1979).

3. William V. Harris, *Restraining Rage: The Ideology of Anger Control in Classical Antiquity* (Cambridge, MA: Harvard University Press, 2001).

4. Harris (*Restraining Rage*, p. 80) has this to say about *aidōs*: 'Another is the heroic virtue of *aidōs*, which is normally translated as "shame" (but in fact even more difficult to translate than *orgē* or *thumos*). This is the "prospective, inhibitory emotion" that, to put it very briefly, leads a person to respect the honour of others'.

5. North, *Sophrosyne*, pp. 14-15.

6. North, *Sophrosyne*, pp. 79-80. Socrates and Critias dialogue over *sophrosyne* (temperance and wisdom), from which these pertinent remarks are taken: 'For self-knowledge would certainly be maintained by me to be the very essence of knowledge, and in this I agree with him who dedicated the inscription, "Know thyself!" at Delphi...the ordinary salutation of "Hail!" is not right, and the exhortation "Be temperate!" would be a far better way of saluting one another... This, however, like a prophet he expresses in a sort of riddle, for "Know thyself!" and "Be temperate!" are the same...and succeeding sages added "Never too much"' (Plato, *Charmides* 164-65, in *The Dialogues of Plato* [trans. B. Jowett; New York: Random House, 1937], pp. 14-15).

Aristotle	
To sobriety of mind (*sōphrosynē*) it belongs not to value highly bodily pleasures and enjoyments, not to be covetous of every enjoyable pleasure, to fear disorder, and to live an orderly life in small things and great alike. Sobriety of mind is accompanied by orderliness, regularity, modesty, caution (*Virt. Vit.* 4.5).	To self-control (*enkrateia*) belongs ability to restrain desire by reason when it is set on base enjoyments and pleasures, and to be resolute, and readiness to endure natural want and pain (*Virt. Vit.* 5.1).

Aristotle may split it into two, but both halves continued to exist and were eventually recombined. Important for us, Aristotle maintained that *sōphrosynē* had much to say about an orderly life, as he is quoted above: '...to live an orderly life in small things and great alike. Sobriety of mind is accompanied by orderliness, regularity, modesty, caution', all of which speak to moderation. Self-control not only restrained desires, but expressed a more active feature, namely, to be 'resolute, ready to endure natural want and pain'. Both *sōphrosunē* and *enkrateia* together provide the virtue needed to stand securely in the middle and to withstand attack.

Over time, 'moderation' (*sōphrosunē*) was seen to have three distinct components: *enkrateia* ('control over the appetites'), *karteria* ('endurance of cold, heat, and toil'), and *autarkeia* ('contentment with little, independence of external things').[7] A person with this virtue always sought moderation (*mēden agan*), based on a certain kind of knowledge (*gnōthi seauton*). *Sōphrosunē*, then, was never solely a virtue of the appetitive part of the soul.

Concerning the importance of 'self-mastery', Helen North observed how it suited the common experience of people, because it expressed, 'The common aim of all Hellenistic philosophies, to render man secure against the blows of chance...in this Cyrenaic attempt to attain steadfast composure under all circumstances'.[8] Accordingly, this required moderation in behavior according to one's self-knowledge.

As Greek rhetoric found its way to Rome, Cicero declared that no particular Latin word adequately translated *sōphrosunē*.[9] Thus, he settled on 'temperance' (*temperantia*). Furthermore, the definition of 'temperance' in Herrenius has proved to be most helpful for this study:

7. North, *Sophrosyne*, pp. 124-25.
8. North, *Sophrosyne*, p. 135.
9. North, *Sophrosyne*, pp. 258-59.

'We will be using the topics of Temperance if we censure the inordinate desire for office, money, or the like; if we restrict each thing to its definite natural bounds; if we show how much is enough in each case, advise against going too far, and set the due limit to every matter' (3.3.5).[10] Here Temperance should control 'the *inordinate* desire for office, money, or the like', including honor and respect—'inordinate' being the key. His comment that 'Temperance' is accompanied by control of ambition for 'office, money, etc.' is a most welcome expansion of the meaning of this virtue. Moderation is clearly on stage. Moreover, when things are 'restricted...to definite natural bounds', praise is awarded for seeking the middle (*mēden agan*). Included is knowing what 'enough' means: 'how much is enough in each case'—'enough' suggesting the avoidance of extremes. Furthermore, it knows how to 'set the due limit to every matter'. Thus 'moderation' sums up what Herennius thinks about Temperance.

This broad definition of 'self-control' provides us with several topics with which to assess Luke's appreciation of this fourth virtue in regard to encomiastic 'accomplishments'. From our sources we know that one cannot approach consideration of this virtue without recognition of the pair, 'self-knowledge' and 'self-restraint'. Self-knowledge' (*gnōthi seauton*) speaks to social knowledge of where a person belongs in terms of rank and status in relationship to others. After that, self-restraint (*mēden agan*) moderates behavior to curb over-reaching actions and so to prevent loss of honor on either side. While the virtue always required control of emotions (food and sex), it depended on knowledge, first knowledge of self and then knowledge of what needs restraint. Thus, we suggest that the following aspects of 'self-control' be kept in mind as we read Luke.

1. Self-mastery of emotions (food and sex, as well as 'inordinate' desires).
2. Self-knowledge in appreciating one's proper social location in terms of role and status.

10. Of 'Temperance', Cicero says: 'Temperance is a firm and well-considered control exercised by reason over lust and other improper impulses of the mind. Its parts are continence, clemency, and modesty' (*Inv.* 2.164). 'Modesty' for Cicero means 'a sense of shame or decency which secures observance and firm authority for what is honorable'. Cicero also stated: 'It is also probable that the temperate man (*temperans*)—the Greeks call him *sôphrôn*, and they apply the term *sôphrosynê* to the virtue which I usually call, sometimes temperance, sometimes self-control, and occasionally also discretion...but our term has a wider meaning, for it connotes all abstinence and inoffensiveness (and this with the Greeks has no customary term, but it is possible to use *ablabeia*, harmlessness; for inoffensiveness is a disposition of the soul to injure no one)' (*Tusc. Disp.* 3.16).

3. Restraint of over-reaching behavior.
4. Pursuit of moderation, nothing to excess; knowing when 'enough' is enough.

Control of Passions, Emotions, and Desires

Nothing is ever simple for us, because as moderns we must be careful when we talk about 'emotions' in antiquity. Their term was *pathos*, a 'passion', which derives from the verb 'to suffer', that is, to experience something. This implies that when someone experiences something, that experience, which is a feeling, is a reaction to some stimulus. This might be translated as 'emotion', only if we accept that it is *caused by something outside of a person*.[11] For the most part, the ancients acknowledged relatively few 'passions', such as anger, hate, fear, shame, indignation, and envy.[12] We accept these; and for the sake of convenience we will name them 'emotions', not 'passions', which facilitates conversation with classical scholarship. But, essential to the following discussion is appreciation of emotions as *caused by some external experience*.

Since our immediate task requires us to think about these emotions as did the ancients, we observe that part of their definition lies in the way they are considered in terms of their opposite. Emotions, Aristotle stated, come in pairs, i.e., binary opposition.[13] The following catalogue is drawn from Aristotle: anger vs. mildness; hate vs. love; fear vs. confidence; shame vs. benevolence; indignation vs. pity; and envy vs. emulation (*Rhet.* 2.2-9). In addition to emotions which are binary opposites, the ancients also juxtaposed virtues with vices, as illustrated by Diogenes Laertius: 'Of the beautiful there are four species: namely, what is just, courageous, orderly and wise... Similarly there are four species of the base or ugly, namely, what is unjust, cowardly, disorderly, and unwise' (*D.L.* 7.100).[14] The

---

11. David Konstan, *The Emotions of the Ancient Greeks: Studies in Aristotle and Classical Literature* (Toronto: University of Toronto Press, 2007), pp. 3-40.

12. Some ancient authors identified innumerable emotions, such as Longinus, *On the Sublime* 22.1; *D.L.* 7.111. 'Emotions', Aristotle states, 'are those things through which, by undergoing change, people come to differ in their judgments and which are accompanied by pain and pleasure, for example, anger, pity, fear and other such things and their opposites' (*Rhet.* 2.1.8).

13. See G.E.R. Lloyd, *Polarity and Analogy: Two Types of Argumentation in Early Greek Thought* (Cambridge: Cambridge University Press, 1966).

14. Goods comprise the virtues of prudence, justice, courage, temperance, and the rest; while the opposite of these are evils, namely, folly, injustice, and the rest' (*D.L.* 7.102).

ancients, moreover, excelled in ranking things in importance. Thus, anger emerged as the monarch of the emotions, a topic thoroughly examined throughout the ancient world.[15] Anger is the emotion most likely to be out-of-control, without the reins of reason to restrain it.

But whose emotions in the gospel are we observing?[16] Those of Jesus? Those of others? We first consider whether Luke portrayed Jesus as 'suffering' any emotions, which ones, and whether they were controlled, i.e., 'moderated'. To begin with, we observe that Luke never uses the words self-knowledge (*sōphrosunē*) and self-control (*enkrateia*), which we have learned is no reason for thinking that Luke ignores this expression of Jesus' virtuous 'accomplishments'. As we have seen time and again, rhetoricians were instructed not to state baldly that so-and-so possessed self-mastery. Instead, they would describe behavior which an audience would immediately grasp as self-mastery. They expected audiences to observe behavior rather than hear labeling. One picture is worth a thousand words.

Jesus' Emotions—Few, Always Reasonably Controlled

If modern readers of Luke think of this canonical virtue at all, they most likely know it from the slanders used to belittle both John and Jesus: 'For John the Baptist has come eating no bread and drinking no wine, and you say, "He has a demon"; the Son of Man has come eating and drinking, and you say, "Look, a glutton and a drunkard, a friend of tax-collectors and sinners!"' (7.33-34). This remark, to be sure, is not a Lukan discussion of virtue, but a controversial remark, intended to insult. Although Lk. 7.31-35 has been much discussed, the treatment by Wendy J. Cotter has emerged as a particularly worthwhile study of it.[17] After identifying the major interpretations of the parable, she carefully examines the precise

15. Harris (*Restraining Rage*, pp. 127-28) concluded his book with 'Appendix: Treatises on Emotions and on Anger', which is a good indication of its importance throughout the ancient world's history.

16. Harris (*Restraining Rage*, p. 110) reports about a time when some Stoics thought that a man should feel no emotion; later Harris (121) quotes Galen that the ideal is to eradicate them: 'I thought the first step was to free oneself from one's *pathē*... And there are *pathē* of the soul which everybody knows: *thumos*, *orgē*, fear, grief, envy, and extreme desire. In my opinion, excessive vehemence in loving and hating anything is also a *pathē*; I think that the expression "moderation is best" is correct, since no immoderate action is good. How, then, could a man eradicate these things if he did not first that he had them?' (Galen, *De propriorum* 3.1-2).

17. Cotter, 'The Parable of the Children in the Market-Place'.

vocabulary used in it[18] and comes to this conclusion: 'We have seen that both the application of the parable (vv. 33-34) and the proverb (v. 35) understand the central issue as one of *unreasonable objection on the basis of wild conclusions* about their (John's and Jesus') eating customs. Verse 35 professes that Wisdom has been maligned but will be proved righteous after all.'[19] This means that,

> ...the application of the parable provides the Q community with a feisty defense of John and Jesus. They take advantage of the parable's image to launch an attack on their own, charging that the denouncing of John and Jesus does not rest on any substantial grounds, but on the self-serving foolishness of puffed-up charlatans who are incapable of recognizing Wisdom.[20]

Thus, ascetic abstinence and ample eating are not vices being discussed here. Jesus did *not* display an uncontrolled passion for food and drink.[21] Although Luke regularly describes Jesus eating with tax collectors and sinners, as well as with Pharisees, no accusation was ever made that he lacked self-control. Jesus, therefore, did not suffer from this emotion, much less lack control over it.

Did Jesus have any emotions? Three times Luke edits his source to excise Mark's notes about Jesus' emotions. First, when the rich man confessed to keeping the commandments all of his life, Mark says 'Jesus loved him' (10.21). But this is omitted in Luke's version of the same story (18.21-22). Second, the king, who was insulted by his nobles when they begged off coming to the king's feast, was overcome with anger and took honorable revenge on those who shamed him: 'The king was enraged. He sent his troops, destroyed those murderers, and burned their city' (Mt. 22.7). But Luke omits this for reasons still unclear. Third, when Jesus attacks the buying and selling in the temple, Mark includes so many details that it becomes high drama (11.15-17), all of which is omitted by Luke (19.45-46). Fourth, Mark says that Jesus experienced 'grief' in the

---

18. For example, the children are *sitting*, not playing games; they *call out* (used in judicial contexts); in a *market place* (where courts are found). See Cotter, 'The Parable of the Children in the Market-Place', pp. 295-302.

19. Cotter, 'The Parable of the Children in the Market-Place', p. 303.

20. Cotter, 'The Parable of the Children in the Market-Place', p. 303.

21. It should be noted, moreover, that Jesus appears to have fasted during the Passover meal recorded in 22.15-38; J.A. Zeisler, 'The Vow of Abstinence', *Colloquium* 5 (1972), pp. 12-14, and Zeisler, 'The Vow of Abstinence Again', *Colloquium* 6 (1973), pp. 49-50; he wrote about a 'vow of abstinence', but this distracted him from considering whether Jesus fasted.

Garden (12.34), which Luke omitted.[22] It would wrong to say that Luke
wants to purge Jesus of any emotions. However, are any emotions shown
to be, in fact, out of rational control?

Jesus occasionally expresses an emotion appropriate to its situation.
When lepers asked Jesus for 'mercy' (*eleēson*, 17.13), he reacted by
cleansing them. Similarly a blind man outside Jericho asks for the same
(18.35-36), and Jesus likewise reacted to his petition. The ancients would
label this 'pity' or (*prautēs*),[23] an emotional response to a situation which
the person did not cause himself, which was the case with the lepers and
the blind man. Jesus displays a similar emotional reaction at the funeral of
a widow's last or only son: 'When the Lord saw her, he had compassion
(*esplagxnisthē*) for her and said, "Do not weep"' (7.13). This emotion is
the same one that the Samaritan showed the wounded Israelite (10.33),
and the father expressed on his son's return (15.20). Literally, this was a
'gut reaction' by Jesus. When people petition Jesus to have 'mercy, pity,
or compassion', they are impinging on Jesus' senses of sight, hearing,
and feeling; they seek to cause an emotional reaction in Jesus. And it
appears that this emotion is appropriate and controlled, and so expresses
self-mastery. Caution: 'mercy' here is not forgiveness of sins, but an act
of compassion.

Pharisees vs. Jesus: 'Inordinate Desires'

We know that virtues are often understood by their opposite, which
suggests that we ask whether Luke presents an extended comparison
between Jesus and the Pharisees. But a comparison over what? To repeat
Herrenius, 'We will be using the topics of Temperance if we censure the
inordinate desire for office, money, or the like' (3.3.3). To this we add Dio
Chrysostom's *Fourth Oration* 'On Kingship', which expands Herrenius's
categories. Dio reports a fictitious conversation between Diogenes and
Alexander, in which the philosopher tries to lead the Warrior-King to
virtuous wisdom. In the course of the exchange, Diogenes informs the
monarch about three ways in which ordinary people manifest desires
out of control. Of course, the philosopher insinuates that his interlocutor
should consider these excesses as things he must master to be a wise king.

---

22. Jerome H. Neyrey, 'The Absence of Jesus' Emotions—the Lucan Redaction
of Lk 22,39-46', *Biblica* 61 (1980), pp. 153-59; reprinted in Neyrey, *The Passion
according to Luke: A Redaction Study of Luke's Soteriology* (Eugene, OR: Wipf &
Stock, 2007), pp. 49-68.

23. David Konstan, *Pity Transformed* (London: Duckworth, 2001).

But for our purposes, his narrative about these 'out-of-control desires' serves as an excellent example of self-control (*sōphrosunē*).

> Now as there are three prevailing types of lives which the majority adopt... the first is *luxurious and self-indulgent as regards bodily pleasures*, the second is *acquisitive and avaricious*, while the third is a more conspicuous and more disordered than the other two—I mean the one *that loves honour and glory*—and it manifests a more evident and violent disorder or frenzy (*Or.* 4.83-84, italics added).

The foolish man lacks rational control over these three emotions which drive ordinary men, but which the wise and virtuous man masters. The master masters them because of the virtue of 'sobriety' (*sōphrosunē*) and 'self-control' (*enkrateia*). These three, which are hardly original with Diogenes, have been conveniently brought together as illustrative of characteristic 'inordinate desires', that is, they are typical emotions outside of reason's control. We propose to describe how Luke compares and contrasts[24] Jesus and the Pharisees in terms of these three excesses: pleasure, wealth, and honor, prominence, and prestige.

About Pleasure

At the beginning of his *De Virtutibus et Vitiis Libellus* (*Virtues and Vices*), Aristotle offers these useful remarks: 'In accordance with Plato the spirit is taken as having three parts, wisdom is the goodness of the rational part, gentleness and courage of the passionate, of the appetitive sobriety of mind (*sōphrosunē*) and self control (*enkrateia*)...' (1.3). The last item, the appetitive part, consists of *sōphrosunē* and *enkrateia*, which are generally thought necessary to control desires concerning sex and food. Luke's narrative is totally silent about sex in Jesus' life, although there is much to say about food and meals. Lukan treatment of meals, foods, and table etiquette has been amply examined, but we bring to the conversation the suggestion that Luke is comparing and contrasting Jesus' opponents with Jesus himself in terms of this virtue. To Herrenius's list of 'inordinate desires' ('for office, money, or the like', 3.3.3), we include concerns by Pharisees over meals. *Sōphrosunē* means that 'we restrict each thing to its definite natural bounds; if we show how much is enough in each case'.

---

24. Readers are referred to the progymnastic rules for 'comparison' or *synkrisis*. Besides maxim, *chreia*, and encomium, Luke would have been taught this genre. Examples of comparison in Luke include: (1) contrast between Zechariah and Mary (1.5-36); (2) obedience to contrasting fathers (2.41-52); (3) etiquette denied but given (7.36-50); (4) Israelites vs. Samaritan (10.29-37) (5) prodigal vs. loyal sons (15.11-32); (6) Pharisee vs. tax collector praying (18.9-14); and the two thieves (23.39-43).

As the following figure indicates, all of the concerns of the Pharisees are explicitly non-concerns for Jesus. Their concerns, Luke implies, are inordinate.

Pharisees and meals	Jesus, disciple, and meals
symposia held in their houses[25] (7.36-50; 11.37-42; 14.1-6).	Jesus and meals: thrice invited to dine with Pharisees in their houses and to participate at symposia
Pharisees' excess over meals: 'There was a rich man who was dressed in purple and fine linen and who feasted sumptuously every day' (16.19).	Jesus' open eating strategy
concern over with whom one eats— their regular criticism of Jesus (5.27-32; 15.1-2; 19.5-7).	no concern over those with whom Jesus eats with: (1) tax collectors and sinners (5.27-32; 15.1-2; 19.5-7); (2) crowds (9.10-17); (3) whom to invite (14.12-14)
meal etiquette (denied: 7.36-50)	new meal etiquette: where to sit (14.7-10)
washing before meals (11.37-40)	non-concern with washing before meals (14.1-6)
concern over how food is produced, i.e., harvest, tithes (11.42)	no concern over how food is produced: food harvested on sabbath, probably un-tithed (6.1-5); eating whatever set before you (10.7-8)
fasting (5.33-35)	no fasting (5.33-35)
roles and statuses confirmed at meals	roles and statuses around meals upset (10.38-42; 12.37; 14.7-10)

As the figure indicates, all of the concerns of the Pharisees are explicitly non-concerns for Jesus. But does Luke want his audience to consider the behavior of the Pharisees as out-of-control, excessive, and lacking in self-control? It can be argued that they represent in a thorough way an extreme,

---

25. Walter Burkert, 'Oriental Symposia: Contrasts and Parallels', in William J. Slater (ed.), *Dining in a Classical Context* (Ann Arbor: University of Michigan Press, 1991), pp. 7-24; Dennis Smith, 'Table Fellowship as a Literary Motif in the Gospel of Luke', *JBL* 106 (1987), pp. 613-38; S. Stein, 'The Influence of Symposia Literature on the Literary Form of the Pesah Haggadah', *JJS* 8 (1957), pp. 13-44.

whether in their banquets-symposia or in their portrayal in the parable about how the rich man dined (16.19-21). Their concerns over how foods were produced or whether they fasted—a very visible claim to honor—or how they washed before meals, are certainly not the concerns of Jesus or his peasant audience, and so should be seen as excessive in their own way. The eating strategy of the Pharisees would restrict, exclude, and so dishonor many people, an extreme narrowing of what constitutes holiness, in contrast to Jesus' eating strategy which contests that in every way. Thus Luke's reporting on food and meals draws very sharp distinctions: closed vs. open groupings, many rules vs. few, ostentation vs. sustenance, and honorable claims vs. shameful criticisms. The distinctions, we argue, are excessive in regard to the Pharisees, sometimes depicted as indulgent and other times as haughty. In light of these sharp contrasts, the Pharisees need *sōphrosunē* and *enkrateia*, as opposed to Jesus.[26]

About Wealth
Jesus expresses no desire for wealth for himself, only that those without it be supported. The following figure juxtaposes what Luke says about the desire for wealth by Jesus' opponents in contrast to his own thoughts and desires.

Pharisees and Wealth	Jesus and Wealth
'The Pharisees, who were lovers of money, heard all this, and they ridiculed him'.[27] 'So give for alms those things that are within; and see, everything will be clean for you' (11.41)	Jesus and wealth, devaluing it (10.3-4; 12.13-21, 22-31, 33; 14.12-14; 18.18-23, 24-27; 19.1-8; 21.1-4)
description of the social position of Pharisees as managers of estates and as would-be brokers who fail their clients[28]	the peasant audience of Jesus was swamped with debit; many of them were day laborers working in the fields managed by the Pharisee managers.
social position of Pharisees as estate managers	parables about taxes and debt; critical remarks about absentee landlords (16.1-8; 20.9-19)

26. In the *progymnasmata*, students were taught to compare persons (*synkrisis*). New Testament writers employ 'comparisons' on a small and large scale. 'Are you greater than our Father Jacob...' (Jn 4.12), and '...greater than our father Abraham' (Jn 8.53); see also Neyrey, 'Encomium versus Vituperation'.

27. For an excellent study of Lk. 16.14, see Halvor Moxnes, *The Economy of the Kingdom: Social Conflict and Economic Relations in Luke's Gospel* (Philadelphia, PA: Fortress Press, 1988).

28. Saldarini, *Pharisees, Scribes and Sadducees*, pp. 50-67, 174-98.

Jesus teaches that wealth is good only when spread around,[29] when taxes are moderated and debts cancelled. As he said, 'You cannot serve God and mammon'. NO, Jesus shows no desire for wealth, much less an 'inordinate one'.

About Honor, Prominence and Prestige

Luke regularly portrays Jesus in flight from fame, reputation, and honor. This material, once called the 'messianic secret', was an hypothesis that Jesus' disciples promoted him posthumously. While subsequent scholarship has demolished this, better explanations of the data can be had though social-science discussions of secrecy.[30] The synoptic evangelists all attest to the phenomenon that Jesus eschewed fame and honor, and regularly sought to avoid it. At the beginning of Jesus' activity, several events occur which have thematic importance, because they establish a pattern illustrating how Jesus did not seek to benefit from honor and fame. When Jesus confronts demons, they are want to challenge him by manipulating his special name, only to be commanded to 'Silence!' (Lk. 3.34-35, 41). Alternately, when Jesus heals a leper, he commands him to perform a public process to be certified 'clean', by going to a person whose public job it was to declare 'unclean' and 'clean', namely, a priest: 'He ordered him to tell no one. "Go", he said, "and show yourself to the priest...for a testimony to them"' (5.14). Jesus 'ordered' him, but his strategy failed: 'But now more than ever the word about Jesus spread abroad; many crowds would gather to hear him and to be cured of their diseases. But he would withdraw to deserted places and pray' (5.15).

Statements such as these argue that Jesus had no desire for honor and fame whatsoever. Moreover, after the report about the popular labeling of Jesus climaxed with Peter's declaration, 'The Messiah of God', Jesus immediately silenced this talk: 'He sternly ordered and commanded them not to tell anyone' (9.21)—'sternly ordered and commanded them', indeed. Furthermore, Jesus replaces the honorable titles given him by men with a new title, which has nothing to do with honor: 'The Son of Man must undergo great suffering, and be rejected by the elders, chief priests, and scribes, and be killed, and on the third day be raised' (9.22). First silence of reputation, then proclamation of shame.

---

29. Luke records Jesus' conclusion to the story about the man who did not share his excessive harvest: 'So it is with those who store up treasures for themselves but are not rich towards God' (12.21); and 'rich with God' is explained later, 'Make friends for yourselves by means of dishonest wealth' (16.9).

30. Pilch, 'Secrecy in the Mediterranean World'; Neyrey, 'The Sociology of Secrecy and the Fourth Gospel'.

Far from seeking or exploiting fame and honor, Jesus foresees for himself the fate of a rejected prophet. Three times in the second half of Luke's narrative Jesus could see with wisdom how his story would end. 'For he will be *handed over* to the Gentiles; and he will be *mocked* and *insulted* and *spat upon*. After they have *flogged* him, they will *kill* him' (18.22-23, italics added). Although Jesus foresees that God will vindicate and honor him ('…and on the third day he will rise again'), that final vindication is but the undoing of shame; so Jesus says in 24.26-27. Confirmation of this is found in Jesus' demands that his disciples follow him in shame and dishonor, because, in his calculus, loss of life means gaining it (9.23-26). In this argument from advantage, whatever benefit will occur comes at a great price.

The following figure once more contrasts Jesus' opponents with himself and his teaching according to the calculus found in Luke's understanding of the ways of God (1.51-52).[31]

'Inordinate' desire for honor in Jesus' Opponents	Dis-valuing the honor in Jesus' world
(Pharisees) 'For you love to have the seat of honour in the synagogues and to be greeted with respect in the market-places' (11.43)	retaliation and defense of honor denied (6.27-31) choice of worst seats urged (14.7-11)
(Scribes) '…who like to walk around in long robes, and love to be greeted with respect in the market-places, and to have the best seats in the synagogues and places of honor at banquets' (20.46)	inversions: – the proud cast down, lowly raised up (1.52) – shameful is honorable, and honorable is shameful (6.20-24) – exalted are humbled, humble exalted (14.11; 18.14) – least is greatest (11.26) – last are first, first are last (13.30)

Jesus' opponents seek recognized signs of honor: 'seats of honor… respectful greetings…clothing…and places of honor at banquets'. His disciples, in contrast, must choose the worst seats (14.7-11), and are denied honorable retaliation (6.27-31). They must live in a world 'turned

---

31. John T. Squires published his Yale dissertation, *The Plan of God in Luke–Acts* (Cambridge: Cambridge University Press, 1993); his focus was on divine providence or plan, but he seems to have ignored the consideration in Luke-Acts that God's ways are not human ways. He has nothing to say about the presentation of God in Lk. 1.51-52.

upside down, where shameful is honorable, least is greatest, and last is first. If the opponents labor for honor and respect, Jesus and his disciples choose the opposite.

Moderation in Jesus' Behavior

We have observed above that, while Jesus' opponents manifest 'inordinate desire' for things such as wealth and honor, he does not. He has mastered what masters his opponents. But other aspects of *sōphrosunē* should be considered, such as *self-knowledge* of one's proper social location in terms of role and status, and *moderation*, nothing to excess, knowing when 'enough' is enough. These will restrain one from over-reaching behavior. In Luke's depiction of how Jesus behaves when confronted by excessive anger, we expect to see moderation operative. We turn now to consider what anger out-of-control looks like and the moderate response of Jesus.

The Anger of Others: The Emotion Most Out-of-Control

This claim hardly needs to be argued.[32] The ancients define anger[33] as the reaction created by the pain caused someone by another: 'A longing...for a real or apparent revenge for a real or apparent slight' (Aristotle, *Rhet.* 2.2.1).[34] Anger is caused by a 'slight', that is, the change in opinion about someone such that he appears valueless in the eyes of others. Divisions naturally follow: 'There are three kinds of slight: disdain, spitefulness, and insult' (2.2.3). Of 'insult' Aristotle says: the sufferer is disgraced, that is, dishonored, because proper respect is not shown. We are again in the cultural realm of honor and shame, as Aristotle continues: 'Men think that

---

32. Harris, *Restraining Rage*, especially pp. 127-28.

33. Harris, *Restraining Rage*, p. 153. See Seneca, *On Anger*, and Plutarch, *On Controlling Anger*. Several modest-sized treatments include, Konstan, *The Emotions of the Ancients Greeks*, pp. 41-76, and William W. Fortenbaugh, 'Aristotle and Theophrastus on the Emotions', in John Fitzgerald (ed.), *Passions and Moral Progress in Greco-Roman Thought* (London: Routledge, 2008), pp. 9-47.

34. This translation is itself problematic, as Harris (*Restraining Rage*, p. 57) observes: 'In the *Rhetoric* he (Aristotle) adopts the dialectician's approach, but he gives a more detailed version of it: anger is "the desire, accompanied by pain, for perceived retaliation [*timōria*] for some perceived slight to oneself or one's own, the slight not having been deserved". (This passage is, by the way, frequently mistranslated—there is nothing in the Greek about a "conspicuous" slight or "conspicuous" retaliation).'

they have a right to be highly esteemed by those who are inferior to them in birth, power, and virtually, and generally, in whatever similar respect a man is far superior to another' (2.2.7). 'Men', he continues, 'are angry with those who ridicule, mock, and scoff at them, for this is an insult' (2.2.12); and 'they are angry with those who have been in the habit of honoring and treating them with respect, if they no longer behave so towards them' (2.2.15-16). The poisonous plant of anger springs from a perceived slight and matures into revenge. Aristotle offers a more refined understanding (*Nich. Eth.* 4.5.1125b27-1126b10) where he talks about being angry with the right people for the right reasons, in the right manner, at the right moment, and for the right amount of time. Nevertheless, for our purposes, anger is the strong reaction to perceived insults and slights; it may grow into a desire for revenge.

Jesus' Moderation when Attacked

We should ask how Luke portrays Jesus as the object of the hostile emotion of anger and so consider his reactions to it. In Luke, only two people are described as being 'angry'. They are fictional characters in narratives that portray great shame inflicted on them. The rich man whose lavish banquet is spurned by his peers is genuinely insulted, and reacts with 'anger' (14.2), but nothing suggests that this is irrational or uncontrolled.[35] The elder son slighted by his father reacts to his shaming by being 'angry' and refusing to celebrate his brother's return (15.28). He reacts to a serious honor insult by his father, and retaliates with strong words, inappropriate for a loyal son. Again, he responds to being seriously shamed.

   Luke's audience was not so naive as to ignore the anger expressed in the exchanges between Jesus and his opponents simply because the word 'anger' is not used. As we noted, 'conflict' is predicted of Jesus by a prophet (2.34), begun in 4.18-30, and increased steadily from the beginning of his public actions. We need to examine this extended conflict in terms of 'anger', by focusing on the growth of this emotion from its beginning, not in Jesus, of course, but in his opponents.

   When Jesus first appears in the synagogue at Nazareth, he makes a striking honor claim (4.16-21). He publicly states his role and status to be that described in Isaiah 61, affirming that 'today this scripture is fulfilled'. In the normal course of the narrative, i.e., apart from Nazareth, Luke's

---

35. Luke omits the king's reaction recorded in Mt. 22.7, which narrates that 'The king was enraged. He sent his troops, destroyed those murderers, and burned their city.' This describes an angry reaction to a serious honor insult.

account of this would tell how Jesus' audience approves of the claim. Luke's audience would know by now that Jesus' presence was prophesied by John (3.15-17), his role and status established by God (3.21-22), and confirmed by Jesus' demonstration of perfect loyalty to God (4.1-12). Moreover, Jesus' claim had already been accepted by 'all the surrounding country' and by other synagogues (4.14-15). On the narrative level, the claim should be accepted as valid, but it is roundly rejected.[36] Jesus counters the rejection by making another claim that, like all prophets, 'No prophet is accepted in the prophet's home town' (4.24). He continues his claims by citing the examples of Elijah and Elisha, which only provoke a more violent reaction: 'All in the synagogue were filled with rage' (4.28). Their reaction confirms one claim, namely, he is a *rejected* prophet. This response, moreover, inflames the town to lethal anger against him, which he sidesteps. According to the choreography of anger, the Nazareth synagogue feels belittled,[37] to which Jesus responds with a re-affirmation of his claim, which provokes them to anger. They display an emotion which is out-of-control, whereas Jesus responds appropriately by trying to moderate their anger with reasons supporting his claim. But what of Jesus' claims? Do they always provoke anger? Luke is using a pattern about the growth and progress of anger against Jesus, which he will use repeatedly in his narrative: a *claim* (expressed or implied) is made, which is felt by some as an *insult* or *slight* (an honor challenge), which prompts them to issue a counter *insult*, which results in the person attacked *attacking the attacker*, etc. Those who feel belittled are shown to increase in anger which grows increasingly out of control.

In theory, the initial response to feeling belittled is to attempt to do the same to the offender, namely, to belittle him in turn. Anger, much less revenge, therefore, is not the initial reaction; first the offender must experience a comparable belittlement before revenge comes on the scene. Those who observed public behavior knew this to be the choreography of anger: perceived provocation or belittlement issues in a reciprocal reaction to belittle the belittler. Jesus' honor claim is interpreted as an insult; he claims status above that of a mere resident of Nazareth, which

36. Operating in the cultural background is the common notion of 'limited good' expressed in a perception of life as a zero-sum game: if someone gains—say, in honor—then someone is losing. See Jerome H. Neyrey and Richard L. Rohrbaugh, '"He Must Increase, I Must Decrease" (John 3:30): A Cultural and Social Interpretation', *CBQ* 63 (2001), pp. 464-83.

37. For a description of the honor quotient in this episode, see Rohrbaugh, 'Luke's Jesus'.

others perceive as diminishing them. They respond the way they were taught: belittling the belittler and then seeking revenge when the belittling increases. Observers and audience know the steps of this dance.

This dynamic should sound familiar to readers of this book, who, by now, are familiar with the rhetorical genre from the *progymnasmata* called a *chreia*. A wise or prominent man already has a reputation for excellence; his prowess in a limited good world is perceived as diminishing the standing of someone else (a belittling), which provokes this belittled person to attempt to belittle the wise or prominent person. Those who feel diminished in honor (insulted or dishonored) ask hostile questions to their belittler to belittle him in turn and so diminish the belittler's honor. This is called an 'honor challenge'. The person thus challenged then attacks his attackers, by asking a counter-question. When he succeeds, the person belittled withdraws, but hardly becomes content with his honor now publicly diminished. Thus, when we examine the dynamics of anger in Luke, we already know the rhetorical choreography of anger because we are familiar with that of the *chreia*.

Returning to Luke, the rejected claims of Jesus are quickly validated. For example, we expect that when Jesus cleansed the leper, this event occurred in public (5.12-16). However wonderful the cleansing itself, it needs to be publicly acknowledged, not simply in the eyes of onlookers, but officially; therefore, the leper himself needs public certification from the proper officials to resume his life. The healed man would achieve this when he offers public sacrifice and obtains certification from the guardians of purity, the priests. An honor claim by Jesus clearly functions in the story, inasmuch as a summary of such healing powers was claimed earlier in 4.18-19, and Jesus compared himself to Elisha who healed a leper. Luke can expect his audience to remember that earlier material, and so appreciate that the authorization previously claimed now applies in the cleansing of this leper as well. The claim here is implicit, but rhetorically evident. The cleansed man, however, did not follow orders, but promoted Jesus' claim: 'Now more than ever the word about Jesus spread abroad; many crowds would gather to hear him and to be cured of their diseases' (5.15). No anger is described because no one has been belittled here.

But Luke immediately tells a series of stories in which certain other groups perceive Jesus' claim to special role and status as belittling them. In the very next story, Jesus recognizes some acceptance of his implicit claims in the efforts made by the paralytic's kin to place him in the lap of Jesus: 'He saw their faith'. Jesus then makes a new claim: 'Friend, your sins are forgiven you' (5.20). This claim, a new access to purity, belittles the scribes and the Pharisees present, who try in turn to belittle Jesus,

'Who is this who is speaking blasphemies? Who can forgive sins but God alone?' (5.22). They clearly perceive that their own role and status as law promoters and law enforcers are challenged by Jesus' claim, and so they seek to redress the slight to their status by belittling their belittler. All of this occurs in public; all present perceive the challenge to the scribes and Pharisees, who must react.

Jesus, however, holds the high cards. He responds cleverly by asking a counter-question about the power of words, asserting that his words can cause an effect which can be verified in the eyes of all, critics as well as public: 'When Jesus perceived their questionings, he answered them, "Why do you raise such questions in your hearts? Which is easier, to say, 'Your sins are forgiven you', or to say, 'Stand up and walk'"' (5.22-23). If he can say and do the harder thing (which requires immediate proof), he can do the lesser thing, where evident proof is not offered. Thus Jesus further belittles those who try to belittle him; and in this Jesus makes a new claim, which makes explicit to all in attendance his very special role and status: 'But so that you may know that the Son of Man has authority on earth to forgive sins...' (5.24). This would seem to exemplify how the person attacked in turn attacks his attackers. Obviously, however, those belittled by Jesus will be all the more insulted, but not everybody is upset. The man who was healed endorses Jesus' claim, 'He went to his home, glorifying God'; and all observers concurred, 'And they glorified God and were filled with awe, saying, "We have seen strange things today"' (5.26). Feelings of belittlement surely remain in the Scribes and Pharisees, but they have to swallow them now. They are not able to seek any kind of revenge.

Except for the attempt to kill Jesus as the conclusion of the incident in Nazareth (4.16-29), Luke is slow to report how subsequent challenge–riposte exchanges end, either for Jesus or for his attackers (6.1-5). But this pattern changes when, at the end of the episode in 6.6-11, the scribes and Pharisees are on the alert 'so that they might find an accusation against him' (to belittle their belittler). The savvy Jesus recognizes this, and once more belittles them; he calls the man with the withered hand to come and stand before all there. Then, Jesus challenges them with a question: 'Is it lawful to do good or to do harm on the sabbath, to save life or to destroy it?' (6.9). This question attacks his attackers, for as he speaks, 'he looked at them all'. Jesus answered his own question by doing good on the sabbath: '"Stretch out your hand". He did so, and his hand was restored' (6.10). But Jesus' attackers, while silenced, are not defeated: 'They were filled with fury and discussed with one another what they might do to Jesus' (6.11). This means that their anger has escalated to a desire for revenge. Their anger, then, is out of control.

The narrative is silent for a while on angry reactions to Jesus, but resumes with the story of the woman bent over. Jesus' healing of her constitutes a powerful claim in a very public place at a very public time: 'He was teaching in one of the synagogues on the sabbath' (13.10). Jesus calls the woman over, probably in the public square, and heals her—the right time and place for her, but not for everyone. 'The leader of the synagogue [was] indignant because Jesus had cured on the sabbath', and while not attacking Jesus directly, he 'kept saying to the crowd, "Come on those days and be cured, and not on the sabbath day"' (13.14). He is, of course, trying to belittle Jesus, who picks up the challenge. Jesus introduces his counter-questions with an insult, 'You hypocrites!' His argument is obvious to all, i.e., ordinary husbandry, even on the sabbath. The second part of his counter-question, moreover, is just as obvious: 'Ought not this woman, a daughter of Abraham whom Satan bound for eighteen long years, be set free from this bondage on the sabbath day?' (13.16). Jesus, then, has attacked his attackers and banished them from the field. Two reactions are noted, which, while they honor Jesus, inflame his belittlers: 'All his opponents were *put to shame* (i.e., "belittled"); and 'the entire crowd was rejoicing at all the wonderful things that he was doing' (13.17). Being 'put to shame' in a public place constitutes an insult of maximum injury; it must, and will be avenged. Thus, anger is out of control.

It has been argued that the Pharisees are also the objects of the parable in 16.1-13. This seems correct when Luke narrates that immediately after it, 'The Pharisees *ridiculed* Jesus' (16.14), to which challenge Jesus replies: 'You are those who justify yourselves in the sight of others; but God knows your hearts; for what is prized by human beings is an abomination in the sight of God' (16.15). When Jesus then tells the story of the rich man and Lazarus, he is still speaking to 'the Pharisees, who were lovers of money' (16.14). This story cannot help but continue belittling those opponents, and thus producing in them anger out of control.

The Pharisees appear one more time when Jesus is teaching in the Jerusalem temple. His charge that they are 'hypocrites' (12.1; 16.15) is sustained here: 'So they watched him and sent spies who pretended to be honest, in order to trap him by what he said, so as to hand him over to the jurisdiction and authority of the governor' (20.20). Their 'pretense' at being honest is hypocritically expressed with public sarcasm: 'Teacher, we know that *you are right in what you say and teach*, and you show deference to no one, but *teach the way of God in accordance with truth*' (20.21, italics added). Hoping that they have deceived Jesus, they ask their question about paying tax to Caesar. But the belittled cannot in turn belittle Jesus, who asks a counter-question. The best testimony comes from the mouth of the accuser, as it does here: '"Whose head and whose title does it bear?" They said, "The emperor's"' (20.24). The one attacked has successfully attacked his attackers. Although they crave revenge, they are impotent here: 'And they were not able in the presence of the people to trap him by what he said; and being amazed by his answer, they became silent' (20.26). Being 'silenced' is equivalent to great shame.[38]

Summary and Conclusions

In summary, we have we learned much about Jesus' dealings with anger and angry people. First, the narrative never states or dramatizes that Jesus was himself ever provoked to anger, namely, that he sought to destroy his opponents, as they sought to do to him. Luke narrates that he was constantly attacked and challenged by angry opponents, whose behavior became out-of-control. In Luke's narrative, Jesus frequently makes claims, which his opponents feel belittle them. Those belittled in turn attempt to belittle their belittler. In the rhetorical genre *chreia*, a challenge is made, whose purpose is to dishonor and discredit a person who enjoys an honorable reputation. The wise man, so challenged, responds in such a way as to send his challengers fleeing. In a *chreia*, however, the challengers are never portrayed as plotting the destruction and/of death of the wise man whom they challenged—because anger is not a player in that genre. But Jesus' reactions here are moderate, because his aim is defensive; he does not plot against his opponents, much less seek their destruction. Contrary to the dynamics of the genre of a *chreia*, Jesus, who is the wise man under attack, keeps his cool, that is, he is not provoked to play the game of anger. His attackers may experience intensified anger and seek revenge, but the man who is attacked stands firm in moderate behavior and is not swept away. Luke's repeated portrayal of Jesus as moderate in the face of the growing anger of his opponents is precisely the behavior which should be attributed to the virtue of self-control/moderation. Actions speak louder than labels.

Moreover, we draw certain conclusions from what we have learned:

1. We now know the ancient conversation about the fourth canonical virtue, however it was named. A definition of it has always been problematic. The word *sōphrosunē* was generally understood as much more than rational control of emotions, although that element was

---

38. Audiences can easily tell winners from losers in the game of challenge and riposte by observing who is 'silenced'. See Neyrey, 'Questions, Chreai, and Challenges to Honor'.

always present. From ancient times, it expressed a sense of moderate behavior which facilitated civic life unimpeded by the tyranny of passions such as love of honor and pursuit of wealth. This moderation constantly included both self-knowledge and seeking the middle way.

2. Ancient rhetoricians and philosophers understood that *sōphrosunē* was based on self- knowledge (*gnōthi seauton*), that is, on knowledge of where one belonged in social terms, that is, who ranked above, alongside, and below oneself. Appreciation of one's role and status in society was essential for controlling one's behavior. Another foundational part of it, 'avoid extremes' (*mēden agan*) referred to the social strategy that directed a person with accurate self-knowledge to maintain his position, neither over-reaching and so dishonoring others, nor allowing oneself to be belittled by others.

3. In the cultural world where honor reigned as the premier value, *sōphrosunē* meant appreciation of one's own social worth as well as that of others. That world, however, was a very agonistic one, blown by winds called 'zero-sum game' and buffeted by other winds expressing 'limited good'. It proved inevitable that men would seek more honor, which was best achieved by diminishing the standing of others.[39]

4. This ubiquitous quest for greater honor at the expense of someone else came to be expressed in the rhetorical genre taught in the *progymnasmata* called the *chreia*. The choreography of a *chreia* was consistently simple: a person with honor/reputation was attacked, generally with an aggressive question, whose sole purpose was to demote the prestige of this wise man. This question must necessarily be rebuffed by the honorable person being questioned if he was to maintain his status. Thus, questions became the primary weapon in trying to belittle someone; a counter-question rebuffed this. The person defending his honor acts with moderation, not in anger.

5. When the emotion of anger is defined, its choreography provides the background—implicit and explicit—for discussions of what anger was and how it functioned: a person who perceived himself to be slighted or insulted would attempt to belittle his belittler. Only when this failed might the person slighted escalate his anger in pursuit of revenge. But initially, a balance of injury was enough: belittle the belittler. Moderation, then, is initially controlling this combat, for it was enough to get even, that is, to belittle the belittler.

---

39. On the relationship of honor and envy/competition, see Cohen, *Law, Violence, and Community*, pp. 61-86.

6. When Luke's narrative is examined, the only emotions out of control are those of the Pharisees, who are concerned with food and meals; they are, however, lovers of money, public respect, distinctive clothing, and other public marks of respect, which Luke would have us consider 'inordinate desires'. If Luke's narrative contains stories about narrative characters who are out of control, there are no such stories about Jesus. While Jesus exhibits no emotions out of control, he does, however, regularly manifest moderation.

7. Luke, whose narrative frequently contrasts characters, presents Jesus juxtaposed to the Pharisees in terms of their 'inordinate desire' for honor. They seek public approval, whereas Jesus is often in flight from fame and glory. Eventually, Luke narrates that Jesus himself accepts as his fate rejection, mockery and shame, which he acknowledges is the 'will of God' for him. If the Pharisees seek to be first or greatest, Jesus' disciples are exhorted to go to the end of the line. Moderation is lacking in the behavior of the Pharisees, but is evident in the behavior of Jesus and his disciples.

8. Because Jesus has accurate self-knowledge as God's anointed, he acts and speaks in ways which the Pharisees interpret as belittling, slighting, and insulting them; he is perceived as diminishing the honor they claim for themselves. They perceive him as belittling their own role and status. As a result, Luke's narrative is frequently peppered with attempts by those belittled to belittle their belittler, which are often called *chreiai* or challenge–riposte exchanges. Although the anger and desire for revenge increase in Pharisees—a loss of moderation and a loss of control—Jesus always operates according to a sense of balanced response, moderation, that is, nothing too much or too little. *Sōphrosunē*, then, is displayed by Jesus in his measured response to the attacking questions. His behavior is presented as defensive, not offensive. It is sufficient that he protect and defend the honorable self-knowledge God had given him. Luke's audience will see *sōphrosunē* in the moderate actions of Jesus.

9. Where does the argument stand regarding Luke's use of the progymnastic encomium as the rhetorical framework of his narrative? Luke's use of the first parts of an encomium, 'origins' and 'nurture/training', have been shown to be the operative literary ways for garnering honor for Jesus from his birth to 'thirty-years old'. The evaluation of Jesus' 'achievements' does not enjoy the same tight and concentrated treatment of virtuous behavior, as did his earlier behavior. But a strong case has been made that Luke portrays Jesus exemplifying the virtues of wisdom, justice and courage. Luke's dramatization of Jesus

according to these canonical virtues should support the probability that Luke portrays Jesus exhibiting the fourth virtue, *sophrosyne* or moderation. The next chapter, on the encomiastic discussion of an honorable man's 'noble death', supports the argument from the other side.

Chapter 8

ENCOMIUM:
THE ACCOMPLISHMENTS OF JESUS:
'NOBLE DEATH'

Their courage in arms...reveals them as the authors of many benefits conferred upon their country and the rest of Greece (Hyperides, *Funeral Speech* 9).

...to those about to die for the preservation and safeguarding of their fathers' way of life, the virtue acquired by them in death would seem far more advantageous than the pleasure of living. For by winning eternal fame and glory for themselves they would be praised by those now living and would leave the ever-memorable (example of their) lives to future generations (Josephus, *Ant.* 17.152).

Even in regard to the end of Jesus' life our interest remains with ancient rhetoric—rhetoric, not the history of the passion narrative, its pre-Markan form, or its redaction by Luke. We want to hear Luke's narrative according to the literary forms with which he and his listeners would be familiar in talking about someone's death. When ancient writers spoke of or wrote about the deaths of honorable people, they had been taught how to tell the story of that death with the explicit rhetorical purpose of honoring such a person, according to their cultural canons. What is called the rhetoric of praise developed out of the funeral orations delivered on the occasion of the civic burial of Athenian soldiers, or the annual memorial of their deaths, or the anniversary of the battle in which they died. These funeral orations created a vocabulary which labeled heroic deaths as 'easy', 'good', 'noble', 'famous', or 'ending well'. This labeling rested on specific cultural reasons for judging that particular death to be considered 'noble'.

For example, in regard to celebration of the death of a soldier who died in combat, Isocrates urged soldiers facing battle to act 'nobly': 'If ever it falls to your lot to face the dangers of battle, seek to preserve your life, but with honor and not with disgrace; for death is the sentence of all mankind, but to die nobly is the special honor which nature has reserved for the good' (*ad Dem.* 43).[1] The rhetorical tradition for praising a 'noble death' developed to the point where orators can be observed following a formula containing regular arguments to honor a deceased soldier or warrior.[2] This topos generally labeled such a death 'noble' according to the following set of six cultural canons, which became commonplaces of a rhetorical topos.

Beneficial Death

A noble death necessarily *benefitted* Athens: 'Their courage in arms... reveals them as the authors of many benefits conferred upon their country and the rest of Greece' (Hyperides, *Funeral Speech* 9; see 15-16, 19, 20-22); '[these soldiers] sacrificed their lives that others might live well' (*Funeral Speech* 26).

Virtuous Death

Athens's fallen heroes were singularly *virtuous*, displaying *exceptional justice*[3] toward Athens by their deaths: 'Now in many ways it was natural to our ancestors...to fight the battles of *justice*: for the very beginning of their life was just... For they deemed that it was the way of wild beasts to be held subject to one another by force, but *the duty of men* to delimit

---

1. More examples may clarify this. Isocrates provides an example of the honorable labeling of certain deaths: 'For we shall find that men of ambition and greatness of soul not only are desirous of *praise* for such things, but prefer a *glorious* death to life, zealously seeking *glory* rather than existence' (*Evag.* 3, italics added). Herodotus frequently speaks of warriors ending their lives well in combat or choosing battle rather than flight. He records how Solon, when asked if he knew of someone truly blest, told him of a certain Tellus of Athens, whose crowning blessing was to die a noble death: '[H]e crowned his life with a *most glorious* death: for in a battle between the Athenians and their neighbors at Eleusis, he attacked and routed the enemy and *most nobly* died; and the Athenians gave him *public burial* where he fell and paid him *great honor*' (*Hist.* 1.30, italics added).
2. Ziolkowski, *Thucydides*; Loraux, *The Invention of Athens*.
3. Justice means duty, a celebrated topic in antiquity: 'First among the claims of justice are our duties to the gods, then our duties to the spirits, then *those to country and parents*, then those to the departed' (Aristotle, *Virt. Vit.* 5.2-3, italics added). The premier aspect of justice celebrated in the annual memorial for Athens's fallen soldiers was the duty they paid to the *polis* and its institutions. For example, many orators rehearsed the history of Athens, in particular its struggles to be free of tyranny and its willingness to fight to preserve the ancestral way of life. The fallen who died were duty-bound to be faithful to that political history at the cost of their lives.

justice by law, to convince by reason, and to serve these two by submitting to the sovereignty of law and the instruction of reason' (Lysias, *Funeral Oration* 17-19).[4]

Voluntary Death

Death which was *voluntarily chosen* distinguished a noble one from that of a victim or slave. Fallen soldiers were often said 'to prefer noble death to a life of servitude' or 'to choose' their death. 'We, who might have ignobly lived choose rather to die nobly before we bring you and those after you to disgrace or before we shame you with our fathers and all our earlier forebearers' (Plato, *Menex.* 246d).[5]

Unconquered in Death

Although warriors died in battle, they were considered to have died *undefeated* or *unconquered*. Lycurgus wrote, 'Unconquered, they fell in the defense of freedom, and if I may use a paradox, they triumphed in their death…neither can we say that they have been defeated whose spirits did not flinch at the aggressor's threat…since by the choosing of a noble death, they are escaping slavery' (*Leocrates* 48-49).

Unique Death

On occasion a death might be considered 'noble' because of some *uniqueness*. An orator might assert that 'no one' else has ever been able to perform this deed and achieve this honor. For example, '*Never before* did men strive for a *nobler* cause, either against *stronger* adversaries or with *fewer* friends, convinced that valour gave strength and courage superiority as no mere numbers could' (Hyperides, *Funeral Speech* 19, italics added).[6]

4. Antigone faced conflicting duties, to bury her brother honorably (kinship) or to obey her uncle to *not* bury him (politics). She died a noble death because of her justice to her brother.

5. Nero inquired whether Seneca, when faced with extreme royal displeasure, was preparing for a 'voluntary death' (*voluntariam mortem*, Tacitus, *Ann.* 15.61).

6. Aristotle remarked: 'A praiseworthy person is…the only one or the first or one of a few or the one who most has done something; for all these things are honorable… and if incitements and honors have been invented and established because of him… and if he was the first one to receive an encomium; and [if for him] statues were set up in the marketplace' (*Rhet.* 1.9.38, italics added). Lysias, an actual orator, wrote: 'They were the first and only people in that time to drive out the ruling classes' (*Funeral Oration* 17-19). On the rhetoric of 'uniqueness', see Jerome H. Neyrey, ' "First", Only, "One of a Few", and "No One Else": The Rhetoric of Uniqueness and the Doxologies in 1 Timothy', *Biblica* 86 (2005), pp. 59-87.

Honored Posthumously

A truly noble death was identified as such by the *posthumous honors* paid to the deceased, including public celebrations of the dead, such as games or monuments.[7] The very funeral orations serve to give glory to the dead, first by promoting a public evaluation of their worth and later by annual burnishing of their reputation. Hence, the purpose of games, monuments, etc., was to give a type of eternal glory to the dead. It was claimed, then, that those being celebrated are like the gods, because their glory, too, is now deathless and everlasting. We know, therefore, that Athenian orators developed a form of epideictic rhetoric based on specific criteria for honoring what they understood as a 'noble death'. This is not in doubt.[8]

Aristotle employed the same criteria in his definition of a 'noble' living person. In his discussion of virtues, he celebrated one virtue which stands alone and dominates the stage: 'nobility'. Although Aristotle had little to say about a noble *death*, in his exposition of epideictic rhetoric, however, he employed the same arguments for a noble *life* to acknowledge someone's honor. His catalogue of criteria bears striking resemblance to the items mentioned in the funeral speeches just mentioned. Thus Aristotle's general material on 'nobility' directly reflects the specific remarks used by orators to eulogize and honor the dead. Aristotle, then, is an important link between praise of a noble *death* and a more generalized description of honor for a virtuous living man. Because the reasons for labeling as noble either a death or a life are ancient, widespread and consistent, we should consider the relevant part of Aristotle's discourse:

7. Greek celebrations of posthumous honors were well known in antiquity, as Dionysius of Halicarnassus notes: 'These writers [Greeks] have given accounts of funeral games, both gymnastic and equestrian, held in honor of famous men by their friends, as by Achilles for Patroclus and, before that, by Herakles for Pelops' (*Ant. Rom.* 5.17.4). Isocrates lists the various posthumous honors that honored Evagoras, including his own speech: 'When I saw you, Nicocles, honoring the tomb of your father, not only with numerous and beautiful offerings, but also with dances, music, and athletic contests, and furthermore, with races of horses and triremes...' (*Evag.* 1). See Ziolkowski, *Thucydides*, pp. 126-28.

8. Dionysius of Halicarnassus claimed that the Athenians instituted the funeral oration 'in honor or those who fought at Artemisium, Salamis, and Plataea, and died for their country, or to the glory of their exploits at Marathon' (*Ant. Rom.* 5.17.2); Thucydides supports this by describing funeral rituals, noting that 'the dead are laid in the public sepulchre in the most beautiful suburb of the city, in which those who fall in war are always buried' (*War* 2.34).

16. Things of which the *reward is honor* are noble; also those which are done *for honor rather than money*. 17. Also, those desirable things which a man does *not do for his own sake*; things which a man has done *for his country*, while neglecting *his own interests*... 18. Those things are noble which it is possible for a man to possess *after death rather than during his lifetime*, for the latter involve *more selfishness*; 19. All acts done *for the sake of others*, for they are *more disinterested*; 20. The successes gained, *not for oneself, but for others*... 24. A courageous man ought *not to allow himself to be beaten*. 25. Victory and honor are noble; *for both are desirable even when they are fruitless... And things worthy of* remembrance, which are more honorable the longer their memory lasts; those which follow us *after death*; those which are *out of the common* (*Rhet.* 1.9.16-26, italics added).

As noted, although Aristotle did not focus on a noble death, his criteria for nobility correspond to those in the topos of 'noble death', a fact worth noting.

Aristotle	Noble Death Tradition
Beneficial (nos. 17, 19, 23)...not done for self-interest (nos. 16, 17, 18).	'Their courage in arms...reveals them as the authors of many *benefits* conferred upon their country and the rest of Greece' (Hyperides, *Funeral Speech* 9)
Virtuous: death is *just* or demonstrates *justice* (no. 23).	'It was natural...to fight the battles of *justice*: for the very beginning of their life was just... For they deemed that it was *the duty of men* to delimit justice by law, to convince by reason, and tov serve these two in act by submitting to the sovereignty of law and the instruction of reason' (Lysias, *Funeral Oration* 17-19).
Productive of *honor*, *glory*, good *reputation*, remembrance (nos. 16, 18, 25).	'For we shall find that men of ambition and greatness of soul not only are desirous of praise for such things, but prefer a *glorious* death to life, *zealously seeking glory* rather than existence' (Isocrates, *Evag.* 3).
Voluntarily chosen (nos. 16, 17, 25).	'We, who might have ignobly lived *choose* rather to die nobly before we bring you and those after you to disgrace' (Plato, *Menex.* 246d).
Victorious; the actor was not defeated (no. 24).	'*Unconquered*, they fell in the defense of freedom... they *triumphed in their death*...neither can we say that they have been *defeated* whose spirits *did not flinch* at the aggressor's threat' (Lycurgus, *Leocrates* 48-49).

Unique to this person (nos. 25-26).	'Never before did men strive for a *nobler cause*, either against *stronger* adversaries or with *fewer* friends, convinced that valour gave strength and courage *superiority as no mere numbers could*' (Hyperides, *Funeral Speech* 19).
Productive of *posthumous honors* (nos. 18, 25).	'When I saw you honoring the tomb of your father, not only with numerous and beautiful offerings, but also with dances, music, and athletic contests, and furthermore, with races of horses and triremes...' (Isocrates, *Evag.* 1).

Finally, in the progymnastic exercise called the encomium, would-be orators were taught this same rhetorical tradition, a clear example of which Aelius Theon reports: '(Fine actions) are also those done *for others rather than for ourselves*; and *done for the sake of the honorable, not the expedient or the pleasant*; and in which the toil is that of the doer but *the benefit is common*; and through which the populace experiences benefits...' (italics added).[9] Therefore, the conventional criteria found in funeral orations about a 'noble' death continued as both the source of praise of the living (Aristotle) and of honoring a 'noble' death (encomium)—hardly an esoteric topos.

The 'Noble Death' Tradition in Israelite Literature

Thus far our information about 'noble death' comes only from Greek rhetorical sources. The authors of the Maccabean literature, however, also used it in their praise of the noble Israelites whose deaths they celebrated.[10] That literature contains both anecdotal reference to this as well as the same criteria found in Greek rhetoric for declaring a death 'noble'.

9. Theon, *Exercises* 110-111 [Kennedy, pp. 50-51].

10. David Seeley, *The Noble Death: Graeco-Roman Martyrology and Paul's Concept of Salvation* (Sheffield: JSOT Press, 1990), pp. 83-112; Arthur J. Droge and James D. Tabor, *A Noble Death: Suicide and Martyrdom among Christians and Jews in Antiquity* (San Francisco: Harper, 1992), pp. 53, 84-96; both comment on the Maccabean literature, the latter with an eye to suicide and the former focusing on the background for Paul's soteriology. Neither bring to their task the rich data from Greek rhetoric. For a full treatment of the motif of noble death in 2 and 4 Maccabees, see Jan Willem Van Henten, *The Maccabean Martyrs as Saviours of the Jewish People* (Leiden: Brill, 1997), pp. 140-50, 157-59, 213-25, who examines the importance of *voluntary* death and death as *benefit*. He appreciates the Judean dependence on motifs made sacred in Greek literature.

Voluntary
Eleazar '...welcomed death with honor rather than a life, and went to the rack of his own accord' (2 Macc. 6.19).

Beneficial
Of one soldier it was said: 'He gave up his life to save his people' (1 Macc. 6.43-44). The dead benefitted the rest by modeling for them noble behavior: 'I will...leave to the young a noble example of how to die a good death willingly and nobly for the revered and holy laws' (2 Macc. 6.28).

Virtuous: Courage and Justice
Concerning courage, Judas exhorted his army, 'If our time has come, let us die bravely for our kindred' (1 Macc. 9.10). Similarly Eleazar eulogized Israelite law by claiming that 'It trains us in courage so that we endure any suffering willingly' (*4 Macc.* 5.23). Justice, however, emerged as the paramount virtue for which Eleazar and the seven sons were praised. Inasmuch as justice refers to one's duty to God, family/fatherland, and ancestors, the story about the old man and the seven brothers regularly noted that they died in fulfilment of their duties: (1) *duty to God*, 'By nobly dying they fulfilled their service to God' (*4 Macc.* 12.14); (2) *duty to the fatherland*, because they endured death for the sake of ancestral laws; so Judas exhorted his army 'to die for their laws and their country' (2 Macc. 8.21); and (3) *duty to kin*: 'Let us bravely die for our kindred' (1 Macc. 9.10).

Unconquered or Victorious
In *4 Maccabees*, the dead were honored, 'By their endurance they conquered the tyrant' (1.11). Thus, Eleazar won a victory, 'Although his sacred life was consumed by tortures and racks, he conquered the besiegers with the shield of his devout reason' (7.4).

Posthumous Honors
This expresses the dominant cultural value: honor, glory, everlasting fame, renown, and the like. Of Eleazar it was said, 'So he gave his life to save his people and to win for himself an everlasting name' (1 Macc. 6.44). Therefore, the Maccabean literature argues that not only did many Israelites know the Greek language, but shared the Greco-Roman canons of honor for a 'noble death'.

Introducing Luke and 'Noble Death'

The purpose of learning the rhetoric about 'noble death' is to have a sure template for examining Luke's narrative of the end of Jesus' life.[11] But special problems arise for modern readers, because this project requires that we identify the strategies we have been taught to examine Luke 22–24, which seem to challenge what we learn from rhetoric. Knowing the topos of 'noble death' and asking whether Luke used it might mean that we are confronted with a disconnect between ancient rhetoric and the scholarly ways we been taught to read that part of the narrative. Rhetoric, in fact, might seem simplistic and naive in contrast to the sophistication of modern scholarship. The following figure attempts a contrast between two different ways of reading Luke. Its value lies in clarifying what each reading presupposes, how it operates, and what benefit it offers.

Rhetoric of Noble Death	Modern Biblical Scholarship
1. cultural label of 'noble death', the last item in a lifetime account of 'accomplishments'	1. scholarly label of 'passion narrative', which privileges a reading focused on end of life
2. a single rhetorical concern: what constitutes a 'noble' death	2. many scholarly concerns: a pre-Markan passion narrative and its sources,[12] pre-Matthean and pre-Lukan sources, and redaction comparisons of synoptic narratives
3. topos on 'noble death' provides cultural labels which are more evaluative than scholarly; a lengthy list of items	3. through form criticism, narrative is atomized into small units and labeled accordingly, such as, arrest, trial before Sanhedrin, trial before Pilate, etc.
4. the cultural, consistent topos used by most ancient writers: what they hold in common	4. search for sources and comparisons of narratives emphasizes distinctiveness

11. For a Johannine example of this, see Neyrey, 'The "Noble" Shepherd in John 10'; he noted that John labels the shepherd who lays down his life for his sheep as 'noble', not 'good'.

12. A. Kolenkow and Robin Scroggs, 'Reflections on the Question: Was There a Pre-Markan Passion Narrative?', *SBLSP* 2 (1971), pp. 503-85; Werner H. Kelber, 'Conclusion: From Passion Narrative to Gospel', in his *The Passion in Mark: Studies on Mark 14–16* (Philadelphia, PA: Fortress Press, 1976), pp. 153-80; and Raymond E. Brown, *The Death of the Messiah: From Gethsemane to the Grave: A Commentary on the Passion Narratives in the Four Gospels* (New York: Doubleday, 1994).

5. only after consideration of 'accomplishments' (virtuous actions) in a hero's life, focus on death; climax of an honorable life	5. focus on 'passion narrative' independent of the full story about Jesus' life or what followed his death; only Luke 22–23 considered
6. cultural bias toward honor; value placed on cultural understanding of virtue	6. ideological bias: value found mostly in atonement theology and *theologia crucis*
7. honor as paramount value	7. 'soteriology' as major norm of worth
8. clear purpose of rhetorical composition: praise and honor for a heroic death	8. many purposes: historical exactitude of events, author's distinctive strategy; satisfaction of scholars paramount, etc.
9. rhetoric common to most people as the unique path for telling a meaningful story	9. historical-critical scholarship— minus rhetoric—as the preferred path for understanding, but for the few scholars
10. topological investigation, concern for evident structures	10. academic archaeology: in-depth analysis of individual items
11. rhetoric reigned in that culture; a culturally sensitive approach	11. rhetoric generally unknown; ethnocentrism ascendant

Inasmuch as we maintain that Luke mastered the traditional form of the encomium as a template for finding materials with which to praise Jesus, we now consider what honor can be found in Jesus' 'noble death'. There was no fixed order in funeral orations for citing this or that reason for a 'noble death'. Alas, we have sinned above by citing the criteria for a noble death in a certain order, which exists only in the mind of this author. Nevertheless, having all of these rhetorical items before us, let us read Luke, identifying each item as it appears in his narrative.

'Noble Death' and Virtue, namely, Justice

The 'innocence' of Jesus in Luke 22–23 has been well discussed.[13] As many have shown, Pilate the judge three times declared of Jesus, 'I find no basis for an accusation against this man' (23.4, 14, 22); a witness says the same, 'This man has done nothing wrong' (23.41); and finally the executioner states the true verdict of this trial: 'Certainly this man was innocent (*dikaios*)' (23.47). Luke's audience would clearly understand

---

13. On the rhetorical purpose of declaring Jesus' innocence, see Richard J. Cassidy, *Jesus, Politics, and Society* (Maryknoll, NY: Orbis Books, 1978); Conzelmann, *The Theology of Luke*; Daryl Schmidt, 'Luke's 'Innocent' Jesus: A Scriptural Apologetic', in Richard J. Cassidy (ed.), *Political Issues in Luke–Acts* (Maryknoll, NY: Orbis Books, 1983), pp. 111-21.

that an unjust trial occurred because the just is condemned, while the guilty goes free. The true judgment should be Pilate's original statement: 'I find no basis for an accusation against this man' (23.4). Jesus was no robber (22.52), nor enemy of Caesar (23.3-4), nor of Herod (23.15). Thus Luke makes evident that all judicial proceedings against Jesus are illegal and unjust. If not guilty of any crime, then Jesus is, as his executioner declared, 'innocent' (23.47), that is, just and virtuous.[14]

Luke repeatedly claims in Acts that 'You killed him, but God raised him', which juxtaposition of earthly shame and heavenly honor became the standard way in Acts for describing God's verdict about Jesus' true virtue. For, God vindicated Jesus[15] and restored his honor, and thus vastly increased his worthiness and glory, which attest that Jesus was indeed, not a sinner, but someone who found favor in God's eyes. Luke's audience knows exactly how God judged Jesus as virtuous.

Which virtue? 'First among the claims of justice are our duties to the gods then our duties to the spirits, then those to country and parents' (Aristotle, *Virt. Vit.* 5.2). We argued earlier in this monograph that Luke derived honor for Jesus from his 'accomplishments', namely, the virtue of justice, showing that Jesus indeed fulfilled his duties to all those owed such. In Jesus' recognition that it is God's will that he undergo the shameful death of a rejected prophet, he attests that he knows his duty-as-obedience to God and fulfils it.

Classical definitions of justice also stated: '…among these claims is piety, which is either a part of justice or a concomitant of it. Justice is also accompanied by holiness and truth and loyalty' (Aristotle, *Virt. Vit.* 5.23). How wonderful would it be if Luke had actually used these words in regard to Jesus. He labels Cornelius a 'devout' man (Acts 10.2), but not Jesus. In regard to Jesus, however, Luke does identify his virtue, although he uses synonyms. First, when in Acts Luke records how Psalm 15 should

---

14. G.D. Kilpatrick, 'The Theme of the Lucan Passion Story and Luke xxiii.47', *JTS* 43 (1941), pp. 34-36; he argued that *dikaios* be understood in support of Luke's concern with Jesus' political innocence. But when scholars attend to how Luke prefaced the executioner's remark, 'He glorified God', a better interpretation suggests praise for a virtue of Jesus, something which would glorify God. See Frank Matera, 'The Death of Jesus according to Luke: A Question of Sources', *CBQ* 47 (1985), pp. 469-85; and D. Sylva, 'The Temple Curtain and the Death of Jesus in Luke', *JBL* 105 (1986), pp. 239-50.

15. Interpreting 'resurrection' as 'vindication' is not a popular move; all the more, then, is George W.E. Nickelsburg's article of significance: 'Resurrection (Early Judaism and Christianity)', in *ABD*, V, p. 688. He uses this in regard to Jesus and Stephen.

be applied to Jesus, he quotes it thus: 'For you will not...let your *Holy One* experience corruption' (2.27); he quoted the same psalm in the same sense in 13.14: 'You will not let your *Holy One* experience corruption'. Yet, Luke also predicates holiness for Jesus by means of another synonym: 'You rejected the *Holy* (*hagion*) and *Just* (*dikaion*) One and asked to have a murderer given to you' (3.14); and 'Both Herod and Pontius Pilate, with the Gentiles and the peoples of Israel, gathered together against your *Holy* (*hagion*) servant' (4.27). The judgment of Peter and the Twelve reflects God's own evaluation of Jesus, for he is the one whom God anointed (Lk. 4.18; Acts 4.27; 10.38). The other two aspects of justice (truth and loyalty) refer to the fixed and constant respect Jesus always showed God (e.g., Lk. 4.3-12), even to his last words, itself a prayer from Ps. 31.5, 'Father, into your hands I commend my spirit' (23.46). Thus, Luke both in explicit words and in narration proclaims Jesus a practitioner of the virtue of justice. It goes without saying that God's vindication of Jesus is the best testimony to the virtue of Jesus.

'Noble Death' Voluntarily Accepted

In contrast with slaves and commoners, heroes died like heroes because they acted as free men, who chose battle, combat and war. Thus Plato reports: 'We, who might have ignobly lived choose rather to die nobly before we bring you and those after you to disgrace or before we shame you with our fathers and all our earlier forebearers' (*Menex.* 246d). While Luke never states that Jesus 'chose' his destiny, he reports, however, many other ways in which Jesus both acknowledged his coming fate and accepted it in obedience. He saw the train coming, but did not step out of the way.

The Fate of Prophets

Although Luke never states that Jesus 'chose' death, in many ways he narrates that Jesus himself talked about the 'necessity' of experiencing the fate of a rejected prophet, even to the point that such *must* happen in Jerusalem: 'I must be on my way, *because it is impossible for a prophet to be killed away from Jerusalem. Jerusalem, Jerusalem, the city that kills the prophets* and stones those who are sent to it!' (13.32-34, italics added). Accordingly Jesus envisions the terminus of his life, i.e., death. He says that it is inevitable for a prophet to be killed outside Jerusalem, which enjoys the terrible reputation of 'killing the prophets and stoning those sent to it'. He knows this; nevertheless, he proceeds on his way to what can only be described as a battle. He voluntarily accepts the events awaiting him.

Thy Will Be Done

Jesus understands that it is God's 'will' that he face Jerusalem, shame, and death. All in Luke's audience are familiar with Jesus' remark: 'The Son of Man *must* undergo great suffering, and be rejected, and killed' (9.22; see also 9.44; 18.32-33).[16] According to Luke, Jesus knows this and so do his disciples. Moreover, Luke narrates the apex of Jesus' voluntary acceptance of his fate in Gethsemane. First, he petitions God to allow him to escape his shameful death: 'Father, if you are willing (*boulei*), remove this cup from me; yet, not my will (*thelēma*) but yours be done' (22.42). The reference to a 'cup' implies that hearers understand it as an allusion to the biblical sense of a cup of destiny, so Jesus is credited with knowing what he asks for. Second, Jesus honors God with his voluntary acceptance of God's will: '...yet, not my will (*thelēma*) but yours be done' (22.42). Two different words are used here, the first one, 'willing' (*boulei*), strongly implies decision, plan, and purpose on the part of another,[17] whereas the second one, 'my will' (*thelēma*), the personal decision of someone, 'what one wishes to bring about by one's own actions'. God has the plan, which Jesus must achieve by voluntarily choosing and performing it. At this point in Luke's narrative, Jesus does not have the full view of God's 'will', which he will express only later in 24.26-27 and in comparable places in Acts. But his obedience here speaks to his voluntary acceptance of God's will.

Expecting and Accepting a Shameful Death

In an earlier chapter on the virtue of 'wisdom', we noted that one aspect of this virtue was the ability of a wise person to assess an action from its beginning to its ending. A wise person can perceive an action in its wholeness, including an understanding of how it proceeds in terms of cause and effect or step-by-step. But there, the wise man is observing the actions of someone else, where he is a wise spectator. In consideration of the voluntary acceptance of danger and death, however, a wise man might also be the protagonist, who correctly appreciates how his own actions will end in conflict and death. Because he can see how his own actions cause reactions in others, he can appreciate how they will result in a certain fate, which will require of him wisdom and courage to face.

16. Cosgrove, 'The Divine *DEI* in Luke–Acts'; he is the rare scholar who stresses the virtuous aspect of obedience embedded in it.

17. BDAG 181 suggests that 'if you *will*' includes the meaning of 'counsel or planning', both divine and human (see Acts 2.23; 4.28; 5.38; 13.36; 20.27); but in BDGA 447, 'my/your will be done' suggests performance or action (see Mt. 6.10; 26.42; Jn 6.39; Acts 21.14; Col. 4.12; and Heb. 10.10).

This, we argue, is another aspect of the voluntary acceptance of the result of one's own actions, and so warrants consideration here. Jesus was wise enough to see how his actions would eventuate in deadly hostility; thus, by expecting it, he accepted it. Prophets should expect rejection and death.

Three times in each of the synoptic gospels the authors record Jesus talking about a shameful death and the vindication that await him in Jerusalem. Although many are wont to call these 'predictions' of his passion, that labeling should be challenged. As just noted, they are the cause–effect assessment of Jesus' own behavior, that is, events which he, a wise man, perceives to be the outcome of his own actions. However, when Jesus' triple remarks are labeled 'predictions', that isolates them from the full narrative in which they are found. In short, they are taken out of context. 'Predictions', once isolated, prejudice a fuller reading of Luke 9, if only because that label represents the words of scholars who are prone to segment the gospel narrative and label each block of material in terms of some scholarly form. We propose an old, but fresh, reading of the initial mention of Jesus' wise assessment of the results of his behavior by reading continuously Luke's narrative in ch. 9, which does not privilege a 'passion prediction'.

As more and more commentators investigate Luke's narrative skills, they become aware of the extent of certain narratives, that is, they come to appreciate how apparently discrete episodes actually fit together to make a larger rhetorical statement. Luke 9 is just one such story. We suggest that 9.7-36 be read continuously in the following manner, which respects the rhetoric of it as a whole.[18] When Joseph Fitzmyer understood Luke 9 in terms of a continuum of questions and answers,[19] he argued that the question asked by Herod, 'Who is this about whom I hear such things?' (9.9), serves as the topic to which various answers are proposed in a sequence of nine connected episodes. This insight proved very persuasive for how a commentator should read Luke 9. Fitzmyer argued that episodes in Luke 9 are connected to the starting point here, the initial question. Because we are examining whether Luke is portraying Jesus in

18. Fitzmyer, *The Gospel according to Luke I–IX*, pp. 794-95; he made the case for reading 9.7-36 as a connected narrative: 'Jesus corrected Peter's acknowledgment of him as God's Messiah by announcing his passion and resurrection. This episode comes along in the Lucan Gospel not so much as a confirmation of the passion, but as a confirmation of the last part of that announcement, viz. that it will not end solely with suffering, repudiation, and death. Luke has sharpened what was in Mark by the introduction of Jesus' 'glory'.' It matters that both Moses and Elijah also appear 'in glory'.

19. Joseph A. Fitzmyer, 'The Composition of Luke, Chapter 9', in Charles H. Talbert (ed.), *Perspectives on Luke–Acts* (Edinburgh: T. & T. Clark, 1978), pp. 139-52.

terms of 'noble death' conventions, we examine Fitzmyer's connected episodes not for how they answer Herod's question ('Who is this...?'), but for what Luke and Jesus tell the audience about Jesus' expecting and accepting a shameful death, i.e., his voluntary acceptance of it. The episodes we consider are: (1) a question: What happened to John? (9.7-9); (2) another question: Who do men say that I am? (9.18-21); (3) contrasting titles, Messiah of God vs. Son of Man (9.21-22); (4) criteria for discipleship (9.24-25); and (5) Moses and Elijah speaking of Jesus' departure (9.28-36).

What Happened to John? (9.7-9)
As the disciples 'went through the villages, bringing the good news', eventually 'Herod the ruler heard about all that had taken place and he was perplexed, because it was said by some that John had been raised from the dead (9.6-7). Herod said, 'John I beheaded; but who is this about whom I hear such things?' One answer, then, cannot be correct: it cannot be John, because 'John I beheaded'. Herod may not like the answer, but many others toy with the idea: '...it was said by some that John had been raised from the dead, by some that Elijah had appeared, and by others that one of the ancient prophets had arisen'. Dead prophets, to be sure; but prophets rejected and killed? Who might have come back from the dead? Prophets, moreover, were never surprised by their violent deaths, for voluntarily facing death was one of their vocational hallmarks. But 'John...raised from the dead' implies much.[20] Moreover, once Luke mentions 'John', he can expect his audience to remember his earlier narrative about John, namely, that this same Herod arrested and executed John because of John's prophetic behavior: 'Herod had been rebuked by him because of Herodias...and because of all the evil things that Herod had done' (3.19). John spoke truth to power and power silenced truth. John spoke with boldness to Herod, knowing that he voluntarily risked death. The rhetorical point here is that a prophet is mentioned who voluntarily faced death ('John I beheaded', 9.9) and who is now narratively linked to Jesus, but in what way? Prophets expect and accept a shameful death.[21] But being raised from the dead?

20. Richard L. Rohrbaugh, 'Gossip in the New Testament', in his *The New Testament in Cross-Cultural Perspective*, pp. 125-46. He brought to our attention the social science model of 'gossip' and would argue that the questions asked in 9.7-9 and 18-19 are an expected cultural search for 'gossip' about Jesus.
21. Although Luke does not explain the significance of prophets in 9.7-9 and 18-19, he does later. Luke records Jesus denouncing the shameful treatment of prophets: 'You build the tombs of the prophets whom your ancestors killed. So you

Very little attention has been given to the crowd's remark that John 'has been raised from the dead'.[22] What does this mean? Fitzmyer understands the remark in 9.7-9 that John 'has been raised from the dead' to mean that John was considered *redivivus*, but he does not explain what this means. In regard to 'one of the prophets of old' who has 'arisen', he cites Lukan parallels to 16.31; 18.33; and 24.46 which explicitly explain this verb as being 'raised from the dead'.[23] Still, he does not suggest what is being claimed in 9.7-9. In general, however, when ancient figures were said to come back to life (*redivivus*), they returned for a purpose, sometimes benevolent, as in the case of Jeremiah who presented a golden sword for battle,[24] and sometimes malevolent, as in the case of Nero, who would return as Beliar the Antichrist. Figures returning from the dead have a function; but does John have one? Does he function as a type of rejected prophet who received posthumous honors,[25] that is, was rejected but vindicated by God?[26] The beheaded John raised from the dead might be establishing a pattern that Jesus will follow, which makes sense to people who claimed the same for John.

---

are witnesses and approve of the deeds of your ancestors; for they killed them, and you build their tombs. Therefore also the Wisdom of God said, "I will send them prophets and apostles, some of whom they will kill and persecute"' (11.47-49). Here, when prophets are killed, this is their only identification tag. In another place, Jesus is not warned off about Herod, because he knows that 'It is impossible for a prophet to be killed away from Jerusalem' (13.33). Moreover, prophets suffer only one fate in Jerusalem: 'Jerusalem, the city that kills the prophets and stones those who are sent to it!' (13.34). Luke expects his audience to connect what was said about John, Elijah, and prophets of old: without exception, they are rejected, shamed, and killed.

22. Francois Bovon, *Luke 1: A Commentary on the Gospel of Luke 1:1–9:50* (Minneapolis, MN: Fortress Press, 2002), p. 350; he goes so far as to deny any significance to the three figures mentioned in 9.7-9. He states, 'The three possible identifications (vv. 7b-8) are of no importance in themselves. Only the christological question is important in the structure of chap. 9.'

23. Fitzmyer, *The Gospel according to Luke I–IX*, 759.

24. 'Jeremiah stretched out his right hand and gave to Judas a golden sword... "Take this holy sword, a gift from God, with which you will strike down your adversaries"' (2 Macc. 15.12-16).

25. No Lukan commentary I have read suggested that the beheaded John 'raised from the Dead' signals anything to explain why this John is related in any way to Jesus. Moreover, I have found no author interested in 9.7-9 and 18-19; and so John 'raised from the dead' is simply ignored.

26. Is the frightened reaction of the disciples at Jesus' appearance in Lk. 24.36-43 an instance of *redivivus*? His presence belongs to a general category of numinous appearances, which typically causes fear and must be quieted by 'Peace!' But when

'Who do the crowds say that I am?' (9.18-21)

Herod's question does not go away, but later functions as an answer to the question Jesus himself asked: 'Who do the crowds say that I am?' (9.18). Re-enter John the Baptizer: 'They answered, "John the Baptist"' (9.19). This John, of course, is the rejected prophet whom Herod beheaded. Other prophets are mentioned, the same as were mentioned earlier: in 9.8 some said, 'Elijah had appeared, and...one of the ancient prophets had arisen', which is repeated in 9.19 'Elijah and...one of the ancient prophets has arisen'. What does Luke presume his audience understands by the mention of Elijah...one of the ancient prophets had *arisen*? Surely more than the prophet who healed a pagan leper (4.26-27). The full answer must wait until 'Moses and Elijah' appear as vindicated prophets in 9.30-31. But Elijah is now twice connected with the beheaded John, suggesting a more ominous meaning. 'Rejected prophets' seems evident, but what does 'arisen' imply? If the discussion in 9.8-9 and 18-19 is about John and prophets, known as figures who were put to death, their having been 'raised from the dead' or 'arisen' implies some sort of vindication of their shameful deaths. Prophets indeed are put to death, but they are also vindicated.

Messiah of God vs. Son of Man (9.21-22)

However one decides what 'Elijah and one of the ancient prophets' means here, Luke once more compares and contrasts them with Jesus. Peter's answer, which is an insider's insight, says something striking: 'The Messiah of God' (9.20). Jesus, however, immediately acts to silence him and the other disciples: 'He sternly ordered and commanded them not to tell anyone' (9.21).[27] This, therefore, is not the proper answer and

---

a 'spirit' appears to people who had denied him and fled from him when arrested, this does not fit the pattern of a benevolent numinous appearance. Why would Jesus return? To take revenge for shameful behavior by the disciples? To shame them as they shamed him? The issue is not what Jesus actually did, but what possible meaning could be given to this returning figure. What is the first thing to come to the disciples' minds?

27. Fitzmyer ('The Composition of Luke', pp. 145-46) argues that Peter's acclamation is very much in line with the narrative answers to Herod's question: 'The real answer to Herod's question is given through another pre-Lukan question asked of Peter, "Who do you say that I AM?" In this case Luke borrows the phraseology word for word from Mark. But the answer differs slightly: "God's Messiah" (or "the anointed one of God"). Luke's account has nothing of the additional Matthean material (16.16b-19) or of the rebuke of Peter found in the earlier Markan source (8.32-33). But Peter's answer, identifying Jesus as "God's Messiah", goes far beyond the answers of the "crowds"...the Son of Man must suffer many things. This pre-Lukan

is taken off the table immediately. Jesus himself definitively answer his own question by identifying himself as a person shamefully treated: 'The Son of Man[28] must undergo great suffering, and be rejected by the elders, chief priests, and scribes, and be killed, and on the third day be raised' (9.22). This name, 'Son of Man', is correctly understood as correcting Peter's 'Messiah of God'; but as a corrective, this suffering 'Son of Man' is indeed linked with the previous mention of the beheaded John (and other prophets who arose from death). Because Jesus speaks it himself, he knows how prophets are rejected. Moreover, he explicitly links it to events which will confront him: rejection and death. And because it is a corrective, it explicitly states that Jesus knows how his life will end, as a wise person would. He volunteers for it because, when he says that this 'must happen', he acknowledges that he is now, as always, paying his dues to his Father. His volunteering, moreover, can be made more evident in his three statements about his approaching shameful death, shown in the following figure:

'The Son of Man must undergo great suffering, and be rejected by the elders, chief priests, and scribes, and be killed...	...and on the third day be raised' (9.22).
'The Son of Man is going to be betrayed into human hands' (9.44).	---------
'Everything that is written about the Son of Man by the prophets will be accomplished. For he will be handed over to the Gentiles; and he will be mocked and insulted and spat upon. After they have flogged him, they will kill him...	...and on the third day he will rise again' (18.31-33)

element serves basically the same purpose in Luke that it has in Mark, as a corrective to the acknowledged messiahship of Jesus. The corrective, however, is far more closely linked to Peter's confession in Luke and provides a still further answer to Herod's question. Put on the lips of Jesus, it says in effect that he may be the Messiah, but he is such as the suffering Son of Man.'

28. Most scholarly considerations of 'Son of Man' are concerned with its antecedents in the literature of ancient Israel; but much less interest is given to Luke's qualification that the Son of Man 'must suffer many things'. Whatever its background, Luke qualifies it as a name expressive of Jesus' approaching death which he expects and voluntarily accepts.

It is one thing for Jesus to speak about his death once, but to repeat it three times and in a formulaic manner speaks to Luke's insistence on Jesus' knowing how his actions will end. This is hardly a 'prediction', so much as a wise understanding of beginnings and endings, that is, the virtue of wisdom.

Criteria for Discipleship (9.23-25)

The voluntary character of Jesus' acknowledgment of his approaching death is confirmed immediately by his exhortation to those who would be his disciples likewise to volunteer and follow him: 'If any want to become my followers, let them deny themselves and take up their cross daily and follow me' (9.23). Inasmuch as Jesus presents himself as a model, he exhorts the disciples to 'follow' him in voluntarily accepting approaching shame; it must be a choice. If the teacher accepts his destiny, so too his disciples must imitate him, not just in the physical humiliation to come, but in the social forbearance of their prized honor. When Jesus said '...take up their cross *daily* and follow me', he is not speaking of physical crucifixion, but of maximum shame (Heb. 12.2); likewise, '...deny themselves'. About himself, Jesus envisioned being 'rejected', i.e., others treating him such, but he tells the disciples that they must 'deny' themselves, which requires them voluntarily to act in a shameful way.[29] Thus, like their teacher who voluntarily faces his own shameful future, the disciple must engage in a calculus about 'save life/lose life for my sake'. This has to be a voluntary choice.

But the stakes are then hyperbolically raised when the choice is between 'gain the world' and 'lose or forfeit himself' (9.25). We should still understand a voluntary quality in 'lose or forfeit', if only because of what follows. The issue is one of respect and honor: those who deny these to Jesus—'who are ashamed of me and of my words'—will experience a reciprocal gesture from Jesus. No prediction here, but a statement of cause and effect. The pejorative term expressing Jesus' censure sums up all of the negative things that await a disciple who denies Jesus any honor or

---

29. Harald Riesenfeld, 'The Meaning of the Verb *arneithai*', *ConNT* 11 (1947), pp. 207-19; he produced a significant study of this verb. At the ending of his article, Riesenfeld urged this translation in regard to 9.23: 'It means abandoning and forsaking one's natural, human being, regarding and treating it as something irrelevant...a negative attitude, directed toward one's own person, one's own pretensions and interests'. One should, then, situates it in its cultural world of honor and shame. But if one asks how this 'denying self' should be understood in social science terms, the premier study is that of Bruce J. Malina, '"Let Him Deny Himself" (Mark 8:34 & par): A Social Psychological Model of Self-Denial', *BTB* 24 (1993), pp. 106-19.

respect—again a voluntary choice. The exhortation in 9.23-27 parallels
9.22; as Jesus voluntarily accepted his own fate, so also his disciples must
voluntarily choose to imitate him in accepting an honorless future.

Moses and Elijah Speaking of his Departure (9.28-36)
The concluding episode in this connected narrative occurs at a specific
time, which relates it directly to 9.22-27, 'Now about eight days *after
these sayings...*' (9.28). Then, Jesus is metamorphosed into an other-
worldly form: 'the appearance of his face changed, and his clothes
became dazzling white'. This, of course, is done by God, itself a singular
honor. Moreover, two noble figures attend him, 'Moses and Elijah,
talking to him', who are also in heavenly appearance ('in glory'). What
could be more opposite to the depiction of Jesus in 9.22 than this? Moses
and Elijah, to be sure, are true prophets, not mere allusions to 'Law and
Prophets'.[30] Luke presumes that his audience would know the gossip
about these two figures in the early church, how they were identified as
prophets rejected on earth by men, but vindicated by God in heaven.[31] To
the point, 'They were speaking of his departure, which he was about to
accomplish at Jerusalem' (9.31). 'Departure' (*exodon*) should be taken to
refer both to Jesus' shameful death and his honorable vindication—after
all, he appears 'glorified'. Jesus in the presence of two rejected/vindi-
cated prophets seems to confirm what we saw earlier, namely, that he is
portrayed as understanding his approaching shameful death; and, as a
wise man, he knows and thus accepts the results of his actions. Because
Moses and Elijah appear 'in glory', that glory must cancel their rejection;
it is God's verdict on their lives as faithful prophets. The wise prophet
Jesus, then, knows how the story ends, both in death and vindication.
    The story climaxes with a second declaration of God's favor of Jesus:
'My Son, my Chosen' (9.35a). But, as has often been noted, the voice is
directed now to the disciples; moreover, it commands them to 'Listen to
him!' If one reads 9.18-36 as a continuous exposition of Jesus' voluntary
facing of his death, then the divine command to 'listen' to Jesus covers all

---

    30. While on occasion, Luke seems to distinguish parts of Scripture into 'Law'
and 'Prophets' (Lk. 24.27 and Acts 26.22), in 9.30, he narrates that two individuals
came to Jesus, 'Moses' and 'Elijah', both in glory. Appearing 'in glory' implies a
heavenly verdict on the life of each; moreover inasmuch as they conversed with Jesus
about a specific topic, Luke intends his audience to understand them as individual
people, not symbols of parts of Scripture.
    31. The fate of Elijah needs no explanation; Moses, as Luke states in Acts 7, was
repeatedly rejected by Israel (7.35, 39); furthermore, in Rev. 11.4-13 we are told that
both Elijah and Moses are killed on earth by men, but vindicated by God in heaven.

of his words from 9.18 on, that is, everything he already said about facing his own shame and death. God's command is a retrospective validation of Jesus' expectation of enduring a shameful death. In the jargon of the encomium, it confirms both Jesus' voluntary acceptance of shame and God's acceptance of Jesus' choice as the way to posthumous glory.[32] In summary, when modern readers listen to the complete story in 9.18-36, they can recognize Jesus' awareness of his inevitable death, namely, that he voluntarily accepted it. All talk about his coming 'passion' expresses his voluntary stance before it and the posthumous honor which awaits him. He faces, then, a 'noble death'.[33]

Revenge Foresworn = Injury Accepted

In the agonistic cultural world of Jesus and Luke, males who were attacked or injured were expected to act honorably, that is, to seek revenge.[34] We know this as 'an eye for an eye, a tooth for a tooth', which validates revenge on one's attacker, even to the dishonoring of his own stage of personal honor, vis. his face (eye, tooth). For a soldier or warrior, the situation will be different, because he engaged in combat to the death, a very different experience than having to live among one's peers with an un-answered insult.

In Luke's narrative of the shameful death of Jesus, he tells his audience three times that Jesus does not engage in revenge, which would culturally balance the scale of insult, attack, and injury. At Passover some participants boast about swords, either for defense or offense. When Jesus cites a scripture that must be fulfilled in his regard, 'And he was counted among the lawless' (22.37/Isa. 53.12), the disciples understand this as an insult that must be prevented or avenged; some say: 'Lord, look, here are two swords' (22.38). One should wonder what a disciple at a Passover meal was doing with a sword in the first place, much less offering it to settle an honor challenge. Nevertheless, swords—two swords, to be exact—are in view. Thus, when Jesus is actually accosted by enemies, some disciples brandish swords to prevent dishonor to Jesus: 'Lord, should we strike with the sword?' (22.49). Before Jesus can speak, one disciple dishonors the slave of the high priest by severing his right ear, a pre-emptive defense of

32. One might say that it labels Jesus' 'departure' as a 'noble death'.

33. Let us not ignore, 'When the days drew near for him to be taken up, he set his face to go to Jerusalem' (Lk. 9.51).

34. Of the nobility of revenge, Aristotle says, 'To take vengeance on one's enemies is nobler than to come to terms with them; for to retaliate is just, and that which is just is noble' (*Rhet.* 1.9.24). Harris, *Restraining Rage*; he traced the history of anger and revenge, indicating how ubiquitous and acceptable revenge was.

Jesus' honor. But Jesus stops this, 'No more of this!' and acts to restore the head and honor of the wounded man. He actually gives a benefit to an enemy, 'He touched his ear and healed him'. Jesus thus restores the balance. In doing this, Jesus modeled for his disciples instructions given much earlier about forswearing revenge and vengeance: 'Love your enemies, do good to those who hate you, bless those who curse you' (6.27-28). The teacher himself practices what he taught his disciples, to accept injury and foreswear revenge. In terms of noble death, both Jesus' foreswearing of revenge and even his remedying of insult, minimally testify to his voluntary acceptance of his fate. He fully accepts the combat into which he is entering: 'But this is your hour, and the power of darkness!' (22.53).

When they deny all power to Jesus by fixing him to a cross, his enemies parade before him to mock him, their consummate shaming of him. 'The leaders *scoffed at* him…the soldiers *mocked him*' (23.35-37, italics added).[35] The poison in this mockery consists on turning against Jesus his own benefactions: 'He saved others; let him save himself' (23.35). Comparably, the soldiers turned against him the honorific claim on the inscription, 'This is the King of the Jews', mocking him with: 'If you are the King of the Jews, save yourself!' (23.37). Both command Jesus to 'save himself', which would indeed be a spectacular revenge against his enemies. But Jesus is silent and does not retaliate, not even with a curse. He voluntarily accepts these insults.

Finally, one criminal dying with him 'kept deriding him'[36] with the same insult, 'Are you not the Messiah? Save yourself and us!' (23.39). The other criminal, not Jesus, answers the insult: 'We indeed have been condemned justly, for we are getting what we deserve for our deeds, but this man has done nothing wrong' (23.41). Jesus remains silent in the face of the insult. But when petitioned by his defender, Jesus finally speaks his first words on the cross: a promise of honorable vindication for standing up for him. 'You will be with me in Paradise' (22.42; cf. 9.26). Luke again makes the point that Jesus does not retaliate or seek any form of revenge. His silence attests to his voluntary acceptance of mockery and insult.

---

35. 'Scoff' literally means 'to turn up one's nose at', a very physical snubbing; 'mocked', 'to make fun of'; both terms should destroy the honor of the person so treated. But, as Jesus has constantly taught, he does not seek revenge, but 'turns the other cheek'.

36. 'Deride' means more verbal abuse, 'to speak in a disrespectful way, denigrate, revile' (BDGA 178).

Although we have culled from various places in Luke's narrative individual items which we label as 'voluntary' acceptance of death, this does not differ from the way in the Maccabean literature that particular items are likewise selected and highlighted. Disparateness is no problem. Moreover, inasmuch as Luke narrates Jesus himself saying much about his coming death, he would have us take this as a fact that Jesus considered this often and that never did he reject it or flee from it. Furthermore, Jesus constantly acknowledges that his shame will be turned into honor, when God raises him from death and honors him. When he accepts vindication, he likewise accepts the shameful death which precedes it. Finally, since Luke is telling his narrative with full awareness of the categories of the encomium, we consider it valid to describe events related to the shame/honor of Jesus in terms of 'noble death', according to two distinctive criteria, voluntary death and post-humous honors. After all, the argument of this book is that Luke is employing the categories of the encomium, rather than that Jesus of Nazareth knew them himself.

Noble Death: Victorious, Unconquered, and Undefeated

In some funeral orations, the orator praising a noble death would claim that the warrior died 'unconquered', or he *'triumphed'*, or he was *'not defeated'*. Luke, of course, makes no such claim for Jesus in his narrative. While the risen Jesus himself declared that 'the Christ must suffer and so enter into his glory', this does not explicitly claim victory over death. Moreover, Luke repeatedly states in Acts that 'you killed him, God raised him', which, in an honor–shame culture, means that Jesus was mocked and shamed on earth, but that God vindicated him and honored him in the heavenly realm. All that is claimed is vindication *after* death or that suffering was the path to glory. But there are several places in Acts where victory over death is explicitly claimed, namely, in the assertion that Jesus *did not see corruption*. In his Pentecost address, Peter explicitly declares that escaping corruption meant that Jesus was victorious over death.

> God raised him up, having *freed him from death*, because it was *impossible* for him to be *held in its power*. For David says concerning him, 'I saw the Lord always before me, for he is at my right hand so that I will not be shaken...my flesh will live in hope. *For you will not abandon my soul to Hades*, or *let your Holy One see corruption*' (2.24-28, italics added).

Jesus was indeed 'freed from death' and death did not 'hold him in its power', which are Lukan expressions of 'triumph'. Confirmation of this comes from the fulfilment of Psalm 15, where David prophesied that God would not 'abandon my soul to Hades, or let your Holy One experience corruption'. Of course, this is a prophecy, because 'David both *died* and was *buried*, and his *tomb* is with us to this day' (Acts 2.29). So the argument goes, 'David spoke of the resurrection of the Messiah, saying, "He was not abandoned to Hades, nor did his flesh experience corruption"' (Acts 2.34). If we may finish Luke's syllogism, David predicted that the Messiah would triumph over death, but Jesus was raised from the dead and saw no corruption, therefore Jesus was victorious over death.

The same argument is made by Paul when he spoke to the synagogue in Antioch in Pisidia. First, Paul states his premise: 'What God promised to our ancestors he has fulfilled for us, by raising Jesus' (Acts 13.32); his proof is Psalm 2, where God's relationship to Jesus is declared: 'You are my Son; today I have begotten you'. Luke's audience would make the connection between 'You are my Son' with the claim at Jesus' baptism, 'You are my Son, the Beloved' (Lk. 3.22), and at his metamorphosis, 'This is my Son, my Chosen' (9.35). Now, when it is repeated, Luke cites how it is set in Psalm 2, 'You are my Son; today I have begotten you'. This unique relationship yields a remarkable result, as is stated in still another Scripture, 'You will not let your Holy One experience corruption' (Ps. 16.10). In a Lukan syncrisis, David, the author of Psalms 2 and 16, is contrasted with Jesus because, while speaking, David was *not* speaking of himself but of someone else, who obviously enjoys a maximally close relationship to God. Paul concludes his argument by repeating the key phrase from the psalm, '...but he whom God raised up *experienced no corruption*' (Acts 13.37/Ps. 16.10). Inasmuch as we argue that Luke was using the rhetorical criteria for a 'noble death', this would amount to honor claimed because of 'victory' over death.

Noble Death and Uniqueness

Praise is due a hero who was the first, the only, one of a few to do something. The mention of Elijah and Elisha or Moses and Elijah in Luke's narrative argue that Jesus was *not* the first prophet to be rejected and even killed. And Jesus' own remarks suggest that he accepted that he was *not* the first or the only or one of a few prophets who died: '...it is impossible for a prophet to be killed away from Jerusalem. Jerusalem, Jerusalem, the city that kills the prophets and stones those who are sent to it!' (Acts 13.33-34). Nor can Luke claim that Jesus was the only one to be vindicated by God. Like many of the criteria for a noble death, uniqueness can only be discerned in hindsight, when *all* of the actions of the hero and their effects can be known. Thus, Luke would have us turn to Acts of the Apostles to see how the disciples identified the uniqueness of Jesus' 'accomplishments'.

In his summary testimony about Jesus before Agrippa and Festus, Paul makes an important statement. He claims that he is saying *nothing novel*, but '...what the prophets and Moses said would take place: that the Messiah must suffer, and that, by being the *first to rise from the dead*, he would proclaim light both to our people and to the Gentiles' (Acts 26.22-23).[37] But this remark appears late in Acts and is credited to Paul, a late disciple. At the beginning of Acts, however, Peter and others began in hindsight to label the accomplishments of Jesus in different terms of uniqueness. Twice they proclaim Jesus 'the Author of life': '...you killed *the Author of life*, whom God raised from the dead' (3.15) and 'God exalted him at his right hand as Author Leader and *Savior*' (5.31). These two different words, 'first' and 'Author/Leader' bespeak uniqueness but in very different ways.

Even if 'first' is only a chronological marker,[38] it speaks to uniqueness. For example, just as Paul in Acts 26.22-23 identified Jesus as the 'first' to rise from the dead, so the other Paul said, 'Christ the first fruits, then at his coming those who belong to Christ' (1 Cor. 15.23), where Jesus is honored by being the first in a series. But 'author/leader' (Acts 3.15; 5.31) surpasses being 'first in time', because it means that this figure is the cause of all that follows.[39] Thus, Luke acknowledges Jesus' uniqueness in being the 'first' to experience posthumous honors as well as the 'cause' of them to others.

Uniqueness is also to be found in the response of Peter to the court, when asked about the healing of the crippled man. Yes, the fate of Jesus was completely reversed; but he is no mere rejected stone, but the 'cornerstone' (Acts 4.11). We suggest that the term 'cornerstone' implies

---

37. 'Nothing novel' means 'what the prophets and Moses said would come to pass'; but what is 'novel', is that '[Jesus] would be first to rise from the dead' (Acts 26.22-23).

38. At the start of his article, Delling lists three vectors of meaning for 'first': (1) spatially, the front, (2) first in time and number, and (3) first in rank and value ('*prōtos*', *TDNT*, VI, p. 865). In his contrast between 'first and last', he cites many Gospel references to claims of hierarchy or preeminence by disciples.

39. BDAG 138 defines 'author/leader' as a reference to 'one who begins something, first in a series'. Similarly Louw and Nida, *Greek–English Lexicon*, I, p. 655 render it as, 'one who causes something to begin, an initiator or founder'. We emphasize that this figure is the 'first' and 'only' one to achieve this distinction, and *causes* a beginning.

uniqueness, that is, it is the 'head' of something. In support, Luke states explicitly how unique is Jesus' name: 'There is salvation *in no one else*, for there is *no other name under heaven* given among mortals by which we must be saved' (4.12).[40] But 'unique' in what sense? Unique in terms of the 'salvation' which comes *only* from him.

We do not claim that the speeches in Acts are funeral orations honoring Jesus, only that in Luke's search for ways to praise the Jesus whom God vindicated, he states that the disciples are discovering in hindsight how Jesus was unique in three ways: (1) in terms of God's vindication of him ('first to rise from the dead'), (2) as cause of salvation, and (3) as having the only name for salvation. Jesus' death, then, is noble because of its uniqueness.

Noble Death and Posthumous Honors

A soldier or warrior would be particularly favored by Fortune if he survived battle and was honored in the *polis* with civic benefactions. Thus, some who went out to win glory, honor, and fame lived to enjoy it. Many funeral orations, however, themselves celebrate posthumously the noble death of a soldier with things representative of honor and glory befitting those who died. The oration itself, a monument, and many other expressions of respect to honor a fallen warrior.[41] Josephus said of Israelite warriors, 'For by winning eternal fame and glory for themselves they would be praised by those now living and would leave the ever-memorable (example of their) lives to future generations' (Josephus, *Ant.* 17.152).

Aristotle, in his definition of nobility states that honor received *after death* is preferable to that awarded while living, a statement that is found in many later rhetoricians: '...and whatever can belong to a person when *dead more than when alive* (for what belongs to a person in his lifetime has more of the quality *of being to his own advantage*' (*Rhet.* 1.9.18, italics added). Where does Luke speak about posthumous glory, honor, might and praise? Twice Jesus is said to be posthumously *exalted*: 'Being

---

40. Again, rare is the commentator who recognizes Peter's words as a claim to uniqueness. Their attention rests on explaining 'name', not the 'only' name.

41. Isocrates lists the various posthumous honors that might be celebrated: 'When I saw you, Nicocles, honoring the tomb of your father, not only with numerous and beautiful offerings, but also with dances, music, and athletic contests, and furthermore, with races of horses and triremes...' (*Evag.* 1). For an extensive catalogue of examples of posthumous glory, see Ziolkowski, *Thucydides and the Tradition of Funeral Speeches at Athens*, pp. 126-28.

therefore "exalted" at the right hand of God' (Acts 2.33), and 'God "exalted" him at his right hand' (5.31). Both citations refer to God's award of posthumous honor. But the dominant expressions of posthumous honor are found in the claims that Jesus is seated 'at God's right hand'.

In his gospel, Luke records few indications that when Jesus faced a shameful death, he had 'honor' as his aim. Twice Jesus' descriptions of the death that awaited him are balanced with a remark about heavenly vindication and honor: '...and on the third day be raised' (9.22; 18.33). Moreover, Jesus' word to the petitioning thief about being with him in Paradise strongly suggest anticipation of posthumous reward and glory after death (23.43). All of these statements come from the lips of Jesus himself. But a word from the risen Jesus is the perfect thematic statement of the argument subsequently made in Acts: 'Was it not necessary that the Messiah should suffer these things and *then enter into his glory?*' (24.6). Now Luke makes an explicit argument: (1) it was the plan and purpose of God that Jesus go to a shameful death; (2) but this was precisely the path to 'glory', that is, to God's vindication and favor, which we label 'posthumous honor'.

It is not, however, in the gospel that we find the clear and complete articulation of Jesus' posthumous honors, but in Acts. No, it is not Athens or any *polis* that honored Jesus after his death. The agent of his honor was none other than the God of Israel, who acted to cancel the shame of his death by 'raising' him up, both raising him *back to life* and raising him *up on high*. From the beginning of Acts, the posthumous honoring of Jesus is repeatedly expressed by the refrain which would become part of the kerygma: 'This man, handed over to you according to the definite plan and foreknowledge of God, you crucified and killed...*but God raised him up*, having freed him from death' (2.24; see also 2.32; 3.15; 5.30). Indeed, God bestowed posthumous honors on Jesus: 'The God of our ancestors has *glorified* his servant Jesus' (3.13). God indeed 'exalted' Jesus (2.33), again, not just by raising from the dead, but especially by *seating* him *at his right hand*, '...exalted at the right hand of God' (2.33; see 5.31 and 7.55). Thus it happens that Jesus of Nazareth is ascribed a new and eminent role of maximum status (see Phil. 2.8-11).

To be at the right side or hand of someone is recognized as being in the premier place of honor and enjoying God's special favor (cf. Mk 16.19). This special session, moreover, can mean two things, both authority/ power and favor. Paul writes that God '*raised* him (Jesus) from the dead and *seated him at his right hand* in the heavenly places, far above all rule and authority...and above every name that is named' (Eph. 1.20-21). In regard to special divine favors, a psalm says: 'The Lord says to my

lord, "Sit at my right hand until I make your enemies your footstool"'
(Ps. 110.1), indicating a most honorable place.[42] Therefore, only posthumously do his disciples understand how Jesus' death and resurrection
became the platform for his becoming pioneer of their salvation. Only
posthumously does God award him a superior role and highest status.

Noble Death and Benefaction

A 'noble' death benefitted others. So spoke Hyperides, 'Their courage
in arms...reveals them as the authors of many benefits conferred upon
their country and the rest of Greece' (*Funeral Speech* 9). We cited earlier
Aelius Theon speaking the same: '(Fine actions) are also those done for
others rather than for self...in which the toil is that of the doer but the
benefit is common; and through which the populace experiences benefits'.
Appreciation of the rhetorical form of 'noble death' might be seen in
competition with the search for the 'soteriology' of Luke. Perhaps it is
better to say that students of ancient rhetoric and modern scholars are
looking for the same thing, but through different lenses. But caution.
Luke is not claiming for Jesus the formal role of Benefactor (*euergetēs*),
which belongs to God alone;[43] Jesus always remains mediator or broker
in a patron–client model.[44]

When investigating the salvific effect of Jesus' death in the gospels
and Paul, scholars are confronted by a library of materials. But in that
library, materials on Luke's account of the salvific character of the death
of Jesus are meager indeed, because he does not advance what many
think is the essentially worthwhile theme of 'atonement' or *theologia
crucis*. Luke, however, has much to say about the beneficial effects of
Jesus' death, but not in the terms made hallowed by scholarship. As we
have been arguing, Luke was trained to write an encomium, a category

42. The 'right hand', moreover, is used for the most important blessings. For
example, when the ancient patriarchs blessed their children and grandchildren, they
blessed with their right hand, as with the case of Jacob: 'Israel stretched out his right
hand and laid it on the head of Ephraim, who was the younger, and his left hand on
the head of Manasseh, crossing his hands (for Manasseh was the firstborn)' (Gen.
48.14; see Isa. 41.13).

43. Jerome H. Neyrey, 'God, Benefactor and Patron: The Major Cultural Model
for Interpreting the Deity in Greco-Roman Antiquity', *JSNT* 27 (2005), pp. 465-92.

44. Jerome H. Neyrey, '"I Am the Door" (John 10:7, 9): Jesus the Broker in the
Fourth Gospel', *CBQ* 69 (2007), pp. 271-91; more recently, Neyrey, 'Was Jesus of
Nazareth a Monotheist? Conversation with Cultural Studies', *BTB* 49 (2019), pp.
132-36.

of which was consideration of a 'noble death'. 'Noble' is predicated according to criteria attested to by ancient rhetoricians, one of which was being of 'benefit to others', which Luke indeed discusses. 'Benefit', yes; 'atonement', no. Gospel only, no; Acts also, yes.

When in Acts Peter claims that the vindicated Jesus is posthumously seated at God's right hand, he explains how this benefits people: 'Being therefore exalted at the right hand of God, and having received from the Father the promise of the Holy Spirit, *he has poured out this that you both see and hear*' (2.33, italics added). Jesus' first benefaction, then, is the gift of Spirit, which will be mentioned continually in Acts. We have seen already that Jesus is acclaimed 'Author of Life' and 'Leader and Savior', which establish him as mediator of God's benefaction to God's people.

There is, moreover, another benefit from Jesus which continues in Acts. John, who called people to 'repent' (Lk. 3.3), prophesied that another would 'baptize with Holy Spirit and fire' (Lk. 3.16), that is, call others to repentance. Jesus performed this beneficial action throughout Galilee (Lk. 5.32; 15.7); moreover, this call to repentance would be continued later by the disciples whom the risen Jesus posthumously commissioned to do this: '…repentance and forgiveness of sins is to be proclaimed in his name to all nations, beginning from Jerusalem. You are witnesses of these things' (Lk. 24.47). And so the apostles did as commissioned: 'Peter said to them, "Repent, and be baptized every one of you in the name of Jesus Christ so that your sins may be forgiven; and you will receive the gift of the Holy Spirit"' (2.38). Thus, posthumously his disciples acknowledged how beneficial Jesus' death proved to be.

Summary and Conclusions

1. Modern readers now know what ancient authors and their audiences knew: the topos of on 'noble death'. Although unfamiliar to us, it was an ancient and common argument for the praise of someone, a form readily recognized, consistent, and clearly articulated. Born in Athenian funeral orations, it was refined over centuries, and eventually employed by the authors of the Maccabean literature. Of interest to us is its presence in the progymnastic genre known as the encomium, as an established form for drawing honor from an honorable man's death. Although we favor materials from the *progymnasmata*, they themselves are but a handbook version of a fully developed genre and rhetorical tradition. Ancient rhetoric provided authors (and audiences) with conventional forms of speaking (and hearing), their typical structures, modes of argumentation, and value systems. There was no other

way to write than to employ rhetorical materials. Either as a whole or in part, the topos on 'noble death' was hardly an esoteric piece of rhetoric known only by rhetoricians, as unfamiliar as it might be to modern scholars.

2. Just the label 'noble' means that such a topos reflects a culture which prized honor, praise, and glory. It was recognized by those who knew this cultural value and how its manifestations argued for a hero's *acquired* honor. This give considerable insight into the criteria of posthumous honors.

3. With great consistency, ancient rhetoricians employed six conventional criteria to argue that a death was 'noble', if it was: (1) beneficial, (2) voluntary, (3) virtuous, (4) victorious, (5) unique, and (6) productive of posthumous honors. These labels are rarely found in the commentaries of modern scholars, which presents a problem for contemporary readers, who might need to learn a new language, which is itself really ancient.

4. Knowledge of the topos on 'noble death' has serious implications. We have argued that Luke began his education by mastering the exercises in the *progymnasmata*, where he would have learned maxim, *chreia*, encomium, comparison, etc., to which we add 'noble death'. Modern scholarship, which accepts the scholarship on the *chreia*, a genre taught in the *progymnasmata*, should also welcome consideration of other genres from those rhetorical handbooks, namely, encomium and 'noble death'.

5. This rhetorical material may force a disconnect between the study of modern scholarship and ancient rhetoric. It remains to be seen whether contemporary studies of the death of Jesus will accept the native criteria for a 'noble' death. Because rhetoric is generally unfamiliar to contemporary scholars, they may well dismiss it as naive and facile. Rhetoric, however, offers what it offers. No ancient author or audience would agree with a negative assessment of its worth. It is not, therefore, shallow scholarship when scholars accept the topos on 'noble death' as a distinctively valuable approach to understanding Luke's account of the end of Jesus' life.

6. With confidence in the rhetoric about 'noble death', we examined Luke's account of the end of Jesus' life, flagging elements in his narrative with appropriate rhetorical labels from the six categories which constitute the topos on 'noble death'. Some elements of the topos prove to be more significant than others—as they were in Athenian funeral orations. Moreover, the labels we propose to identify certain deeds and words of Jesus are not those generated in modern criticism, but those from ancient rhetoric.

7. However, when we read Luke's narrative of the end of Jesus' life according to the topos on 'noble death', we learn things which we would likely never otherwise recognize in the story. We appreciate how Luke articulated Jesus' death as voluntary; he died like an obedient son, not a slave. Moreover, although his accusers and judges labeled Jesus as sinner, the topos on 'noble death' urged us to consider Jesus' virtues, in particular, how he was just and fulfilled his duties to his heavenly Father. Despite a famine of material in Luke's gospel about the beneficial character of Jesus' death, that is amply remedied by the extensive articulation of it in the posthumous reflection on Jesus' death in Acts. Moreover, no modern scholar has ever thought to consider the posthumous honors awarded Jesus, not simply the fact of them, but their significance as *posthumous honors*, a significant aspect of the 'noble death' topos.

8. It must be admitted that the exact terminology for the criteria for a 'noble death' is not explicitly used by Luke. But the concepts and topics are present in Luke's narrative, as has been shown. Moreover, ancient rhetoricians instructed authors to use behavior to express virtue, rather than to tag something by a familiar label. It matters what an audience hears being described. Luke told a narrative to a non-literate audience; he was not writing about philosophy or rhetoric for an elite circle. Moreover, we argue that Luke's audience fully appreciated encomiastic materials narrated earlier in his story, such as 'origins' and 'nurture and training', although *he did not label* these data with encomiastic labels. Then Luke and his audience may be presumed to know the other encomiastic categories commonly used to find honor for a person in his 'accomplishments', namely, the canonical virtues and 'noble death'. One does not know just this or that element of an encomium. No one in antiquity would fault Luke's use of the topos of 'noble death' for drawing praise for Jesus. Nor would they fail to recognize what Luke was doing.

9. Employing the rhetoric about 'noble death' necessarily means that we look backward and forward in the Lukan narrative for clues about Jesus' death.[45] It is a mistake, therefore, to focus only on Luke 22–23. Some of Jesus' sayings alert readers to his awareness of his impending shame and so his voluntary acceptance of it. But consideration of Jesus' end of life requires the same readers also to study the interpretation of his death in the Acts of the Apostles, where many of the criteria are more explicitly treated, especially, Jesus' posthumous

---

45. The encomium was formally intended to cover the whole of a man's life, from origins to death.

honors. Thus, the Lukan material about the end of Jesus' life cannot be restricted to chs. 22–23, but must include Luke 24 and the Acts of the Apostles. The extent of the topos on 'noble death' requires a very broad investigation, as it did in the original oratory on 'noble death'. The story of the end of Jesus' life, then, does not begin with his entry into Jerusalem, nor end with his burial.

10. Therefore, our appreciation of Luke's use of the encomiastic instructions about declaring a death 'noble' is not the imposition of an alien form on Luke's narrative, but the recognition of Luke's education and his skill in writing. Our use of those encomiastic instructions constitutes for us merely an emic template which surfaces and identifies what is already there. Progymnastic authors are our native informants.

11. The success of arguing that Luke employed the topos on 'noble death' must be taken alongside his use of other elements from the progymnastic encomium. The accurate assessment of each topic in the encomium supports the judgment that other topics are also present. And, as noted above about 'origins' and 'nurture and training', Luke *used* them, but *never labeled them*. Moreover, it would indeed be strange if Luke successfully used encomiastic topics such as 'origins' and 'nurture and training', but ignored the others, in particular the topos on 'noble death'. Success in one place argues well for success in other areas.

12. It would seem, then, that the hypothesis of this monograph has proved to be well argued. Luke began his education with the study of the rhetorical handbooks called the *Progymnasmata*. Evidence for this, we have seen, is his success in employing various genres taught in them. His further rhetorical education, moreover, would position him among the few literate elites of his day (in terms of wealth and social location), something that can be further argued by identification of the many rhetorical topoi and topics he employs, such as historical prologues, forensic defense speeches, and the like. Luke, then, can be seen as an urbanite, educated to perform public things of importance, such as writing sophisticated prose. Most important for this book, Luke was well trained in classical rhetoric, in particular, how to write an encomium.

APPENDIX
GRECO-ROMAN RHETORIC THAT LUKE KNOWS

Types of Rhetoric

'We must distinguish between…the three kinds of Rhetoric, deliberative, epideictic, and forensic' (Aristotle, *Rhet.* 1.3.9).

1. *Epideictic*:

> Duane F. Watson, 'Paul's Speech to the Ephesian Elders (Acts 20:17-48: Epideictic Rhetoric of Farewell', in Duane Watson (ed.), *Persuasive Artistry: Studies in New Testament Rhetoric in Honor of George A. Kennedy* (Sheffield: JSOT Press, 1991), pp. 184-208.

2. *Forensic*:

> Jerome H. Neyrey, 'The Forensic Defense Speech and Paul's Trial Speeches in Acts 22-26: Form and Function', in C.H. Talbert (ed.), *Luke-Acts: New Perspectives from the Society of Biblical Literature Seminar* (New York: Crossroads, 1984), pp. 210-24; Fred Veltman, 'The Defense Speeches of Paul in Acts', in Charles H. Talbert (ed.), *Perspectives on Luke–Acts* (Edinburgh: T. & T. Clark, 1978), pp. 243-56; Craig Evans, '"Speeches" in Luke-Acts', in Albert Descamps and Andre de Halleux (eds.), *Melanges Biblique en homage au R.P. Beda Rigaux* (Gembloux: Duculot, 1970), pp. 298-311.

Argument from Enthymeme

> William S. Kurz, 'Hellenistic Rhetoric in the Christological Proof of Luke-Acts', *CBQ* 42 (1980), pp. 171-95.

Formal Elements of a Speech

> Bruce Winter, 'The Importance of *captatio benevolentiae* in the Speeches of Tertullus and Paul in Acts 24:1-2', *JTS* 42 (1991), pp. 505-31.

Progymnasmata

Michel A. Parsons, 'Luke and the *Progymnasmata*', in Todd Penner and Caroline Vander Stichele (eds.), *Contextualizing Acts: Lukan Narrative and Greco-Roman Discourse* (SBLSymS, 20; Atlanta, GA: SBL Press, 2003), pp. 43-63; Michael W. Martin, 'Progymnastic Topic Lists: A Compositional Template for Luke and Other *Bioi*?', *NTS* 54 (2008), pp. 18-41; Mikeal C. Parsons and Michael W. Martin, *Ancient Rhetoric and the New Testament* (Waco, TX: Baylor University Press, 2018).

Progymnastic Genres

1. *Fable*

Parsons and Martin, *Ancient Rhetoric and the New Testament*, pp. 45-70.

2. *Maxim*

John Nolland, 'Classical, and Rabbinic Parallels to "Physician, Heal Yourself" (LK. IV 23)', *NovT* 21 (1999), pp. 193-209; John Dominic Crossan, *In Fragments: The Aphorisms of Jesus* (San Francisco, CA: Harper & Row, 1983), pp. 180-245; John S. Kloppenborg, *The Formation of Q* (Philadelphia, PA: Fortress Press, 1987), pp. 180-245.

3. *Chreia*

Ronald F. Hock and Edward N. O'Neil, *The Chreia in Ancient Rhetoric. I. The Progymnasmata* (Atlanta, GA: Scholars Press, 1986); Jerome H. Neyrey, 'Questions, Chreai, and Challenges to Honor: The Interface of Rhetoric and Culture in Mark's Gospel', *CBQ* 60 (1998), pp. 657-81; Thomas D. Stegman, 'Reading Luke 12:13-34 as an Elaboration of a Chreia: How Hermogenes of Tarsus Sheds Light on Luke's Gospel', *NovT* 49 (2007), pp. 328-51.

4. *Syncrisis*

Parsons and Martin, *Ancient Rhetoric and the New Testament*, pp. 231-74.

5. *Encomium*

Michel A. Parsons, 'Luke and the *Progymnasmata*', in Penner and Vander Stichele (eds.), *Contextualizing Acts*, pp. 43-63.

6. *Ecphrasis*

G.B. Miles and G. Trompf, 'Luke and Antiphon: The Theology of Acts 27–28 in the Light of Pagan Beliefs about Divine Retribution, Pollution, and Shipwreck', *HTR* 69 (1976), pp. 259-67; David Ladouceur, 'Hellenistic

Preconceptions of Shipwreck and Pollution as a Context for Acts 27–28',
HTR 73 (1980), pp. 435-49.

Rhetorical Topoi and Genres

1. *Preface in Greek Historical Writing* (Lk. 1.1-4; Acts 1.1-5)

Loveday Alexander, 'Luke's Preface in the Context of Greek Preface-
Writing', *NovT* 28 (1986), pp. 48-72; Vernon K. Robbins, 'Prefaces in
Greco-Roman Biography and Luke-Acts', *PRS* 6 (1979), pp. 94-108.

2. *Biographies*

Richard A. Burridge, *What Are the Gospels? A Comparison with Graeco-
Roman Biography* (Waco, TX: Baylor University Press, 2018); Charles H.
Talbert, 'Prophecies of Future Greatness: The Contribution of Greco-Roman
Biographies to an Understanding of Luke 1:5–4:15', in James L. Crenshaw
and Samuel Sandmel (ed.), *The Divine Helmsman* (New York: KTAV,
1984), pp. 129-41.

3. *Symposia meals*

Oswyn Murray, *Sympotica: A Symposium on the Symposium* (Oxford:
Clarendon Press, 1991); E. Springs Steele, 'Luke 11:37-54—A Modified
Hellenistic Symposium', *JBL* 103 (1984), pp. 479-94.

4. *Farewell address*

Duane Watson, 'Paul's Speech to the Ephesian Elders (Acts 20:17-38:
Epideictic Rhetoric', in Duane Watson (ed.), *Persuasive Artistry: Studies
in New Testament Rhetoric in Honor of George A. Kennedy* (Sheffield:
JSOT Press, 1991), pp. 184-208; William S. Kurz, S.J., 'Luke 22:14-38
and Graeco-Roman and Biblical Farewell Addresses', *JBL* 104 (1985), pp.
251-68; Jerome H. Neyrey, 'Jesus' Farewell Speech (LK 22:14-38)', in his
The Passion according to Luke: A Redaction Study of Luke's Soteriology
(Eugene, OR: Wipf & Stock, 1985), pp. 5-48.

5. *Roman trial*

Jerome H. Neyrey, 'The Forensic Defense Speech and Paul's Trial Speeches
in Acts 22-26', in Talbert (ed.), *Luke–Acts*, pp. 210-24; Neyrey, 'The Trials
of Jesus in Luke–Acts', in his *The Passion according to Luke*, pp. 69-107.

6. *'We' Passages*

Henry J. Cadbury, '"We" and "I" Passages in Luke–Acts', *NTS* 3 (1956),
pp. 128-45; Vernon K. Robbins, 'By Land and By Sea: The We-Passages

and Ancient Sea Voyages', in Talbert (ed.), *Perspectives on Luke Acts*, pp. 215-42.

6. *'Noble Death'*

Tradition: John E. Ziolkowski, *Thucydides and the Tradition of Funeral Speeches at Athens* (Salem, NH: The Ayer Company, 1981); Jerome H. Neyrey, 'The "Noble" Shepherd in John 10: Cultural and Rhetorical Background', *JBL* 120 (2001), pp. 267-91.

BIBLIOGRAPHY

Alexander, Loveday, 'Luke's Preface in the Context of Greek Preface-Writing', *NovT* 28 (1986), pp. 48-72.

Arius Didymus, *Epitome of Stoic Ethics* (ed. Arthur J. Pomeroy; Atlanta, GA: Society of Biblical Literature, 1999).

Aune, David E., 'Greco-Roman Biography', in his *Greco-Roman Literature and the New Testament: Selected Forms and Genres* (Atlanta, GA: Scholars Press, 1988), pp. 140-65.

Balch, David J., 'Two Apologetic Encomia: Dionysius on Rome and Josephus on the Jews', *JSJ* 13 (1982), pp. 102-22.

Baldwin, C.S., *Medieval Rhetoric and Poetic* (New York: Sedgwick, 1928).

Batey, Richard A., 'Jesus and the Theatre', *NTS* 30 (1986), pp. 563-74.

Belfiore, Elizabeth, 'Harming Friends: Problematic Reciprocity in Greek Tragedy', in Gill, Postlewaithe, and Seaford (eds.), *Reciprocity in Ancient Greece*, pp. 139-51.

Betlyon, John W., 'Coinage', in *ABD*, I, p. 1086.

Betz, Hans Dieter, *The Sermon on the Mount: A Commentary on the Sermon on the Mount, including the Sermon on the Plain (Matthew 5:3–7:27 and Luke 6:20-49* (Minneapolis, MN: Fortress Press, 1995).

Billings, Bradley, 'At the Age of 12: The Boy Jesus in the Temple (Luke 2:41-52), the Emperor Augustus, and the Social Setting of the Third Gospel', *JTS* 60 (2009), pp. 70-89.

Blundell, Mary Whitlock, *Helping Friends and Harming Enemies: A Study in Sophocles and Greek Ethics* (New York: Cambridge University Press, 1989).

Bonner, Stanley F., *Education in Ancient Rome* (Berkeley, CA: University of California Press, 1977).

Bourdieu, Pierre, 'The Attitude of the Algerian Peasant toward Time', in *Mediterranean Countrymen: Essays in Social Anthropology of the Mediterranean* (ed. Julian Pitt-Rivers; Paris: Mouton, 1963), pp. 55-72.

Bovon, Francois, *A Commentary on the Gospel of Luke 9:51–19:27* (Minneapolis, MN: Fortress Press, 1981).

Bovon, Francois, *Luke 1: A Commentary on the Gospel of Luke 1:1–9:50* (Minneapolis, MN: Fortress Press, 2002).

Brown, Raymond E., *The Birth of the Messiah* (New York: Doubleday, 1993).

Brown, Raymond E., *The Death of the Messiah: From Gethsemane to the Grave: A Commentary on the Passion Narratives in the Four Gospels* (New York: Doubleday, 1994).

Buchanan, George W., 'The Age of Jesus', *NTS* 41 (1995), p. 297.

Burkert, Walter, 'Oriental Symposia: Contrasts and Parallels', in *Dining in a Classical Context* (ed. William J. Slater; Ann Arbor: University of Michigan Press, 1991), pp. 7-24.

Burridge, Richard A., *What Are the Gospels? A Comparison with Graeco-Roman Biography* (Waco, TX: Baylor University Press, 2018).

Burrows, Theodore, 'Epideictic Literature', *Studies in Classical Philology* 3 (1902), pp. 89-261.

Cadbury, Henry J., '"We" and "I" Passages in Luke–Acts', *NTS* 3 (1956), pp. 128-45.

Cassidy, Richard J., *Jesus, Politics, and Society* (Maryknoll, NY: Orbis Books, 1978).

Clausen, John A., *Socialization and Society* (Boston, MA: Little, Brown & Co., 1968).

Cohen, David, *Law, Violence, and Community in Classical Athens* (Cambridge: Cambridge University Press, 1995).

Conzelmann, Hans, *The Theology of Luke* (New York: Harper & Brothers, 1960).

Cosgrove, Charles H., 'The Divine *DEI* in Luke–Acts', *NovT* 26 (1984), pp. 168-90.

Cotter, Wendy J., C.S.J., 'The Parable of the Children in the Market-Place, Q (Lk) 7:31-35: An examination of the Parable's Image and Significance', *NovT* 29 (1987), pp. 289-304.

Couroyer, B., 'De la mesure vous mesurez il vous sera mesuré', *RB* 77 (1970), pp. 366-70.

Cribiore, Raffaella, *Writing, Teachers, and Students in Graeco-Roman Egypt* (Atlanta, GA: Scholars Press, 1996).

Crossan, John Dominic, *In Fragments: The Aphorisms of Jesus* (San Francisco, CA: Harper & Row, 1983).

Dahl, Nils A., 'The Parables of Growth', *ST* 5 (1951), pp. 140-47.

Darton, Michael, *Modern Concordance to the New Testament* (London: Longman & Todd, 1976).

De Jonge, H.J., 'Sonship, Wisdom, and Infancy: Luke ii:41-51a', *NTS* 24 (1978), pp. 317-54.

Derrett, J. Duncan M., 'An Apt Student's Matriculation (Lk 2,39-52)', *Estudios Biblicos* 58 (2000), pp. 101-22.

Derrett, J. Duncan M., 'Birds of the Air and Lilies of the Field', *DR* 105 (1978), pp. 181-92.

Derrett, J. Duncan M., 'Christ and Reproof (Matthew 7,1-5/Luke 6,37-42)', *NTS* 34 (1988), pp. 271-81.

Derrett, J. Duncan M., *Jesus' Audience. The Social and Psychological Environment in which He Worked* (New York: Seabury Press, 1974).

Donahue, John R., 'Tax Collectors and Sinners: An Attempt at Identification', *CBQ* 33 (1971), pp. 39-61.

Dover, K.J., *Greek Popular Morality in the Time of Plato and Aristotle* (Berkeley, CA: University of California Press, 1974).

Droge, Arthur J., and James D. Tabor, *A Noble Death: Suicide and Martyrdom among Christians and Jews in Antiquity* (San Francisco: Harper, 1992).

Dungan, David L., and David R. Cartlidge, *Sourcebook of Texts for the Comparative Study of the Gospels* (Missoula, MT: Scholars Press, 1974).

Edwards, M.J., 'Not Yet Fifty Years Old', *NTS* 40 (1994), pp. 449-54.

Elliott, John H., 'Temple versus Household in Luke–Acts: A Contrast in Social Institutions', in *The Social World of Luke–Acts: Models for Interpretation* (ed. Jerome H. Neyrey; Peabody, MA: Hendrickson, 1991), pp. 211-40.

Emmons, Robert A., *Is Gratitude Queen of the Virtues and Ingratitude King of the Vices?* (2017). Published as https://scottbarrykaufman.com/wp-content/uploads/2017/09/Emmons-paper-for-Gratitude-Complaint-consultation-September-2017.pdf.

Evans, Craig, '"Speeches" in Luke–Acts', in *Melanges Biblique en homage au R.P. Beda Rigaux* (ed. Albert Descamps and Andre de Halleux; Gembloux: Duculot, 1970), pp. 298-311.

Feldman, Louis, 'Hellenizations in Josephus', *Jewish Antiquities*: The Portrait of Abraham', in *Josephus, Judaism and Christianity* (ed. Louis Feldman and Gohei Hata; Detroit, MI: Wayne State University Press, 1987), pp. 133-53.

Feldman, Louis, 'Josephus as an Apologist to the Greco-Roman World: His Portrait of Solomon', in *Aspects of Religious Propaganda in Judaism and Early Christianity* (ed. Elizabeth Schüssler-Fiorenza Notre Dame, IN: University of Notre Dame Press, 1976), pp. 69-98.

Feldman, Louis, 'Josephus' Portrait of David', *HUCA* 60 1989), pp. 129-74; 'Josephus' Portrait of Hezekiah', *JBL* 111 (1992), pp. 597-610.

Feldman, Louis, 'Josephus' Portrait of Jacob', *JQR* 79 (1988), pp. 101-51.

Fitzgerald, John T., *Cracks in an Earthen Vessel: An Examination of the Catalogues of Hardships in the Corinthian Correspondence* (Atlanta, GA: Scholars Press, 1988).

Fitzmyer, Joseph A., *The Gospel according to Luke I–IX* (Garden City, NY: Doubleday, 1981).

Fitzmyer, Joseph A., 'The Composition of Luke, Chapter 9', in Talbert (ed.), *Perspectives on Luke–Acts*, pp. 139-52.

Forkman, Göran, *The Limits of Religious Community* (Lund: C. W. K. Gleerup, 1972).

Fortenbaugh, William W., 'Aristotle and Theophrastus on the Emotions', in *Passions and Moral Progress in Greco-Roman Thought* (ed. John Fitzgerald; London: Routledge, 2008), pp. 9-47.

Foster, Paul, 'Educating Jesus: The Search for a Plausible Context', *Journal for the Study of the Historical Jesus* 4 (2006), pp. 7-33.

George, A., 'Le parallèle entre Jean-Baptiste et Jésus en Lc 1–2', in *Mélangaes bibliques en hommage au R. P. Béda Rigaux* (ed. A. Descamps and A. De Halleux; Gembloux: Duculot, 1970), pp. 147-71.

Gerhardsson, Birger, *The Testing of God's Son* (Lund: Gleerup, 1966).

Gill, Christopher, Norman Postlewaithe, and Richard Seaford (eds.), *Reciprocity in Ancient Greece* (Oxford: Oxford University Press, 1998).

Golden, Michael, '*Pais*, "Child", and "Slave"', *L'Antiquité Classique* 54 (1985), p. 93.

Goodman, Martin, 'The First Jewish Revolt: Social Conflict and the Problem of Debt', *JJS* 33 (1982), pp. 417-27.

Gould, John, 'Law, Custom and Myth: Aspects of the Social Position of Women in Classical Athens', *JHS* 100 (1980), pp. 38-59.

Hamilton, Niell Q., 'Temple Cleansing and Temple Bank', *JBL* 83 (1964), pp. 365-72.

Hall, Edward T., *Beyond Culture* (New York: Doubleday, 1981).

Hanson, K.C., '"How Honorable! How Shameful!" A Cultural Analysis of Matthew's Makarisms and Reproaches', *Semeia* 68 (1996), pp. 81-112.

Hanson, K.C., and Douglas E. Oakman, *Palestine in the Time of Jesus: Social Structures and Social Conflicts* (Minneapolis, MN: Fortress Press, 1998).

Hare, D.R.A., *The Theme of Jewish Persecution of Christians in the Gospel according to St. Matthew* (Cambridge: Cambridge University Press, 1967).

Harris, William V., *Ancient Literacy* (Cambridge, MA: Harvard University Press, 1989).

Harris, William V., *Restraining Rage: The Ideology of Anger Control in Classical Antiquity* (Cambridge, MA: Harvard University Press, 2001).

Henderson, Ian H., 'Quintilian and the *Progymnasmata*', *Antike und Abendland* 36 (1934), pp. 82-99.

Henten, Jan Willem van, *The Maccabean Martyrs as Saviours of the Jewish People* (Leiden: Brill, 1997).

Herzfeld, Michael, '"Law" and "Custom": Ethnography *of* and *in* Greek National Identity', *Journal of Modern Greek Studies* 3 (1985), pp. 167-85.

Hezser, Catherine, *Jewish Literacy in Roman Palestine* (Tübingen: Mohr/Siebeck, 2001).

Hock, Ronald, and Edward O'Neil, *The Chreia in Ancient Rhetoric*. I. *The Progymnasmata* (Atlanta, GA: Scholars Press, 1986).

Humphreys, Sally, 'Law, Custom and Culture in Herodotus', *Arethusa* 20 (1987), pp. 211-20.

Kaster, Robert A., 'Notes on "Primary" and "Secondary" Schools in Late Antiquity', *TAPA* 113 (1983), pp. 323-46.

Kee, Howard Clark, 'The Terminology of Mark's Exorcism Stories', *NTS* 14 (1978), pp. 242-46.

Kelber, Werner H., 'Conclusion: From Passion Narrative to Gospel', in his *The Passion in Mark: Studies on Mark 14–16* (Philadelphia, PA: Fortress Press, 1976).

Kennedy, George A. *Progymnasmata: Greek Textbooks of Prose Composition and Rhetoric* (Atlanta, GA: Society of Biblical Literature Press, 2003).

Kilpatrick, G.D., 'The Theme of the Lucan Passion Story and Luke xxiii.47', *JTS* 43 (1941), pp. 34-36.

Kindstrand, Jan F., 'Diogenes Laertius and the Chreia Tradition', *Elenchos* 7 (1986), pp. 219-43.

Kloppenborg, John S., *The Formation of Q* (Philadelphia, PA: Fortress Press, 1987).

Kluckhohn, Florence, and Fred Strodbeck, *Variations in Value Orientations* (Evanston, IL: Row & Peterson, 1961).

Kolenkow, A., and Robin Scroggs, 'Reflections on the Question: Was There a Pre-Markan Passion Narrative?', *SBLSP* 2 (1971), pp. 503-85.

Konstan, David, *The Emotions of the Ancient Greeks: Studies in Aristotle and Classical Literature* (ed. Toronto: University of Toronto Press, 2007).

Konstan, David, *Pity Transformed* (London: Duckworth, 2001).

Konstan, David, 'Reciprocity and Friendship', in Gill, Postlewaithe, and Seaford (eds.), *Reciprocity in Ancient Greece*, pp. pp. 279-301.

Kurz, William S., 'Hellenistic Rhetoric in the Christological Proof of Luke–Acts', *CBQ* 42 (1980), pp. 171-95.

Kurz, William S., 'Luke 3:23-38 and Greco-Roman and Biblical Genealogies', in Talbert (ed.), *Luke–Acts*, pp. 169-87.

Ladouceur, David, 'Hellenistic Preconceptions of Shipwreck and Pollution as a Context for Acts 27–28', *HTR* 73 (1980), pp. 435-49.

Loraux, Nicole, *The Invention of Athens: The Funeral Oration in the Classical City* (Cambridge, MA: Harvard University Press, 1986).

Lee, Thomas R., *Studies in the Form of Sirach 44–50* (SBLDS, 74; Atlanta, GA: Scholars Press, 1986).

Louw, Johannes, and Eugene Nida, *Greek–English Lexicon of the New Testament based on Semantic Domains* (New York: American Bible Society, 1986).

Lloyd, G.E.R., *Polarity and Analogy: Two Types of Argumentation in Early Greek Thought* (Cambridge: Cambridge University Press, 1966).

Lyons, George, *Pauline Autobiography: Toward a New Understanding* (SBLDS, 73; Atlanta, GA: Scholars Press, 1985).

Mack, Burton, 'Decoding the Scripture: Philo and the Rules of Rhetoric', in *Nourished with Peace: Studies in Hellenistic Judaism in Memory of Samuel Sandmel* (ed. Frederick E. Greenspahn, Earle Hilgert, and Burton L. Mack; Chico, CA: Scholars Press, 1984), pp. 81-115.

Mack, Burton, and Vernon Robbins, *Patterns of Persuasion in the Gospels* (Sonoma, CA: Polebridge Press, 1989).

Magie, David, *Roman Rule in Asia Minor, to the End of the Third Century after Christ* (Princeton, NJ: Princeton University Press, 1950).

Malina, Bruce J., 'Apocalyptic and Territoriality', in *Early Christianity in Context: Monuments and Documents. Essays in Honour of Emmanuel Testa* (ed. Fredrick Manns and Eugenio Alliata; Jerusalem: Franciscan Printing, 1993), pp. 369-80.

Malina, Bruce J., 'Christ and Time: Swiss or Mediterranean?', *CBQ* 51 (1989), pp. 1-31.

Malina, Bruce J., *Christian Origins and Cultural Anthropology* (Atlanta, GA: John Knox Press, 1986).

Malina, Bruce J., 'Humility', in Pilch and Malina (eds.), *Handbook of Biblical Social Values*, pp. 99-100.

Malina, Bruce J., '"Let Him Deny Himself" (Mark 8:34 & par): A Social Psychological Model of Self-Denial', *BTB* 24 (1993), pp. 106-19.

Malina, Bruce J., 'Love', in Pilch and Malina (eds.), *Handbook of Biblical Social Values*, pp. 106-108.

Malina, Bruce J., *The New Testament World: Insights from Cultural Anthropology* (Louisville, KY: Westminster/John Knox Press, 3rd edn, 2001).

Malina, Bruce J., *On the Genre and Message of Revelation. Star Visions and Sky Journeys* (Peabody, MA: Hendrickson, 1995).

Malina, Bruce J., and Jerome H. Neyrey, *Calling Jesus Names: The Social Value of Labels in Matthew* (Sonoma, CA: Polebridge Press, 1988).

Malina, Bruce J., and Jerome H. Neyrey, 'Honor and Shame in Luke–Acts: Pivotal Values of the Mediterranean World', in *The Social World of Luke–Acts: Models for Interpretation* (ed. Jerome H. Neyrey; Peabody, MA: Hendrickson, 1991), pp. 25-65.

Malina, Bruce J., and Jerome H. Neyrey, *Portraits of Paul: An Archaeology of Ancient Personality* (Louisville, KY: Westminster/John Knox Press, 1996).

Malina, Bruce J., and Richard L. Rohrbaugh, *Social Science Commentary on the Synoptic Gospels* (Minneapolis, MN: Fortress Press, 1992).

Marrou, H.I., *A History of Education in Antiquity* (Madison WI: University of Wisconsin Press, 1982).

Martin, Michael W., 'Progymnastic Topic Lists: A Compositional Template for Luke and Other *Bioi*', *NTS* 54 (2008), pp. 18-41.

Matera, Frank, 'The Death of Jesus according to Luke: A Question of Sources', *CBQ* 47 (1985), pp. 469-85.

Maxwell, Kathy Reiko, *Hearing Between Lines: The Audience as Fellow-Worker in Luke–Acts and its Literary Milieu* [Waco, TX: Baylor University Press, 2007).

McHardy, Fiona, *The Ideology of Revenge in Ancient Greek Culture: A Study of Ancient Athenian Revenge Ethics* (1999), published at https://www.academia.edu/28361076.

Miles, G.B., and G. Trompf, 'Luke and Antiphon: The Theology of Acts 27–28 in the Light of Pagan Beliefs about Divine Retribution, Pollution, and Shipwreck', *HTR* 69 (1976), pp. 259-67.

Millett, P., *Lending and Borrowing in Ancient Athens* (Cambridge: Cambridge University Press, 1991).

Momigliano, Arnaldo, *The Development of Greek Biography* (Cambridge, MA: Harvard University Press, 1971).

Mowrey, R.L., 'The Divine Hand and the Divine Plan in the Lukan Passion', *SBLSP* (1991), pp. 558-75.

Moxnes, Halvor, *The Economy of the Kingdom: Social Conflict and Economic Relations in Luke's Gospel* (Philadelphia, PA: Fortress Press, 1988).

Munn, Nancy D., 'The Cultural Anthropology of Time: A Critical Essay', *Annual Review of Anthropology* 21 (1992), pp. 93-123.

Murray, Oswyn, *Sympotica: A Symposium on the Symposium* (Oxford: Clarendon Press, 1991).

Nadeau, Ray, 'The Progymnasmata of Aphthonius in Translation', *Speech Monographs* 19 (1952), pp. 264-85.

Neusner, Jacob, 'Money-changers in the Temple: The Mishnah's Explanation', *NTS* 35 (1999), pp. 287-90.

Neyrey, Jerome H., 'The Absence of Jesus' Emotions—the Lucan Redaction of Lk 22,39-46', *Biblica* 61 (1980), pp. 153-59; reprinted in Neyrey, *The Passion according to Luke*, pp. 49-68.

Neyrey, Jerome H., 'Bewitched in Galatia: Paul in Social Science Perspective', *CBQ* 50 (1988), pp. 72-100.

Neyrey, Jerome H., 'Deception, Ambiguity, and Revelation: Matthew's Judgment Sciences in Social-Science Perspectives', in *When Judaism and Christianity Began* (ed. Alan Avery-Peck, Daniel Harrington, and Jacob Neusner; Leiden: Brill, 2004), pp. 199-230.

Neyrey, Jerome H., 'Encomium versus Vituperation: Contrasting Portraits of Jesus in the Fourth Gospel', *JBL* 126 (2007), pp. 529-52.

Neyrey, Jerome H., '"First", Only, "One of a Few", and "No One Else": The Rhetoric of Uniqueness and the Doxologies in 1 Timothy', *Biblica* 86 (2005), pp. 59-87.

Neyrey, Jerome H., 'The Footwashing in John 13:6-11: Transformation Ritual or Ceremony?', in *The Social World of the First Christians: Essays in Honor of Wayne A. Meeks* (ed. L.M. White and O.L. Yarbrough; Minneapolis, MN: Fortress Press, 1995), pp. 198-213.

Neyrey, Jerome H., 'The Forensic Defense Speech and Paul's Trial Speeches in Acts 22–26: Form and Function', in Talbert (ed.), *Luke–Acts*, pp. 210-24.

Neyrey, Jerome H., 'God, Benefactor and Patron: The Major Cultural Model for Interpreting the Deity in Greco-Roman Antiquity', *JSNT* 27 (2005), pp. 465-92.

Neyrey, Jerome H., *Honor and Shame in the Gospel of Matthew* (Louisville, KY: Westminster/John Knox Press, 1998).

Neyrey, Jerome H., '"How Does This Man Have Learning, since He is without Education?" (John 7:15), *BTB* 48 (2018), p. 90.

Neyrey, Jerome H., '"I Am the Door" (John 10:7, 9): Jesus the Broker in the Fourth Gospel', *CBQ* 69 (2007), pp. 271-91.

Neyrey, Jerome H., 'In Conclusion...John 12 as a Rhetorical *Peroratio*', *BTB* 37 (2007), pp. 101-13.

Neyrey, Jerome H., 'Jesus' Farewell Speech (LK 22:14-38)', in his Passion according to Luke, pp. 5-48.

Neyrey, Jerome H., 'Josephus' Vita and the Encomium: A Native Model of Personality', *JSJ* 25 (1994), pp. 177-206.

Neyrey, Jerome H., 'Loss of Wealth, Loss of Family and Loss of Honor: A Cultural Interpretation of the Original Four Makarisms', in *Modelling Early Christianity: Social-Scientific Studies of the New Testament in its Context* (ed. Philip F. Esler; London: Routledge, 1995), pp. 139-58.

Neyrey, Jerome H., 'Nudity', in Pilch and Malina (eds.), *Handbook of Biblical Social Values*, pp. 118-22.

Neyrey, Jerome H., 'The "Noble" Shepherd in John 10: Cultural and Rhetorical Background', *JBL* 120 (2001), pp. 267-91.

Neyrey, Jerome H., *The Passion according to Luke: A Redaction Study of Luke's Soteriology* (Eugene, OR: Wipf & Stock, 1985).

Neyrey, Jerome H., 'Questions, Chreiai, and Honor Challenges: The Interface of Rhetoric and Culture in Mark's Gospel', *CBQ* 60 (1998), pp. 657-81.

Neyrey, Jerome H., 'The Social Location of Paul: How Paul Was Educated and What He Could Compose as Indices of His Social Location', *Fabrics of Discourse: Essays in Honor of Vernon K. Robbins* (ed. David B. Gowler, L. Gregory Bloomquist, and Duane F. Watson; Harrisburg, PA: Trinity Press International, 2003), pp. 126-64.

Neyrey, Jerome H., 'The Sociology of Secrecy and the Fourth Gospel', in *What Is John?* II. *Literary and Social Readings of the Fourth Gospel* (ed. F. Segovia; Atlanta, GA: Scholars Press, 1998), pp. 79-109.

Neyrey, Jerome H., 'The Trials of Jesus in Luke–Acts', in his *The Passion according to Luke*, pp. 69-107.

Neyrey, Jerome H., 'Was Jesus of Nazareth a Monotheist? Conversation with Cultural Studies', *BTB* 49 (2019), pp. 132-36.

Neyrey, Jerome H., 'Witchcraft Accusations in 2 Cor 10–13: Paul in Social Science Perspective', *Listening* 21 (1986), pp. 160-70.

Neyrey, Jerome H., and Richard L. Rohrbaugh, '"He Must Increase, I Must Decrease" (John 3:30): A Cultural and Social Interpretation', *CBQ* 63 (2001), pp. 464-83.

Neyrey, Jerome H., and Eric Rowe, 'Telling Time in the Fourth Gospel', *HvTSt* 64 (2008), pp. 291-322.

Nickelsburg, George W.E., 'Resurrection (Early Judaism and Christianity)', in *ABD*, V, p. 688.

Nolland, John, 'Classical, and Rabbinic Parallels to 'Physician, Heal Yourself' (LK. IV 23)', *NovT* 21 1999), pp. 193-209.

Nolland, John, *Luke 1–9:20* (Dallas, TX: Word Books, 1989).

North, Helen, *From Myth to Icon: Reflections of Greek Ethical Doctrine in Literature and Art* (Ithaca, NY: Cornell University Press, 1979).

North, Helen, *Sophrosyne: Self-Knowledge and Self-Restraint in Greek Literature* (Ithaca, NY: Cornell University Press, 1966).

Oakman, Douglas E., 'Jesus, Q, and Ancient Literacy in Social Perspective', in his *Jesus and the Peasants* (Eugene, OR: Cascade Books), pp. 298-308.

O'Fearghail, Fearghus, 'Rejection at Nazareth', *ZNW* 75 (1985), pp. 60-72.

Ogg, George, 'The Age of Jesus When He Taught', *NTS* 5 (1959), pp. 291-98.

Osborne, Robin, 'Law in Action in Classical Athens', *JHS* 105 (1985), pp. 40-58.

Parker, Robert, 'Pleasing Thighs: Reciprocity in Greek Religion', in Gill, Postlewaithe, and Seaford (eds.), *Reciprocity in Ancient Greece* (Oxford: Oxford University Press, 1998), pp. 105-26.

Parsons, Michel A., 'Luke and the *Progymnasmata*', in *Contextualizing Acts: Lukan Narrative and Greco-Roman Discourse* (ed. Todd Penner and Caroline Vander Stichele; SBLSymS, 20; Atlanta, GA: SBL Press, 2003), pp. 43-63.

Parsons, Mikeal C., and Michael Wade Martin, *Ancient Rhetoric and the New Testament* (Waco, TX: Baylor University Press, 2018).

Pelling, Christopher, *Character and Individuality in Greek Literature* (Oxford: Clarendon Press, 1990).

Pilch, John J., *A Cultural Handbook to the Bible* (Grand Rapids, MI: Eerdmans, 2012).

Pilch, John J., *Healing in the New Testament* (Minneapolis, MN: Fortress Press, 2000).

Pilch, John J., 'Lying and Deceit in the Letters to the Seven Churches: Perspectives from Cultural Anthropology', *BTB* 22 (1992), pp. 126-34.

Pilch, John J., 'Secrecy in the Mediterranean World: An Anthropological Perspective'. *BTB* 24 (1994), pp. 151-57.

Pilch, John J., 'Sickness and Healing in Luke–Acts', in *The Social World of Luke–Acts: Models for Interpretation* (ed. Jerome H. Neyrey; Peabody, MA: Hendrickson, 1991), pp. 200-209.

Pilch, John J., and Bruce J. Malina (eds.), *Handbook of Biblical Social Values* (Eugene, OR: Cascade Books, 2012), pp. xxvi-xxxvii.

Plato, *The Dialogues of Plato* (trans. B. Jowett; New York: Random House, 1937).

Ramsaran, Rollin A., 'Living and Dying, Living Is Dying (Philippians 1:21): Paul's Maxim and Exemplary Argumentation in Philippians', in *Rhetorical Argumentation in Biblical Texts: Essays from the Lund 2000 Conference* (ed. Anders Eriksson, Thomas Olbricht, and Walter Übelacker; Harrisburg, PA: Trinity Press International, 2002), pp. 325-39.

Rawson, Beryl, *Children and Childhood in Roman Italy* (Oxford: Oxford University Press, 2003).

Reden, Sitta von, 'The Commodification of Symbols: Reciprocity and its Perversions in Mendander', in Gill, Postlewaithe, and Seaford (eds.), *Reciprocity in Ancient Greece*, pp. 255-61.

Riesenfeld, Harald, 'The Meaning of the Verb *arneithai*', *ConNT* 11 (1947), pp. 207-19.

Robbins, Vernon K., 'By Land and By Sea: The We-Passages and Ancient Sea Voyages', in Charles H. Talbert (ed.), *Perspectives on Luke Acts*, pp. 215-42.

Robbins, Vernon K., 'Classifying Pronouncement Stories in Plutarch's Parallel Lives', *Semeia* 20 (1981), pp. 33-42.

Robbins, Vernon K., 'Introduction: Using Rhetorical Discussions of the Chreia to Interpret Pronouncement Stories', *Semeia* 64 (1994), pp. vii-xvii.

Robbins, Vernon K., *Jesus, the Teacher: A Socio-rhetorical Interpretation of Mark* (Philadelphia, PA: Fortress Press, 1984).

Robbins, Vernon K., 'Prefaces in Greco-Roman Biography and Luke–Acts', *PRS* 6 (1979), pp. 94-108.

Robbins, Vernon, 'Pronouncement Stories and Jesus' Blessing of the Children: A Rhetorical Approach', *Semeia* 29 (1983), pp. 43-74.

Robinson, J.A.T., 'The Baptism of John and the Qumran Community', in his *Twelve New Testament Studies* (London: SCM Press, 1962), pp. 11-27.

Rohrbaugh, Richard L., 'Gossip in the New Testament'. in his *The New Testament in Cross-Cultural Perspective*, pp. 125-46.

Rohrbaugh, Richard L., 'Honor: Core Value in the Biblical World', in *Understanding the Social World of the New Testament* (ed. Dietmar Neufeld and Richard E. DeMaris; London: Routledge, 2010), pp. 109-25.

Rohrbaugh, Richard L., 'Legitimating Sonship—A Test of Honour: A Social-scientific Study of Luke 4:1-30', in *Modelling Early Christianity: Social-scientific Studies in the New Testament and its Context* (ed. Philip F. Esler; London: Routledge, 1994), pp. 183-97.

Rohrbaugh, Richard L., *The New Testament in Cross-Cultural Perspective* (Eugene, OR: Cascade Books, 2007).

Rohrbaugh, Richard L., 'The Social Function of Genealogies in the New Testament and its World', in *To Set at Liberty: Essays on Early Christianity and its Social World in Honor of John H. Elliott* (ed. Stephen K. Black; Sheffield: Sheffield Phoenix Press, 2014), pp. 311-27.

Russell, D.A., and N.G. Wilson, *Menander Rhetor* [Oxford: Clarendon Press, 1981).

Saburin, Richard A., 'The Growing of Christ: Understanding Luke 2:40, 52, in the Light of the Structural Pattern of Luke–Acts', *Journal of Asia Adventist Seminary* 10 (2007), pp. 15-25.

Saldarini, Anthony J., *Pharisees, Scribes, and Sadducees in Palestinian Society: A Sociological Approach* (Wilmington, DE: Michael Glazier, 1988).

Schmidt, Daryl, 'Luke's 'Innocent' Jesus: A Scriptural Apologetic', in *Political Issues in Luke–Acts* (ed. Richard J. Cassidy; Maryknoll, NY: Orbis Books, 1983), pp. 111-21.

Seeley, David, *The Noble Death: Graeco-Roman Martyrology and Paul's Concept of Salvation* (Sheffield: JSOT Press, 1990).

Shuler, Philip L., *A Genre for the Gospels: The Biographical Character of Matthew* (Philadelphia, PA: Fortress Press, 1982).

Sylva, D., 'The Temple Curtain and the Death of Jesus in Luke', *JBL* 105 (1986), pp. 239-50.

Smith, Dennis, 'Table Fellowship as a Literary Motif in the Gospel of Luke', *JBL* 106 (1987), pp. 613-38.

Squires, John T., *The Plan of God in Luke–Acts* (Cambridge: Cambridge University Press, 1993).

Steele, E. Springs, 'Luke 11:37-54—A Modified Hellenistic Symposium', *JBL* 103 (1984), pp. 479-94.

Stegman, Thomas D., 'Reading Luke 12:13-34 as an Elaboration of a Chreia: How Hermogenes of Tarsus Sheds Light on Luke's Gospel', *NovT* 49 (2007), pp. 328-51.

Stegemann, W., 'Theon', *RE* 5A (1934), pp. 2037-54.

Stein, S., 'The Influence of Symposia Literature on the Literary Form of the Pesah Haggadah', *JJS* 8 (1957), pp. 13-44.

Stock, Augustine, 'Jesus, Hypocrites, and Herodians', *BTB* 16 (1986), pp. 3-7.

Talbert, Charles H., *Literary Patterns, Theological Themes, and the Genre of Luke–Acts* (Missoula, MT: SBL Press, 1975).

Talbert, Charles H., 'Prophecies of Future Greatness: The Contribution of Greco-Roman Biographies to an Understanding of Luke 1:5–4:15', in *The Divine Helmsman* (ed. James Crenshaw and Samuel Sandmel; New York: KTAV, 1980), pp. 129-41.

Talbert, Charles H. (ed.), *Luke–Acts: New Perspectives from the Society of Biblical Literature Seminar* (New York: Crossroads, 1984).

Talbert, Charles H. (ed.), *Perspectives on Luke–Acts* (ed. Charles H. Talbert; Edinburgh: T. & T. Clark, 1978).

Thaniel, Katherine, 'Quintilian and the Progymnasmata' (unpublished dissertation, McMaster University, 1973).

Unnik, W.C. van, *Tarsus or Jerusalem* (London: Epworth Press, 1962).

Veltman, Fred, 'The Defense Speeches of Paul in Acts', in Talbert (ed.), *Perspectives on Luke–Acts*, pp. 243-56.

Wallace-Hadrill, Andrew, *Suetonius* (London: Duckworth, 2004).

Watson, Duane F., 'Paul's Speech to the Ephesian Elders (Acts 20:17-48: Epideictic Rhetoric of Farewell', in *Persuasive Artistry: Studies in New Testament Rhetoric in Honor of George A. Kennedy* (ed. Duane Watson; Sheffield: JSOT Press, 1991), pp. 184-208.

Wees, Hans van, 'The Law of Gratitude: Reciprocity in Anthropological Theory', in Gill, Postlewaithe, and Seaford (eds.), *Reciprocity in Ancient Greece*, pp. 13-49.

Winter, Bruce, 'The Importance of *captatio benevolentiae* in the Speeches of Tertullus and Paul in Acts 24:1-2', *JTS* 42 (1991), pp. 505-31.

Wuellner, Wilhelm, 'The Rhetorical Genre of Jesus' Sermon in Luke 12:1–13:9', in *Persuasive Artistry: Studies in New Testament Rhetoric in Honor of George A. Kennedy* (ed. Duane F. Watson; JSNTSup, 50; Sheffield: Sheffield Academic Press, 1991), pp. 93-118.

Zeisler, J.A., 'The Vow of Abstinence', *Colloquium* 5 (1972), pp. 12-14.

Zeisler, J.A., 'The Vow of Abstinence Again', *Colloquium* 6 (1973), pp. 49-50.

Ziolkowski, John E., *Thucydides and the Tradition of Funeral Speeches at Athens* (Salem, NH: The Ayer Company, 1981).

INDEX OF REFERENCES

INDEX OF AUTHORS

Index of Subjects

Abraham 25, 45, 149, 157
agonism, agonistic 129, 136, 138, 159,
  181
angels 61, 86, 89
anger 129, 139, 140, 143-45, 152-60, 181
apostles 59, 176, 185, 189
artisan 69, 125

banquet 149, 151, 153
  see food/meals
baptism 46, 67, 74, 86, 100, 127, 184
  baptism by John 46, 74, 86
  baptism of Jesus 184
body 13, 43, 50-52, 61, 65, 97
body parts
  ears 72, 83, 183
  eyes 27, 67, 68, 79, 90, 92, 99, 124,
    125, 136, 155, 156, 167, 171, 181
  face 73, 179-81
  feet 39, 69, 136, 188
  hand 63, 65, 79-81, 156, 157, 172,
    176, 183, 185, 187-89
  head 23, 80, 128, 182, 186
bread 63, 70, 134, 144

Caesar 23, 56, 90, 111, 120, 130, 157,
  171
challenge–riposte 34, 36, 38, 65, 68, 73,
  75, 129, 130, 156-60
    see *chreia*, below
chreia 1-3, 6-8, 35-38, 129, 130, 155,
  158, 159, 190, 194
clothing 11, 30, 46, 61, 79, 97, 107, 126,
  133, 151, 160
  courage 117-38, 162-64, 166-68, 173,
    188
  as attacking attackers 120-22, 155-58
  as attacking kinship institution 123
  as attacking political institution 132
  as boldness of speech 130

as defense 120, 138
facing death 175
labor, endurance 117-20, 127, 135,
  138
  see virtues, canonical, below

David
  as ancestor 24, 25, 27, 44, 45
  as example 70, 83
  as prophet 183, 184
disciples 101, 103-107, 109, 120, 123-30,
  135, 136, 150-52, 177-82,

Elijah 70, 115, 154, 174-77, 180, 181,
  184
  John as Elijah 45, 59, 115, 175, 176
Elisha 70, 154, 155, 184
Elizabeth 16, 25, 44, 45, 96
encomium, topics of
  origins 2-5, 7, 10, 17-28, 39, 40, 44,
    49-51, 53-55, 79, 86, 160, 191, 192
  nurture and training 7, 11, 29, 31, 33-
    35, 37-41, 43-49, 55, 191, 192
  deeds of body, soul, and fortune 9,
    10, 13, 43, 50-52
  achievements 43, 52, 185, 186
  death 2-4, 7, 9, 10, 14-15, 17, 118,
    137, 138, 158, 161-92
    see Noble Death, below

fable 7, 194
family 32, 34, 35, 43-47, 90, 91, 110,
  120, 168
  see courage, attacking kinship, below
  see encomium origins, generational,
    above
  see institutions, kinship, below
  see justice, duties to parents below
fasting 70, 86, 111, 148
funeral orations 8, 14, 15, 162-92